When Novels Perform History

D1795626

PETER LANG
Oxford • Bern • Berlin • Bruxelles • Frankfurt am Main • New York • Wien

When Novels Perform History

Dramatizing the Past
in Australian and Canadian Literature

Rebecca Waese

PETER LANG

Oxford • Bern • Berlin • Bruxelles • Frankfurt am Main • New York • Wien

Bibliographic information published by Die Deutsche Nationalbibliothek
Die Deutsche Nationalbibliothek lists this publication in the Deutsche
Nationalbibliografie; detailed bibliographic data is available on the Internet at
http://dnb.d-nb.de.
A catalogue record for this book is available from the British Library.

Library of Congress Control Number: 2017945167

Cover image: *Red Land Warrior* by Carmel Debreuil. Reproduced with
permission.

Cover design: Peter Lang Ltd.

ISSN 1660-6205
ISBN 978-1-906165-84-0 (print) • ISBN 978-1-78707-832-1 (ePDF)
ISBN 978-1-78707-833-8 (ePub) • ISBN 978-1-78707-834-5 (mobi)

© Peter Lang AG 2017

Published by Peter Lang Ltd, International Academic Publishers,
52 St Giles, Oxford, OX1 3LU, United Kingdom
oxford@peterlang.com, www.peterlang.com

This publication has been peer reviewed.

Printed in Germany

Contents

vi

Acknowledgements

My deep thanks go to my family and friends across the globe who have been such wonderful sources of support and encouragement. Thank you, first, and a thousand times to my mother, Linda Waese, and to my father, Stan Waese, who have believed in me since the beginning and made every effort to help me achieve my goals. I am grateful for the love and support of my grandmother, Estelle Kuchar; my incredible siblings, Jessica Shifman and Adam Waese; and my siblings-in-law, Jessie Gibson, Kate Gibson, Jolene Waese, Alan Shifman, Matt Dri, Steve Balmforth, Andrew Stevens, and Katrina Lacey, for your encouragement, warmth, humour, and wisdom. Thank you to Robyn and Den Gibson for your loving support and giving my kids 'Grandma and Pa' time when I needed to write. The final stretch of nitpicking by the family will always be appreciated. Thank you to Wayne Stevens and Irene Gibson.

Thank you to my mentors, Terry Goldie, Linda Hutcheon, and Sue Thomas for your professional guidance and long-standing championing of my work. I am grateful for the support of the Disciplinary Research Program in Drama, Theatre, and English from La Trobe University. Versions of previously published articles appear with permission: 'Dramatic Modes and the Feminist Poetics of Enactment in Daphne Marlatt's *Ana Historic*' from *Studies in Canadian Literature* and 'Film and Drama in Guy Vanderhaeghe's *The Englishman's Boy*' from *Journal of American Studies of Turkey*. Thank you to Suzi Hayes and Nicholas Cowley for research assistance, Caryn Rae Adams for copy-editing, and fellow Canadian-Australian, Carmel Debreuil, for the use of the *Red Land Warrior*, for the cover art. Many thanks to colleagues from La Trobe University who have offered advice and friendship: Sue Martin, Alison Ravenscroft, Paul Salzman, Alexis Harley, Catherine Padmore, Kelly Gardiner, Claire Knowles, Anneli Bjorasen, and a special mention to Rob Conkie for your support and encouragement. Thank you to my friends who have helped in so many ways, and, particularly, to Sarina Sherlock, Andrea Ditoro, Kate East, Mina Jane, Chris

Benz, Maha Sidaoui, Adrienne Guthrie, Janna Press, Dayna Simon, Mandy Thomson, Sarah Henstra, Sharyn Myer, and my Torquay family. I would like to thank some of my most inspirational teachers: Marilyn Eisenstat, Stan Dragland, Jim Schaefer, Charlie Tomlinson, Lawrence Garber, Susan Popplewell, Paul Comeau, Douglas Kneale, and Lisa Zeitz. Thank you to Bev Richardson who first inspired me to pursue writing when I was seven.

My deepest thanks go to my family, Mark, Zach, and Ivy Stevens, who have given me love, inspiration, and pure joy. Zach, you have a happy, loving spirit and soul and an incredible intellect. You've helped me with two-square ball breaks in the backyard, awesome hugs, and delicious tea. Ivy, you are funny, kind, and wise far beyond your years. I thank you for the love and the advice you gave me when you were four: 'Just do your best, Mum. That's all you can do.' To Mark, my husband and loving partner, thank you so much for helping me through this journey. You have been here every step of the way with patience, generosity, encouragement, vision, and wise strategic advice to help me achieve this goal. I look back to when I felt like the beetle climbing up the mountain backwards in *Cosmos*, and, at last, with your love and support, we've reached the top of this one. Thank you with all my heart.

Exploring History in Australian and Canadian Literature through Dramatic Modes

This book presents new scholarship on how Australian and Canadian writers use dramatic modes to represent, engage with, and interrogate history and historiography in a selection of novels published between 1985 and 2010. Dramatic modes in fiction about the past often heighten perceptions of immediacy and sensory awareness by creating a sense of immersion or embodiment in a particular historical scene. Alternatively, dramatic modes may establish reflexive and critical distances between readers and constructions of history in ways that break through familiar forms and patterns of narrative expression to highlight the illusory nature of representation and create sites of resistance, decolonization, and inquiry. Some novels use dramatic modes that alternate between providing readers with sensations of immersion and estrangement, thereby continually re-positioning readers as they examine how they accept or resist nationalistic and hegemonic representations of history in fiction.

When Novels Perform History examines various dramatic modes which bring the body and a sense of the reader's presence and engagement to the fore in the novels discussed, as well as performative ways of writing about history. Its methodology combines a close analysis of text and form, performance and postcolonial theory and reflection on strategies used to engage readers. Through a close examination of selected texts, the book points to ways in which dramatic modes in fiction can direct attention to aspects of history that are not often recorded, explore subjective and physical experiences of characters responding within historical contexts, and prompt inquiry into how these stories can be represented effectively and evocatively. A number of novels that utilize dramatic modes engender what Ross Gibson calls a 'palpable' sense of an encounter with events or characters constructed from the past, which gives an affective reaction so potent that it can be felt in the body, potentially answering Gibson's call for 'new cultural forms [in which] to think about tendencies of history' and the need to create historiographies that engage readers through the senses.[1] Dramatic modes are well suited to Australian and Canadian novels where characters rehearse and perform newly established roles in settler/ invader contexts, and the comparative structure of the book, alternating between Australian and Canadian texts, considers the respective histories of both countries, which, among significant differences, share a history of British colonization, the dispossession and unconstitutional mistreatment of indigenous peoples, and the emergence of multicultural populations.

While there have been a few other comparisons of the literature and culture of these two countries,[2] this study extends the comparative approach beyond these books to explore the performative and theatrical aspects of selected novels from these countries and identify a range of techniques that are used to convey a compelling and evocative sense of postcolonial history within them. Despite theoretical groundwork on performativity in postcolonial theatre by Joanne Tompkins, Helen Gilbert, and Gary Boire,[3] there has been surprisingly little analysis of dramatic modes in Australian and Canadian fiction about history even as the field has grown in recent years.[4]

1   Ross Gibson, 'Palpable History', *Cultural Studies Review* 14/1 (March 2008), 179.
2   Examples of comparative literary analyses include Charlotte Sturgess, ed., *The Politics and Poetics of Passage in Canadian and Australian Culture and Fiction* (Nantes: University de Nantes CRINI/CEC, 2006); Terry Goldie, *Fear and Temptation: The Image of the Indigene in Canadian, Australian, and New Zealand Literatures* (Kingston: McGill-Queen's University Press, 1989); and Ronald Blaber's and Marvin Gilman's *Roguery: The Picaresque Tradition in Australian, Canadian and Indian Fiction* (Springwood, NSW: Butterfly, 1990).
3   Helen Gilbert and Joanne Tompkins, *Post-Colonial Drama: Theory, Practice, Politics* (London: Routledge, 1996); and Gary Boire, 'Inside Out: Prison Theatre from Australia, Canada, and New Zealand', *Australian-Canadian Studies* 8/1 (1990), 21–30.
4   Peter Pierce observes melodrama in a few works of Australian fiction in *Australian Melodramas: Thomas Keneally's Fiction* (St Lucia: University of Queensland Press, 1995), 159–77; see also, Peter Brooks, *The Melodramatic Imagination: Balzac, Henry James, Melodrama, and the Mode of Excess* (New Haven, CT: Yale University Press, 1976), 4.

Graham Huggan examines dramatic modes in three postcolonial novels that perform history in *The Post-Colonial Exotic* on Salman Rushdie's *The Satanic Verses*, V. S. Naipaul's *The Enigma of Arrival*, and Hanif Kureishi's *The Buddha of Suburbia*, in which he posits that performativity might usefully become 'a central concept for understanding colonial strategies of physical oppression and postcolonial identity formation'.[5] There have been some publications on theatricality in nineteenth-century English novels[6] and performativity in Indian and Caribbean novels which will be considered in the concluding chapter that looks beyond Australian and Canadian contexts at two other evocative applications of dramatic modes in novels about history.[7] *When Novels Perform History* explores a range of dramatic modes, including metatheatre, melodrama, and narrative strategies that alternately immerse readers in or estrange readers from representations of Australian and Canadian history in fiction to increase an understanding of how postcolonial identities are constructed and how new roles and formulations of power are rehearsed in settler-invader contexts.

Each of the six chapters in this book is arranged thematically around specific dramatic and performative modes that are used to explore history and historiography in Australian and Canadian fiction for various strategic aims. In each of the selected novels, there are mediated experiences of theatre and performative explorations for readers. In some novels, representations of contemporary melodrama convey affect, reflexivity, and nostalgia; in others, dramatic techniques such as those developed by

5   Graham Huggan, 'Staged Marginalities', in *The Post-Colonial Exotic: Marketing the Margins* (London: Routledge, 2001), 277.

6   Joseph Litvak, *Caught in the act: theatricality in the nineteenth-century English novel* (Oakland: University of California Press, 1992); Emily Allen, *Theater Figures: The Production of the Nineteenth-Century British Novel* (Columbus: Ohio State Press, 2003); Special issue of *Victorian Network* 13/2 (Winter 2011).

7   See Maria-Sabina Draga Alexandru, *Performance and Performativity in Contemporary Indian Fiction in English* (Boston: Brill Rodopi, 2015); Simon Gikandi, *Maps of Englishness: Writing Identity in the Culture of Colonialism* (New York: Columbia University Press, 1996); Parama Sarkar, 'Performing Narrative: The Motif of Performance in Arundhati Roy's *The God of Small Things*', *South Asian Review* 28/2 (2007), 217–36.

Constantin Stanislavski,[8] for example, draw a reader into an understanding of a character's inner desires and motivations. Some novels use versions of estrangement techniques, such as those developed by Bertolt Brecht, to create reflexive moments in fiction which are designed to position readers to interpret critically rather than to experience an emotional release.[9] Plays-within-novels provide critical distance that results in alternate and counter-hegemonic views of history that can illuminate the shortcomings of certain representational modes. Dramatic modes may prompt readers to envision historical possibilities through imaginative speculation or to perceive incomprehensible violence through familiar structures from the theatre. Rather than establishing a single dramatic mode, this book explores a range of the uses of dramatic modes in contemporary Australian and Canadian historically based fiction. Each dramatic mode is analysed through a close examination of a primary text (or two), and delivers an analysis of performative writing and postcolonial and historiographic theory. The novels in question demonstrate ways in which dramatic and performative modes contribute to new understandings of power relations, postcolonial identities, and how history in fiction is constructed over a twenty-five-year period to resonate with, engage, and challenge contemporary readers. The Australian novels discussed include Thomas Keneally's *The Playmaker* (1987),[10] David Musgrave's *Glissando: A Melodrama* (2010),[11] Peter Carey's *Illywhacker* (1985)[12] and Richard Flanagan's *Gould's Book of Fish: A Novel in Twelve Fish* (2001).[13] The novels from Canada include Tomson Highway's *Kiss of the Fur Queen* (1998),[14] Daphne Marlatt's *Ana*

---

8   Constantin Stanislavski, *An Actor Prepares*, trans. Elizabeth Reynolds Hapgood [1936] (London: Methuen Drama, 1986).

9   Bertolt Brecht, *Brecht on Theatre: The Development of an Aesthetic*, ed. and trans. John Willett (New York: Hill and Wang, 1964), 93.

10   Thomas Keneally, *The Playmaker* (London: Hodder and Stoughton, 1987).

11   David Musgrave, *Glissando: A Melodrama* (Collingwood: Sleepers Press, 2010).

12   Peter Carey, *Illywhacker* (St Lucia: University of Queensland Press, 1985).

13   Richard Flanagan, *Gould's Book of Fish: A Novel in Twelve Fish* [2001] (Sydney: Picador Pan Macmillan Australia, 2002).

14   Thomson Highway, *Kiss of the Fur Queen* (Toronto: Doubleday/Random House, 1999).

Historic (1988),[15] and Guy Vanderhaeghe's *The Englishman's Boy* (1996).[16] Observations on Richard Flanagan's *The Narrow Road to the Deep North* (2014)[17] and Daphne Marlatt's *The Gull: The Steveston Noh Project* (2009)[18] extend the scope of the relevant chapters in which they appear.

All of the Australian and Canadian authors whose novels feature prominently in this book are prolific in more than one genre, collectively spanning poetry, stage plays, screenplays, short stories, novels, children's books, and opera; this speaks to the authors' varied interests in and proclivities toward creative expression through interdisciplinary means. Conceivably, the authors' expertise of working in other performative genres enriches these genre-crossing novels that merge performance and history in literature and each author has won major prizes for his or her respective work. Richard Flanagan, novelist, historian, and Tasmanian environmental activist, won the Commonwealth Writers Prize for *Gould's Book of Fish* (2001), the Man Booker Prize for *The Narrow Road to the Deep North* (2014), and was the director and scriptwriter of the film adaptation of his novel *The Sound of One Hand Clapping* (2008). Thomas Keneally, born in Sydney and well known for his prolific and popular historical fiction, won the Booker Prize for *Schindler's Ark* (1982), the Order of Australia (1983), and is also a playwright. David Musgrave, a Sydney-based poet, critic, founder of an independent press, and novelist of *Glissando* (2010) has won many poetry prizes including the Newcastle Poetry prize. Peter Carey, from Bacchus Marsh, Australia and now a New York resident, has twice won the Booker Prize for *Oscar and Lucinda* (1988) and *True History of the Kelly Gang* (2001). Carey has written short stories, screenplays, and was awarded the Order of Australia (2012). Tomson Highway, a Cree Canadian playwright, musician, librettist, and novelist won the Governor-General's award in 1989 for

---

15   Daphne Marlatt, *Ana Historic* (Toronto: Coach House Press, 1988).

16   Guy Vanderhaeghe, *The Englishman's Boy* [1997] (London: Anchor/Transworld Publishing, 1998).

17   Richard Flanagan, *The Narrow Road to the Deep North* (North Sydney, NSW: Random House Australia, 2013).

18   Daphne Marlatt, *The Gull: The Steveston Noh Project*, trans. Toyoshi Yoshihara (Vancouver: Talonbooks, 2009).

his play, *Dry Lips Oughta Move to Kapuskasing* and has written children's books in English and Cree. Guy Vanderhaeghe, Saskatchewan-born, best known for his trilogy of novels set in the American and Canadian West, has also written plays and screenplays and won the Booker Prize in 1996 for *The Englishman's Boy* and Governor General Awards for his fiction (1982, 1996, and 2015). Daphne Marlatt, a poet, novelist, essayist, playwright, and feminist critic, born in Melbourne, Australia and raised in British Columbia, Canada, won the Order of Canada in 2006 and the George Woodcock Lifetime Achievement award in 2012 for her founding work on literary journals *TISH* and *tessera* and her writing defined by its feminist, lesbian, and postcolonial poetics.

The novels under discussion – only one of which is written by a woman and only one by an indigenous author – are not in and of themselves representative of the vast scope of Australian and Canadian literature, but, rather, exemplify the use of dramatic modes that expand the possibilities for the writing of history and historiography in fiction in the two countries.[19] The theoretical implications of the book's findings are not limited to the focus texts within it; the book's central premise of how novels perform history can be extended beyond Australian and Canadian novels to other nations and the concluding chapter therefore invites readers to consider the dramatic modes that can also be seen to be operating within Arundhati Roy's *The God of Small Things* (1997) and Wilson Harris' *The Infinite Rehearsal* (1987).

The central concern of this book, however, is the dramatization in fiction of those aspects of the postcolonial condition that are common to Australia and Canada. In *Decolonising Fictions*, Diana Brydon and Helen Tiffin observe the similarities between the postcolonial conditions of Australia and Canada, two countries where 'English language and culture were transported [...] to [...] foreign territor[ies] where the indigenous inhabitants were either annihilated or marginalized'.[20] Alan Lawson describes the shared 'position of ambi/valence' of non-indigenous writers in 'Second World' countries, such as Australia and Canada, who

19   The scope of this study is limited to novels written in English.
20   Diana Brydon and Helen Tiffin, *Decolonising Fictions* (Sydney: Dangaroo Press, 1993), 12.

experience a doubleness in their perspective and emplacement as they look backwards to countries of origin while perceiving the land in which they live.[21] These 'Second World' countries have in common what George Manuel and Michael Posluns, in *The Fourth World: An Indian Reality*, call the 'Fourth World', referring to indigenous populations, and indigenous writers in these countries have different stories and viewpoints than writers who have come to inhabit these lands. Tomson Highway's *Kiss of the Fur Queen* will be considered closely in Chapter 2 in a specific study of performative strategies arising from Cree and Western traditions. Before outlining the chapters, the introduction provides an examination of the origins of this performative and historical fiction genre, with its roots in the height of postmodernism and postcolonialism in the mid-1980s. It examines current debates underlying the subjective expression of history in performative fiction between historical evidence and fictional liberties designed to create affective responses in the reader and study the emergence of the 'performative turn' in history and the humanities. It introduces the theorists whose writing on dramatic and performative modes and reflexivity can be usefully connected with novels that engage with history, including Joanne Tompkins, Greg Dening, Richard Hornby, Bertolt Brecht, Constantin Stanislavski, and Peter Brook and shows, in a summary of chapters, where their theories are applied to examine aspects of performative history novels.

The Emergence of Dramatic Modes in Australian and Canadian Historical Novels

The significant emergence of Australian and Canadian novels that invoke a dramatic mode to represent and engage with history can be traced to the mid-1980s when postmodernism and postcolonialism were the defining

---

21   Alan Lawson, 'A Cultural Paradigm for the Second World', *Australian-Canadian Studies* 9/1–2 (1991), 69.

cultural discourses of the day. Linda Hutcheon's 'Canadian Historiographic Metafiction' (1984) identified a major shift in the narrative forms of many historical novels which moved from early realist accounts to more self-reflexive narratives, reflecting changes in the ways Canadian writers understood themselves and their histories and examining ways in which they perceived they belonged or did not belong to their nation.[22] Hutcheon contrasts early Canadian nineteenth-century realist historical novels that were constructed with imported European forms and aesthetics with Canadian historiographic metafictions written by Ruby Wiebe, Timothy Findley, George Bowering, and other novels from the 1970s and 1980s that explored the authors' understandings of the 'mimetic connection between art and life'; these later novels highlighted the processes of constructing historical narratives and the decision-making involved with the production of national historical narratives in fiction.[23] Hutcheon draws on the thinking of Roland Barthes to demonstrate how historiographic metafictions foster relationships between writers and readers, who engage in creating historical interpretations that become meaningful and resonant through collaborative processes. From the 1980s onward, as governments in Canada and Australia were beginning to legislate historical advances for women, minorities, and indigenous peoples – the legalization of abortion with the Morgentaler decision in Canada (1988), the Canadian Multicultural Act (1988), the Aboriginal Land Rights Act in Australia (1983), and the Mabo decision in Australia (1992) – a growing number of writers began incorporating dramatic modes and theatrical strategies in novels that engaged with history, which allowed for multiple perspectives and voices, and for national narratives that were counter-discursive to earlier models.

In novels that engage with dramatic modes to explore history, hallmark traits of postmodernism including self-reflexivity and irony are prominent and lead readers to interrogate and deconstruct the grand narratives often associated with traditional perceptions of history, such as notions of a nation's 'progress' and 'destiny'. Such performative texts provide alternatives

---

22   Linda Hutcheon, 'Canadian Historiographic Metafiction', *Essays on Canadian Writing* 30 (1984), 228–38.
23   Hutcheon, 'Canadian Historiographic Metafiction', 228.

to more conventionally constructed historical novels, which, as Pierre Nora writes in *Memory and History*, arise from a long-standing tradition of writing history as 'the reconstitution of a past *without lacunae or faults*'.[24] In *The Canadian Postmodern*, Hutcheon introduced the term 'historiographic metafiction' in her identification of fiction that shows a heightened awareness of the process and complexities of writing history as it produces reflexive art.[25] Hutcheon's writing on historiographic metafiction informs this book to some degree, as each of the focal novels, drawn from postcolonial contexts, combines in some way notions of historiographic reflexivity within dramatic and theatrical modes, and many of them feature parody and irony to challenge authoritative versions of history. Other contemporary views of historiography are examined, including Frederic Jameson's assertion that it is a sign of the late capitalist times in postmodern society that the only historical representations we can have of the past are mediated through 'our own pop images and stereotypes' and are shot through with nostalgia; in the end, Jameson suggests, we are bound to live 'in a perpetual present where the past is only accessible through a nostalgic gaze that reveals more about our own time than about the history being represented'.[26] Jameson's view highlights the nature of the challenges that face novelists who attempt to access the past through performative modes in fiction with the inevitable blurring of past and present that representative modes bring, along with the common desire of writers to acknowledge the limitations of representation. Wolfgang Iser's theory in *The Play of the Text*, where the text is perceived as an arena for transformative play and the reader has an active role in making meaning,[27] can be usefully applied to performative novels that revisit history, as Iser emphasizes the idea that

---

24   Pierre Nora, 'Memory and History: Les Lieux de Mémoire', *Representations* 26 (Spring 1989), 9.

25   Linda Hutcheon, *The Canadian Postmodern: A Study of Contemporary English-Canadian Fiction* (Toronto: Oxford University Press, 1988), 14.

26   Frederic Jameson, 'Postmodernism and Consumer Society', *Postmodernism and its Discontents: Theories and Practices*, ed. Ann Kaplan (London: Verso, 1988), 117–18.

27   Wolfgang Iser, 'The Play of the Text', *Languages of the Unsayable: The Play of Negativity in Literature and Literary Theory*, ed. Sanford Budick and Wolfgang Iser (New York: Columbia University Press, 1989), 328–9.

a text does not deliver any singular or static view of the past but invites a reader into an 'ongoing event' of deciphering and interpretation.[28]

One of the most significant concerns of authors who re-work historical material into literary representations of history is the need to address the complex negotiation between historical evidence and fictional liberties. Some writers create texts that, as Herb Wyile describes, focus on emotional truths that arise from historical experiences rather than representations that depict 'the letter of the record' derived from historical sources.[29] Ross Gibson takes this view further, into the body, when he advocates a call for a kind of historiography that brings about a sense of 'felt conviction' where the 'perceiver gets convinced "in the bones" rather than in the portions of our sensibility that manage linguistic, textual argument'.[30] These more subjective approaches to representing historiography and history in novels do not generally represent a writer's desire to denounce existing historical evidence but rather to develop a considered crossing-over between dramatic modes and experimental ways of writing history in literature in order to create affective and embodied readings. When affective speculation is brought to bear on historical evidence and the boundaries between the two become less distinct, it can result in aesthetic forms that offer something valuable to readers and writers who long for more embodied alternatives to conventional historical fiction. Canadian writer Daphne Marlatt asks, in *Ana Historic*, what if speculation and imagination allow us to recover or inhabit marginalized women's history?[31] Dramatic acts of speculation and imagination extending from existing historical evidence in novels can help bridge omissions in historical records that, particularly in Australian and Canadian history, do not provide a comprehensive representation of people from minority groups in cultures where a significant portion of historical testimonial evidence is oral or contested by people in positions of power and influence. Ross Gibson clarifies why such a practice of creating

28   Iser, 'The Play of the Text', 336.
29   Herb Wyile, *Speaking in the Past Tense: Canadian Novelists on Writing Historical Fiction* (Waterloo: Wilfrid Laurier University Press, 2007), 13.
30   Ross Gibson, 'Palpable History', *Cultural Studies Review* 14/1 (March 2008), 179.
31   Daphne Marlatt, *Ana Historic* (Toronto: Coach House Press, 1988), 55.

'palpable history' is so important in Australia (and this can be extended to Canada as well) when he observes that 'conventional historiographical protocols often come up short when we try to get the fullest possible comprehension of the past that has whelped our present'.[32] In Australia, he maintains, 'we need to imagine across gaps and quandaries in the evidence; we need to venture out past the vestiges or documented ruses that have been allowed some visibility, past what is accepted as admissible for discursive conviction'.[33]

Subjective history-telling, in fiction and in the genre of history itself, is hotly debated and rightly so, with a view to avoiding revisionist histories with little relation to what happened in the past. J. L. Granatstein, in *Who Killed Canadian History?* (1998), upbraids the movement towards subjectivity in the teaching of and transcribing of history and identifies it as what he calls a 'dumbing down' effect caused by historians who focus on subjective and personal histories as they sacrifice the 'macro scale' vision to the 'micro scale', which Granatstein suggests erodes the 'unifying traditional narratives of the past' (56–7).[34] While Granatstein speaks from a context of history proper, and not fiction that engages with history or historiography, the 'unifying traditional narratives' of the past to which he refers are inherently patriarchal, with other multiple blind spots of race, class, ethnicity, and gender, and typify an earlier realist model of Canadian history-telling. For contemporary novelists who use dramatic modes to explore history in Canada and Australia, the 'micro' views of women, indigenous people, and immigrants make invaluable contributions to national narratives that tell diverse stories of the past. These views work to deconstruct certain patriarchal, colonial, and racialized traditions and values that are embedded in what Granatstein calls the 'unifying traditional narratives'. For histories that have previously gone unrecorded or are poorly preserved, the novelist's conundrum of how to balance fictive liberties with known and unknown facts in representing an experience of history is inevitable.

32   Gibson, 'Palpable History', 186.
33   Gibson, 'Palpable History', 186.
34   J. L. Granatstein, *Who Killed Canadian History?* (Toronto: HarperCollins Publishers, 1998), 56.

Hayden White makes a useful distinction in *Rethinking History* (2005) between the way in which historical discourse is primarily concerned with what is 'true', while fiction about history and/or historiography is primarily concerned with conveying what is 'real' – which includes not just known facts but also what might be 'possible or imaginable'.[35] White writes,

> [A] simply true account of the world based on what the documentary record permits one to talk about what happened in it at particular times, and places can provide knowledge of only a very small portion of what 'reality' consists of. However, the rest of the real, after we have said what we can assert to be true about it, would not be everything and anything we could imagine about it. The real would consist of everything that can be truthfully said about its actuality plus everything that can be truthfully said about what it could possibly be.[36]

White grants that historians are typically interested in what is real but suggests they are not motivated 'by the question of the *reality* of the past' as many writers who work with history in fiction are, and therein lie some of the crucial differences between the genres.[37] White suggests that the literary devices in the writing of history in fiction – 'the topoi, tropes and figures, schemata of thought, characterization, personification, emplot-ment', as in the case of Primo Levi's *Survival in Auschwitz* – can make the difference between 'a merely truthful account of an event' and 'an artistic treatment of a real event in [the] past which transcends the truth-reality distinction'.[38] White reminds readers of Aristotle who conceived of history and poetry as potentially complementary forces that, along with philoso-phy, could allow humans 'to represent, imagine and think the world in its

---

35   Hayden White, 'Introduction: Historical Fiction, Fictional History, and Historical Reality', *Rethinking History* 9/2–3 (2005), 147 <http://dx.doi.org/10.1080/13642520500149061> accessed 10 August 2016.

36   White, 'Introduction: Historical Fiction, Fictional History, and Historical Reality', 147.

37   White, 'Introduction: Historical Fiction, Fictional History, and Historical Reality', 147.

38   White, 'Introduction: Historical Fiction, Fictional History, and Historical Reality', 149.

totality, both actual and possible, both real and imagined, both known and only experienced'.[39]

White shows the close and often blurred relationship between historical narratives and drama through some historians' use of dramatic devices in historical discourse, such as the emplotment of characters into dramatic scenes with rising and falling actions and finite closures, which indicate that components of dramatic narrative are firmly embedded within some historical accounts.[40] This is evident in the kind of historical writing Paul Carter refers to as 'imperial recording' where action is factual, completed, and staged theatrically before the reader, as employed in *A History of Australia* by nineteenth-century historian Manning Clark who described historical scenes with an emphasis on theatrical re-enactment unfolding in front of readers.[41] Hayden White in 'The Historical Event' unpacks the terms 'event' and 'destiny' that are often used in historical narratives and shows how they are 'translated into the elements of a drama with a presumed beginning, middle, and end, a denouement, and a falling off of action after the scene of recognition (anagnorisis)'.[42] White suggests that when a sequence of historical events is 'periodized' or 'parsed into acts and scene' in a text, it follows a dramatic mode that is imposed upon it, complete with recognizable teleologies which prompt readers to make sense of the story and what it endeavours to tell us about the past.[43] From White's discussion of historical narratives that incorporate drama and theatre to convey a broader sense of the totality of the past, both real and imaginable, this book will examine where dramatic conventions and components are particularly effective in fiction about history, represented in Keneally's *The Playmaker*, with colonials rehearsing new societal roles on

39 White, 'Introduction: Historical Fiction, Fictional History, and Historical Reality', 147.
40 White, 'Introduction: Historical Fiction, Fictional History, and Historical Reality', 147.
41 Paul Carter, *The Road to Botany Bay: An Essay in Spatial History* (New York: Knopf, 1988), xiv.
42 Hayden White, 'The Historical Event', *differences: a Journal of Feminist Cultural Studies* 19/2 (2008), 23.
43 White, 'The Historical Event', 23.

what they perceive to be an empty 'stage', in Musgrave's *Glissando*, where melodramatic conventions are used to depict scenes with high emotion, and in Flanagan's *Book of Fish*, where dramatic and artistic frames are used in an attempt to convey the full enactment of history, although the novel suggests that history escapes representation despite a range of aesthetic methods designed to portray it.

The 'Performative Turn' and Performative Writing in History and the Humanities

Before studying the particular performative elements and their effects in the selected novels, it is useful to consider some of the key developments in performative writing and in the 'performative turn', which have gained traction in the humanities from the late twentieth century until the present. The 'performative turn' is an elusive concept to define as it has multiple applications in the humanities, with well-known examples in the fields of anthropology, sociology, gender studies, history, linguistics, and literature. It has developed from an earlier dramaturgical model of viewing culture and society as performance and has spread widely across disciplines, as Peter Burke demonstrates comprehensively in 'Performing History: The Importance of Occasions', showing how the concept of the 'performative turn' has emerged in cultural contexts alongside the rise of postmodernism since the 1980s with its emphases on fluidity and the deconstruction of traditions, fixed forms, and the politics of identity.[44] Early references to the dramaturgical model in linguistics and anthropology appear in the 1940s and 1950s, with literary theorist Kenneth Burke proposing a 'dramatistic approach' in his 1945 behavioural study *A Grammar of Motives* and anthropologist Victor Turner coining the term 'social drama' in his work describing

44   Peter Burke, 'Performing History: The Importance of Occasions', *Rethinking History: The Journal of Theory and Practice* 9/1 (2003), 38–9.

the rituals and symbols used to resolve conflict among Ndembu villagers.[45] John Austin developed his watershed concept of 'performative utterances' in *How To Do Things With Words* (1955) where words make things happen rather than merely describe action as in the celebrant's pronouncement of marriage at a wedding ceremony.[46] Austin's work foregrounded performative models in anthropological studies of gossip and ritual and also performativity models in gender studies as developed by Judith Butler in *Gender Trouble*.[47] Dramaturgical models were also employed by Michel Foucault in his philosophical conception of executions as 'theatres of terror'[48] and in Foucault's view of history as a discontinuous series of interpretations that 'must be made to appear as events on the stage of historical progress'.[49]

Early references to dramaturgical models by Kenneth Burke and Victor Turner in the 1940s and 1950s evoke a sense of a staged performance *for* or *before* an audience or readers rather than a performative collaboration *with* them in a shared world as the late twentieth-century usage of the term 'performative turn' came to suggest. The shift in terminology from 'dramatistic' (Burke) to 'performative' across the humanities occurred during the late twentieth century as postmodern studies, theories of gender performance and notions of affect began to permeate critical thinking. Performance studies grew as an independent discipline in universities in 1980s, particularly in America, where Peter Burke notes how its practitioners attempted to deconstruct traditional binaries of 'art' and 'life' as shown in studies of performative anti-war demonstrations.[50] The last decade of the twentieth century and the first decade of the twenty-first brought with them a turn to performative writing in fiction that engaged with history with Brian Massumi's 'autonomy of affect' examining the expectation and intensity of

---

45 Burke, 'Performing History: The Importance of Occasions', 36.
46 John Austin, *How To Do Things With Words* (Boston: Clarendon Press, 1962).
47 Judith Butler, *Gender Trouble; feminism and the subversion of identity* (New York: Routledge, 1990).
48 Foucault qtd in Burke, 'Performing History: The Importance of Occasions', 37.
49 Michel Foucault, *Surveiller et punir* (Paris: Gallimard, 1975), 154.
50 Burke, 'Performing History: The Importance of Occasions', 38.

affect in writing (1995),[51] and Greg Dening's views in *Performances* (1996) on enlivening Australian history through dramatic modes.[52] Dening suggests all history-making is theatrical to some extent and points to the fallacy of representing history as a closed book or a *fait accompli* when such a view of the past – ordered and 'hindsighted' – contradicts how we perceive life as we live it, where it is 'always filled with possibilities [...] always processual and unfinished'.[53] To write 'History' presupposes that the past is 'text-able',[54] or possible to contain in narrative, when, as Dening elaborates:

> The past is everything that has happened – every heartbeat, every sound, every molecular movement. This totality is both objectively specific (it happened in a particular way) and infinitely discrete (the happenings are not connected). Mozart writes a sonata on a cold day in a spiteful mood; Pomare, high chief of Tahiti, at the same moment distractedly 'eats' the eye of a human sacrifice. Yet we have a common-sense confidence that the 'real' past, like the 'real' present, is much more connected and ordered.[55]

Like Annie, the contemporary writer in Marlatt's *Ana Historic*, who recognizes how difficult it is to represent herself with her plurality of inner contradictions let alone someone else from a century earlier, dramatic modes in novels about history not only admit but accommodate uncertainty and the unknown under the auspices of imaginative possibility. Evelyn Hinz in 'Mimesis: the Dramatic Lineage of Auto/Biography' writes: 'In drama and life writing what we delight in is a sense that the subject can never be pinned down'.[56] As readers imagine bodies performing and rehearsing historical possibilities, they may glimpse, through the mind's eye, historical possibilities too amorphous and unwieldly to be tamed into text. If a

---

51   *Brian Massumi*, 'The Autonomy of Affect', *Cultural Critique* 31, The Politics of Systems and Environments, Part II (Autumn 1995), 83–109.

52   Greg Dening, *Performances* (Melbourne: Melbourne University Press, 1996), 110.

53   Dening, *Performances*, 17.

54   Dening, *Performances*, 41.

55   Dening, *Performances*, 41.

56   Evelyn Hinz, 'Mimesis: The Dramatic Lineage of Auto/Biography', in Marlene Kadar, ed., *Essays on Life Writing: From Genre to Critical Practice* (Toronto: University of Toronto Press, 1992), 199.

narrative is too flat or textually complete, readers cannot enter. Dramatic modes animate the gaps and silences, the myriad versions of history that haunt the text, glimmer briefly, yet remain, for the most part, untold.

Dening uses the term 'force' to describe the quality of human experience that is present in life and in theatre and is often missed by historians and ethnographers in their texts.[57] The idea of force in history and storytelling is as ancient as Greek civilization. In *Poetics*, Aristotle described how skilled rhetoricians used *energeia* (force) and *enargeia* (shining forth) to make objects appear before their listeners' eyes.[58] The energy of human presence has tremendous power; as Scott Magelssen puts it, it makes for a 'more forceful mode of creating and disseminating narratives about the past'.[59] Magelssen refers to stage dramatizations of history, summarizing Freddie Rokem's notion of the force of narrative in *Performing History*. This force, or dramatic energy, can also be perceived to some degree in novels that convey dramatizations of history. It appears in Keneally's *The Playmaker* as Ralph Clark's players rehearse their new roles in the colony viewed doubly by an internal audience and the reader who witness live moments of theatre. It is what Carey's *Illywhacker* evokes through Badgery's picaresque storytelling that guides the reader's gaze and what Highway develops in *Kiss of the Fur Queen* through Jeremiah's vibrant Cree storytelling and sensual theatrical performances of 'Chachagathoo, the Shaman'. Flanagan's *Gould's Book of Fish*, Musgrave's *Glissando* and Vanderhaeghe's *The Englishman's Boy* use multi-discursive art forms (visual art, music, and film, respectively) along with dramatic modes to have their narrators latch onto something physical and embodied in history through language. Marlatt's *Ana Historic* and Vanderhaeghe's *The Englishman's Boy* each show the struggles of their writer protagonists to represent their explorations of history in ways that are true to the subjects whose stories they attempt to tell with a sense of vitality and being there.

57   Dening, *Performances*, 115.
58   Artistotle qtd in Freddie Rokem, *Performing History: Theatrical Representations of the Past in Contemporary Theatre* (Iowa City: University of Iowa Press, 2000), 189.
59   Scott Magelssen, 'Making History in the Second Person: Post-touristic Considerations for Living Historical Interpretation', 303.

Performative writing plays a central role in this book as the authors of the selected novels engage in various dramatic modes to invite readers to explore intimate, arresting, and genre-crossing representations of colonial and postcolonial history and historiography. Della Pollock's essay 'Performing Writing' (1998) explores the potentiality of performative writing as social action that is an often welcome and radical disruption within social and cultural discourses that are saturated with textuality.[60] Pollock posits performative writing as a practice rather than a genre that makes an 'important, dangerous and difficult intervention into routine representations of social/performative life'.[61] Performative writing calls attention to the ongoing relationship between writer and reader and the worlds around the signs and referents that are difficult to convey. Pollock argues that performative writing has the ability to shift the discursive paradigm from '"what if" [...] to its performative counterpart, "as if"'[62] and to write in the 'breaks and ruptures' that constitute history to draw 'one charged moment into another'.[63] In Pollock's view, performative writing is subjective, not in the way that it refers to personal individual unrecorded stories or what Granatstein calls the 'micro' view of exploring subjective experience, but in the way that tends 'to *subject* the reader to the writer's reflexivity' with a critical and immediate intimacy.[64] Performative writing explores the relation between the shifting, contextual selves that are created through reflections and the re-positioning of the reader and writer through the text. Full of subversive and active possibilities to connect with readers and bring acute awareness of the processes of writing, performative writing becomes a central practice in this emerging interdisciplinary genre of Australian and Canadian novels that invites readers to explore the sensory, confronting, and dynamic literary representations of colonial and postcolonial history through dramatic modes in fiction.

---

60   Della Pollock, 'Performing Writing', in Peggy Phelan and Jill Lane, eds, *The Ends of Performance* (New York: New York University Press, 1998), 73–103.

61   Pollock, 'Performing Writing', 75.

62   Pollock, 'Performing Writing', 81–2.

63   Pollock, 'Performing Writing', 91.

64   Pollock, 'Performing Writing', 86.

Linking Dramatic Theories to Australian and Canadian Literature about History

While numerous theorists have influenced this project, there are a few whose writings on theatre and drama have been formative to my discussion of dramatic modes and their employment in Australian and Canadian historically based fiction. In particular, Joanne Tompkins's writings on re-visioning, resistance, and mimicry in the context of postcolonial metatheatre have served for me as a launching pad towards other explorations of how novelists transpose these dramatic modes to Australian and Canadian fiction to construct particular self-reflexive connections between writers and readers, and how they create charged moments of 'being' or 'presence' in the texts. In 'Spectacular Resistance', Tompkins observes how metatheatre can be used as a politically powerful strategy of resistance in postcolonial contexts:

> If metatheatre 're-uses' or 're-cycles' theatre, then in the post-colonial context it should be possible to see metatheatre as a strategy of resistance. While theatre generally replays the present or the past to celebrate it, remember it, or decipher it, metatheatre in post-colonial plays is often a self-conscious method of re-negotiating, re-working – not just re-playing – the past and the present.[65]

Tompkins' discussion of the split gaze of the audience in postcolonial metatheatre can be usefully applied to some fiction that incorporates metatheatrical content in order to explore the shifts in a reader's positionality and identifications as he or she examines the representations of history for subtle insights that may be derived from a reflexive mode. In metatheatre, Tompkins suggests that while audience members watch characters watching a play their gaze is split but also magnified to some degree, which foregrounds the actions of questioning and 'revisioning'.[66] In novels with metatheatrical content, as in Keneally's *The Playmaker* in Chapter 1,

65   Joanne Tompkins, '"Spectacular Resistance": Metatheatre in Post-Colonial Drama', *Modern Drama* 38/1 (1995), 42.
66   Tompkins, '"Spectacular Resistance": Metatheatre in Post-Colonial Drama', 45.

where the reader watches a character watching a play, the reader's interpretive vision is split and also intensified as a reader sees characters interpreting
other characters who are performing their nation's stories – both overtly and
subversively – within the novel. Tompkins refers to Homi Bhabha's concept of the 'sign of a double articulation', where the words of the colonized
subject 'speak twice', and argues that 'these plays demonstrate a specular-
ity that is at least split and is the location of difference, ambivalence and
resistance in metatheatre'.[67] In postcolonial fiction with a metatheatrical
mode, readers are drawn to characters in novels who speak doubly as they
perform scenes from their history as strategic interpreters of it.

In *Drama, Metadrama and Perception*, Richard Hornby draws attention to a number of overlapping fields of reality at work when an audience
watches a play-within-a-play or a play that contains metatheatrical elements.
Hornby observes, 'When a character says, "no one dies in the second act,"
audience identification ceases.'[68] A process of identification and separation
occurs as the audience alternates between absorption in the play and an
awareness of its constructedness. This technique of estrangement, related
in part to what Bertolt Brecht calls the *Verfremdungseffekt*, interrupts the
dramatic flow of action and produces an estranging effect between the
spectators and the spectacle they are watching.[69] In Brecht's epic theatre,
this technique prevents the viewer from experiencing an emotional catharsis
and creates critical distance so that analytical thought and, ideally, social
action will occur beyond the performance. When Brecht's theory of theatre
is applied to works of fiction that engage with history through dramatic
modes, as it is in this book, related yet different processes of identification
and separation emerge in the selected texts. Authors use similar patterns
of engaging and estranging techniques to draw readers in and out of the
representation of historical events even though all the 'performances' are
mediated through the written word. The estrangement effect is actually at
work in a literary form as readers are drawn in and out of dramatic frames

67   Tompkins, '"Spectacular Resistance": Metatheatre in Post-Colonial Drama', 45.
68   Richard Hornby, *Drama, Metadrama, and Perception* (Cranbury, NJ: Associated
     University Press, 1986), 115.
69   Brecht, *Brecht on Theatre: The Development of an Aesthetic*, 93.

and are prompted to confront their own complicity in the ways in which they perceive the 'performances' of history. This dramatic technique of estrangement, which is examined in detail in the analysis of Flanagan's *Gould's Book of Fish* in Chapter 5, highlights new possibilities of representing aspects of history evocatively and provocatively through reflexive modes of performance and theatricality.

Rather than estranging, Daphne Marlatt's writing, which is discussed in Chapter 4, provides opportunities for readers to become intimately drawn into the dramatizations of certain characters and creates experiences through performative language itself rather than having language represent or frame a particular experience from a critical distance. While Marlatt cannot escape textual representation on some level, her dramatizations reduce the critical distance from which readers typically analyse a novel. Following a line of thought closer to Stanislavski's method than Brecht's, Marlatt invites readers to embody characters and draw upon their own lived experiences to dramatize the lives of characters from history. Marlatt strives like a number of writers and theorists including Roland Barthes, Samuel Beckett, and Peter Brook, to bring the body and sensory experience into the text.[70] Barthes asks in *The Pleasure of the Text*, 'How can a text, which consists of language, be outside language?'[71] and suggests junctures where the sensual and the physical pierce through prose to arrest the reader. Beckett proposes a revolution against all language that makes

---

70 See Roland Barthes' *The Pleasure of the Text*, trans. Richard Miller (London: Lowe and Brydone, 1975); Samuel Beckett's *Disjecta: Miscellaneous Writings and a Dramatic Fragment*, ed. Ruby Cohn (London: John Calder, 1983); Walter Benjamin's *Illuminations*, ed. Hannah Arendt, trans. Harry Zorn [1955] (London: Pimlico, 1999); and *Reflections: Essays, Aphorisms, Autobiographical Writings*, ed. Peter Demetz, trans. Edmund Jephcott (New York: Schocken Books, 1978); and Peter Brook's *The Empty Space* [1968] (London: Penguin, 1990). Laura U. Marks' *The Skin of the Film: Intercultural Cinema, Embodiment, and the Senses* (Durham: Duke University Press, 2000) also provides excellent commentary on embodied texts and films.

71 Barthes, *The Pleasure of the Text*, 30.

no effort to accommodate Being, or a living presence, inside of it.[72] In *The Empty Space*, Peter Brook writes,

> A word does not start as a word – it is an end product which begins as an impulse, stimulated by attitude and behaviour which dictates the need for expression. This process occurs inside the dramatist; it is repeated inside the actor. Both may only be conscious of the words, but both for the author and then for the actor the word is a small visible portion of a gigantic unseen formula [...]. [They know] the only way to find the true path to the speaking of a word is through a process that parallels the original creative one.[73]

While Brook describes a process that seeks the body (or traces of a body) behind a dramatic text, a similar process of seeking bodily or sensory presences occurs in novels that incorporate dramatic modes. The emphasis on the presence of bodies in the text disrupts the Cartesian hierarchy of mind over body; words do more than express ideas, they also translate gestures and oral and extralinguistic stories.

Summary of Chapters

Chapter 1, 'Melodrama in Thomas Keneally's *The Playmaker* and in David Musgrave's *Glissando*', examines the use of melodrama as an engaging and critically relevant representational mode for examining nineteenth-century colonial Australian society and exploring concepts of history, identity, and historiography in two Australian novels. In *The Playmaker* (1987), Keneally's use of melodrama and other comic dramatic frames reflects the author's optimism towards the nation in a work published just before Australia's Bicentennial in 1988. Keneally's dramatic mode shares qualities with the imperial dramatic mode of representing history, employed by

---

72   Samuel Beckett, *Disjecta: Miscellaneous Writings and a Dramatic Fragment*, ed. Ruby Cohn (London: John Calder, 1983), 172.

73   Peter Brook, *The Empty Space* [1968] (London: Penguin, 1990), 115.

Manning Clark and other Australian historians, with a sense of destiny and the desire to create heroes for the nation. Homi Bhabha's thinking on colonial hybridization and Joanne Tompkins's concept of the split gaze of the audience in postcolonial metatheatre provide a theoretical foundation for the chapter. I apply Tompkins' discussion of the split gaze in postcolonial metatheatre[74] to Keneally's novel to explore how the dramatic act of witnessing can foreground the action of questioning and re-visioning conceptions of history. In a contrasting case of melodrama, David Musgrave's *Glissando* (2010) engages with melodramatic modes in a satirical and ironic manner to examine key moments from Australian history: the orphan motif of growing up without parents in a new land; the dispossession of indigenous peoples; and the murder of innocent indigenous people. The novel incorporates melodrama, satire, and music in its content and form, and melodic and comic tones infuse the narrative and accompany profound political questions surrounding colonialism and its representation in fiction.

Chapter 2, 'Performing Identity in Tomson Highway's *Kiss of the Fur Queen*', focuses on the hybrid structure and content of Highway's first novel, which conveys a semi-autobiographical story that examines historical and political realities for Cree Canadians through mediated dance, oral storytelling, and musical and theatrical performances. The novel demonstrates Highway's resistance against the fixity of text through the incorporation of Cree storytelling, traditionally related in an oral form, and a musical structure where each section of the novel is given a title based on an Italian term from classical music and the main content of each section develops thematically to fit the mood and expression suggested by the musical term. The novel explores a critically significant historical event in Canadian history, which had its parallel in Australia with the Stolen Generations, when thousands of indigenous children were taken from their families in the mid-twentieth century and put in residential schools. *Kiss of the Fur Queen* tells the story of two young Cree brothers who are sexually abused in a residential school in Winnipeg in the 1950s and grow up to develop cultural identities as artists and performers. The brothers' complex and hybridized

---

74   Tompkins, '"Spectacular Resistance": Metatheatre in Post-Colonial Drama', 45.

cultural identities, which are performed, parodied, and interrogated at different points in the novel, are studied in this chapter through an application of four theoretical approaches: Frantz Fanon's identity theory from *Black Skin, White Masks*; Maria Campbell's insights on representing indigenous spirituality in the arts;[75] Angela Van Essen's research on the dialectic particularities of Highway's Cree and the re-appropriation of cultural memory through Cree in-jokes that inspire empowerment; and Gerald Vizenor's concept of 'Native survivance'.[76] Highway engages dramatic structures and performative modes from indigenous and non-indigenous cultures in the text, in what Rachid Belghiti calls 'a counter-movement' that disrupts 'Canada's historiography of exclusion'.[77] The chapter explores how art is integral to life in indigenous cultures rather than an imitation of it as it is often perceived in non-indigenous cultures.[78]

Chapter 3, 'Performing the Nation in Peter Carey's *Illywhacker*', examines a variety of performances of Australian national identity and cultural stereotypes in *Illywhacker* (1985) and positions readers within the narrator's imaginative and meta-theatrical historiography from 1919 to 2025. Displaying the qualities of an Australian picaro, the book's narrator, showman, and con artist, Herbert Badgery uses second-person addresses to call upon readers as spectators within the narrative, encouraging them to take up calls to action as active witnesses. This chapter demonstrates how nationalism is portrayed as a theatrical construct in the novel, and how this effect is rehearsed and sustained through convincing performances by members of the hegemonic majority who shape their Australian identities according to British and American models. It reveals how *Illywhacker*

---

75   Maria Campbell, 'Interview', in Harmut Lutz, ed., *Contemporary Challenges: Conversations with Canadian Native Writers* (Saskatoon: Fifth House Publishing, 1991), 48–56.

76   Angela Van Essen, 'nêhiyawaskiy (Cree Land) and Canada: Location, Language, and Borders in Tomson Highway's *Kiss of the Fur Queen*', *Canadian Literature* 215 (Winter 2012), vi.

77   Rachid Belghiti, 'Choreography, Sexuality, and the Indigenous Body in Tomson Highway's *Kiss of the Fur Queen*', *Postcolonial Text* 5/2 (2009), 3.

78   Belghiti, 'Choreography, Sexuality, and the Indigenous Body in Tomson Highway's *Kiss of the Fur Queen*', 7.

exposes theatrical underpinnings of postcolonial identity politics in Australian culture: how Australian-born characters emulate the British, how first-generation Chinese-Australian immigrants exploit racial stereotypes as 'camouflage', in the manner that Homi Bhabha describes,[79] and how Australian stereotypes are manufactured for export to American and Japanese investors. The chapter ends with an examination of Carey's final image of the 'Best Pet Shop in the World', which contains live human exhibits of Australian stereotypes in relation to which readers are cast as spectators invited to consider a postmodern pastiche of recurring historical types in a dystopic future.

Chapter 4, 'Dramatic Modes and the Feminist Poetics of Enactment in Daphne Marlatt's *Ana Historic*', explores how dramatic modes in this Canadian novel endeavour to make readers feel as though they are immersed in particular moments of history rather than before representations of it. *Ana Historic* draws readers into inhabiting the minds and virtual bodies of a few characters, particularly strong female roles, in ways similar to how Stanislavski's system guides actors to develop characters based on the text and their own lived bodily experiences. Both Della Pollock's and Roland Barthes' theories are influential in this chapter's analysis of how the body and sensory experiences are brought into text, and I apply Barthes' notion of the *punctum* from *Camera Lucida*[80] – the force that pierces through a photo to arrest and enliven a spectator – to Marlatt's work and identify affective junctures where sensual and physical elements rise beyond the words on the page to connect with readers.

Chapter 5, 'Performing History, Violence, and the Unsayable in Richard Flanagan's *Gould's Book of Fish*', explores experimental and performative approaches to representing key events in Australian colonial history, since *Gould's Book of Fish* exposes the limitations of more traditionally linear narrative fictions about history. Flanagan incorporates dramatic distancing strategies, theatrical metaphors, framing devices, satire, and visual art in his narrator's search for compelling forms through which to represent

79   Homi K. Bhabha, *Nation and Narration* (London: Routledge, 1990), 131.
80   Roland Barthes, *Camera Lucida: Reflections on Photography* [1981], trans. Richard Howard (New York: Hill and Wang, 2000).

the life of Gould and the colonization of Aboriginal Tasmanians. This
novel experiments with incorporating presence, or what Samuel Beckett
calls 'Being', inside the writing in order to break out of what Beckett calls
the 'prison' of representational language.[81] This chapter makes connections
between the novel's performative modes of distancing and Bertolt Brecht's
techniques of *Verfremdungseffekt* (estrangement effect) from epic theatre.[82]
Wolfgang Iser's theories of imaginative play in the text also provide a framework for understanding a reader's necessarily active and participatory role
that is required in reading the novel.[83] A close examination of *Gould's Book
of Fish* suggests there are some spaces of trauma from Australian history
that cannot be traversed through any representational modes in fiction.

Chapter 6, 'Filmic and Dramatic Modes in Guy Vanderhaeghe's *The
Englishman's Boy*', examines techniques and narrative structures borrowed
from film and drama and the oscillation between dramatic and cinematic
modes transposed to literature in a Canadian novel set in the American
Wild West in the late 1800s and in Hollywood in the 1930s. Vanderhaeghe
immerses readers in dramatic and sensory representations of history, and
switches between these and cinematic descriptions as the protagonist,
screenwriter Harry Vincent, narrates the process of creating a film based
on Shorty McAdoo's recollections of an historic rebellion at Cypress Hills.
The Englishman's Boy integrates a counterpoint strategy that alternates
between immersion and estrangement as it dramatizes moments based on
history while reminding readers of the inevitable limitations of representation. Dramatic rituals and ceremonies are integrated into the prose, and
film inspires narrative structures in the novel, including crosscuts between
chapters, literary versions of panoramic shots, close-ups and flashbacks. This
chapter explores how the modern and technological modes used to represent stories effectively shape and re-conceive the stories themselves. Walter
Benjamin's 'The Work of Art in the Age of Mechanical Reproduction'[84]
provides a starting point for exploring how the sense of presence found

81   Beckett, *Disjecta: Miscellaneous Writings and a Dramatic Fragment*, 172.
82   Brecht, *Brecht on Theatre: The Development of an Aesthetic*.
83   Iser, 'The Play of the Text', 325–39.
84   Walter Benjamin, 'The Work of Art in the Age of Mechanical Reproduction', 211–44.

in theatre is approximated in the novel's search for the aura of bodies and objects from history that can be sensed but, perhaps, never truly re-captured.

The concluding chapter, 'Taking It Further: Novels that Perform History Inside and Beyond Australian and Canadian Contexts', articulates key points arising from the use and effects of dramatic modes in Australian and Canadian novels that explore history and historiography in fiction, and extends the focus to a few additional novels that integrate dramatic modes in order to consider aspects of history in postcolonial nations outside of Australia and Canada. It examines, for example, in *The God of Small Things* (1997) Arundhati Roy's inclusion of kathakali theatre and dramatic frames around traumatic memories, and in *The Infinite Rehearsal* (1987) Wilson Harris' use of an extended metaphor of a never-ending rehearsal of postcolonial identity. It considers how dramatic processes are approached in the selected novels through mediated means and ends with some final reflections on the possibilities and limitations of dramatic modes these novels deploy.

Dramatic modes in fiction generate a range of ways of interpreting postcolonial history, from positioning readers to take a hopeful, intimate or nostalgic view or one that is more despairing, removed, or ironic. This book will study novels that bring an energetic force, borrowed from theatre, to the texts. Some novels are enlivened through theatrical techniques of Stanislavski's embodiment of character, as in in Marlatt's *Ana Historic*, and others are animated by Brecht's estrangement techniques, seen in *Gould's Book of Fish*, and melodramatic conventions, deployed in Musgrave's *Glissando*. Dramatic modes highlight role-playing that is such a pervasive feature in colonial and postcolonial contexts, seen in Carey's *Illywhacker*, where the picaresque model of narration brings out and challenges stereotypes of race and culture through role-playing and directing the reader's gaze. *When Novels Perform History* examines how the energetic force we find in the theatre is translated into novels, using mediated versions of melodrama, reflexive staging, immersive and distancing techniques, and considers the varied creative and political effects, appeals, and challenges of these interdisciplinary modes.

While the dramatic, performative, and theatrical modes explored here exist through texts – not intended for performance – the application of dramatic modes to colonial and postcolonial fiction creates new stirrings; some novels are enhanced with animated intensity, others benefit from theatrical frames that result in reflexive and parodic re-visioning as a way of conveying extra-textual connotations. In a range of incarnations, the dramatic modes in fiction about history and historiography invite readers to take an imaginative leap and collaborate as participants in creative interdisciplinary forms that explore, in ground-breaking ways, the sensory, resonant, confronting, and dynamic experiences of colonial and postcolonial pasts through fiction, drama, and the imagination.

CHAPTER I

Melodrama in Thomas Keneally's *The Playmaker* and in David Musgrave's *Glissando*

Although melodrama has been criticized since its golden age in the nineteenth century for its sentimentalism, stock characters, and predictable happy endings, it has in recent years begun to be redefined as a useful field of study by contemporary critics, particularly in film and drama, for its ability to give rise to affective revelations and portray emotional depths,[1] and for its genre-crossing propensities.[2] Melodrama is employed in some Australian history books to explore dramatic conflict, hardship, and morality, as in Manning Clark's popular six-volume series, *A History of Australia*.[3] In addition to its uses on stage, in film, and in history books, melodrama has engaging and evocative applications in literature and this chapter identifies how melodrama is used to great effect in two contrasting novels that explore significant aspects of Australia's history: Thomas Keneally's *The Playmaker* (1987) and David Musgrave's *Glissando* (2001). Outside of this book, readers will also find observations of melodrama in

1   See Jeremy Maron, 'Affective Historiography: Schindler's List, Melodrama and Historical Representation', *Shofar* 27/4 (2009), 66–94; Linda Williams, 'Melodrama Revised', in Nick Browne, ed., *Refiguring American Film Genres* (Berkeley: University of California Press, 1998). Also useful is Veronica Kelly, 'Melodrama, an Australian Pantomime, and the Theatrical Constructions of Colonial History', *Journal of Australian Studies* 17/38 (1993), 51–61, which looks at the connection between theatrical melodrama and the construction of Australian colonial identities.

2   See Marcie Frank, 'At the Intersections of Mode, Genre, and Media: A Dossier of Essays on Melodrama', *Criticism* 55/4 (Autumn 2013), 535–45, on the intermediality of melodrama and its connection to modernity.

3   Manning Clark, *A History of Australia*, 6 vols [1963–1987] (Carlton: Melbourne University Press, 1998).

Australian novels by Marcus Clarke, Christina Stead, Kate Grenville, and Patrick White.[4] Melodrama is a representational mode that is particularly well suited to exploring some of the key characteristics of early Australian colonial society that contained moral conflicts, emotional excesses of feeling and a shift toward secular society. Melodrama provides a means for readers to imagine key moments of Australian history through a stylized and dramatic mode that appeals to emotional truths and may reveal insightful underlying counter-narratives. This chapter considers the uses and effects of melodrama and the various melancholic, ironic, secular, and comic versions of history it generates in Australian fiction. While a number of novels using melodrama can be drawn from Australia (or from Canada or other postcolonial countries in a larger study), I have limited the discussion to Keneally's *The Playmaker* and Musgrave's *Glissando* to explore the contrast between the authors' distinct representations of history that reflect prevalent attitudes from their times using melodramatic modes in novels written approximately twenty-five years apart.

Thomas Keneally, born in Sydney and best known for his historical fiction, is a prolific, provocative figure in Australian literature. He has written more than thirty novels, non-fiction, drama, and a children's book. Keneally is a popular author, drawn to history and various modes of representing it to celebrate his vision of his country. His novels have won prestigious national and international literary prizes including the Miles Franklin Award for *Three Cheers for Paraclete* in 1968 and the Booker Prize for *Schindler's List* in 1982. *The Playmaker* is Keneally's third and brightest version of a colonial and convict tale that he has written over a period of thirty years and it was published one year before the celebration of Australia's Bicentenary in 1988. Keneally tells the story of the settlement of the first colony in New South Wales in melodramatic and comedic modes and celebrates the transformation of convicts coming together as colonials to perform a play as a symbol of creative harmony and, through this, he shows the possibilities for a bright future. Two reviewers of *The Playmaker* declare, 'This is Mr. Keneally

4   Peter Pierce studies a few melodramatic fictions by these authors in *Australian Melodramas: Thomas Keneally's Fiction* (St Lucia: University of Queensland Press, 1995), 159–77.

at his best' (The Daily Telegraph) and 'Keneally shows all his usual skill in breathing life into bare facts' (New Statesman).⁵ However, Keneally's presentation of the colonial settlement which is viewed so optimistically in the story of the colony's first play in *The Playmaker* has attracted a fair amount of negative attention from literary critics for its revisionary and conservative tone, which will be examined in this chapter. Keneally's *The Playmaker* reinforces a particular imperial view of colonial history, similar to what Paul Carter identifies in early Australian historical narratives as 'imperial history' or the 'staging of history',⁶ where historians portrayed the destiny of white colonials unfolding in a new and empty land, centre stage, and indigenous people functioned as either extras or backdrop. While much of *The Playmaker* portrays Keneally's white, paternalistic, conservative attitude that does not look particularly critically into the past, the use of dramatic modes in the novel suggests to readers, specifically in the epilogue, a crack in the authoritative impression Keneally constructs that history can be known fully and presented as a *fait d'accompli*. Keneally's uses of metatheatre and melodrama in the novel show a formal innovation in that they incorporate the energy of theatre to animate a version of history that has within it a multitude of enactment and interpretive possibilities of colonial life, not all of which can be revealed in a single telling.

David Musgrave, a celebrated Sydney poet, publisher, academic, and short story writer, engages with melodrama in several ways in *Glissando*, his first and highly acclaimed novel, and displays dexterity in alternating between satire and melodrama in a fictive but familiar version of Australian history. Georgie Williamson in *The Australian* praised 'the care [Musgrave] takes in balancing scholarly fastidiousness with a poet's luminous prose, high comedy with mortal seriousness'.⁷ *The Weekend Australian* called it 'an Australian classic, a satirical romp of epic proportions' and another critic

---

5   Keneally, *The Playmaker*, ii.
6   Paul Carter, *The Road to Botany Bay: An Essay in Spatial History* [1987] (New York: Knopf, 1988).
7   Geordie Williamson, 'A Spiritual Superiority: Glissando Review', *The Australian*, Arts, 24 April 2010 <http://www.theaustralian.com.au/arts/books/review-musgrave-glissando/story-e6frg8nf-1225856027192> accessed 10 August 2016.

focuses on its use of melodrama as a fitting literary reflection of Australian tall tales and one that facilitates self-reflection: 'the melodramatic style – filled with music, exaggerated characters, and improbable events – echo[es] the great Australian yarn to brilliantly satirize the chequered history of art in this country' (*Bookseller and Publisher*).[8] Some of the melodrama in *Glissando* is mournful and wrought with melancholy as Musgrave engages with expressive musical and melodramatic conventions that lift the novel beyond the conventional limitations of a more static or traditional text. More of the melodrama found in *Glissando*, however, is satirical and exaggerated so far as to reach the realm of the absurd. In both of its usages in the novel, melancholic and exaggerated, melodrama helps to expose injustices towards indigenous people, crises in Australian identity, and the need for a representational form that examines the past with an awareness of embodied histories. It considers performativity as a powerful tool for examining and imagining Australian identities from the past.

Before taking a closer look at melodrama at work in the two novels and examining melodrama's capacity to explore aspects of Australian history in fiction, it is useful to examine the origins of melodrama and its characteristics. The genre of melodrama has a long history of boundary-crossing. Marcie Frank describes how melodrama was first used to signify 'dramatic speech accompanied by music' in Paris with Rene-Charles Guilbert de Pixerecourt's *Ceolina, ou l'Enfant du mystère* (1800), which was translated into English by Thomas Hocroft as *The Tale of Mystery: A Melo-drame* (1802) and performed at Covent Garden.[9] Melodrama later grew to include elements from dance and pantomime and used elaborate sets and mechanical 'multimedia performance elements' which consolidated its connection with modern technology.[10] In *Melodrama and Modernity* (2001), Ben Singer positions melodrama as a 'cluster concept' of elements

---

8   Both reviews qtd in *Glissando Reviews* <http://sleeperspublishing.com/2011/produ
     ct-1/> accessed 10 August 2016.
9   Frank, 'At the Intersections of Mode, Genre, and Media: A Dossier of Essays on
     Melodrama', 536–7.
10   Frank, 'At the Intersections of Mode, Genre, and Media: A Dossier of Essays on
     Melodrama', 536–7.

whose composition typically contains some of the following basic features: pathos, heightened emotion, moral polarization between good and evil, sensationalism, spectacle, and a non-classical structure of implausible plots and solutions.[11] Singer includes Lea Jacobs' idea of 'situation' as an essential element of melodrama where twists of fate, deadly peril, startling reversals and suspense typically define melodramatic plots.[12]

There are productive connections to be made between the genre of melodrama – with its capacity to enact a range of intense emotions – and how it can be used in fiction to examine the construction of Australian colonial identities that derive from a context of conflict between settlers and indigenous people, lost child narratives, battles with nature, alienation, and coming to terms with the past in an uncertain future. In a study of the role of melodrama in the construction of Australian colonial identities in theatre, Veronica Kelly argues that melodrama 'carries a more formidable libidinal charge than the spectacular or comic forms: a charge which is, typically, ambivalently utopian and dystopic'[13] and is well suited as a representational mode for a society defined by its 'mythic narratives' and 'deadly struggle' between settlers and indigenous people.[14] Kelly maintains that much of the libidinal charge generated by melodrama is due to the tension delivered by its at once utopian and dystopic qualities.[15] In a melodrama in theatre, Kelly observes, the conclusion may offer salvation but 'the ghostly outlines of the potential alternative outcomes remain to shadow the particular scripted conclusion and lend it resonance, ambiguity, and a sense of provisory unease'.[16] Melodrama delivers this dramatic

11 Ben Singer, *Melodrama and Modernity: Early Sensational Cinema and Its Contexts* (New York: Columbia University Press, 2001), 44–9.
12 Singer, *Melodrama and Modernity: Early Sensational Cinema and Its Contexts*, 41.
13 Veronica Kelly, 'Melodrama, an Australian pantomime, and the theatrical constructions of colonial history', *Journal of Australian Studies* 17/38 (1993), 53.
14 Kelly, 'Melodrama, an Australian pantomime, and the theatrical constructions of colonial history', 51.
15 Kelly, 'Melodrama, an Australian pantomime, and the theatrical constructions of colonial history', 53.
16 Kelly, 'Melodrama, an Australian pantomime, and the theatrical constructions of colonial history', 53.

tension in certain novels, and a charge, even as it is mediated through text on the page. Melodrama, in some instances, signals the novelists' desires to cross boundaries in search of a genre that is inherently embodied, even as the melodrama is operating within a novel. This chapter will investigate alternate possibilities of salvation and despair that haunt the melodramatic contexts of Keneally's *The Playmaker* and Musgrave's *Glissando* and discover how melodrama can be used to convey the elusive energies and psychological anxieties of the colonial past filtered through the authors' individual perspectives.

Keneally's Optimistic View of History in *The Playmaker*

The Playmaker, published in 1987, creates an overall optimistic portrayal of relations between colonial officials and convicts in the first criminal colony in New South Wales in 1789, focusing on the white characters and their potential in the new world with the indigenous characters in the background. Melodrama and metatheatre are key components of Keneally's dramatic mode which emphasizes role-playing and rehearsing as metaphors for the formative stages of colonial society and depicts how convicts and colonial officials rehearse their futures and transform their fantasies into reality. Readers may be moved to feel emotional undercurrents and become drawn in as reflexive spectators before certain melodramatic representations of history in *The Playmaker*.

Keneally's *The Playmaker* engages with drama in its content and its form. The novel describes the performance of the first European play in what later became Australia, in the New South Wales convict colony in 1789. Theatre is not restricted to the stage in the novel: hangings, ghosts, secret love affairs and murders occur in the convicts' everyday lives and blur the lines between performance and reality. Theatre also structures the form of the novel. Keneally arranges the chapters in five parts, as in a five-act play, with the convicts' performance of George Farquhar's *The Recruiting Officer*, directed by Lieutenant Ralph Clark, providing the finale in the fifth part. The first few pages of *The Playmaker* include an advertisement for the play, a cast list and a programme listing the actors' crimes and former occupations, which place a reader in the role of a spectator who has come to watch *The Recruiting Officer*. The information about the convicts is listed in these opening pages in detail, suggesting historical authenticity, although there are discrepancies surrounding some fictionalized characters in Keneally's novel who do not exist in comprehensive historical documents and databases such as *The Journal and Letters of Lt. Ralph Clark 1787–1792*, or who appear under different names in the journals of Watkin Tench or Davy Collins.[17]

In the Author's Note, Keneally stipulates that the novel is based on 'rich material' from the historical evidence in First Fleet journals, where a list of historical sources is acknowledged,[18] yet his selectively bright view of colonization has prompted some critical debate in line with discussions of revisionist history in fiction. Keneally appears to select facts from historical journals that contribute to an overall positive and hegemonic view of colonial history in *The Playmaker*. Peter Quartermaine suggests Keneally puts on a skilled performance as a 'Bookmaker' with his obsession about 'staging the scene' with 'facts' from history.[19] Ruth Brown accurately identifies Keneally's vision of Australian history as 'conservative' and 'resembl[ing] that of an earlier period'.[20] Brown criticizes the confident ease with which Keneally refers to the knowability of history as if it was 'unearthed and shaped by [...] historians', requiring only to be brought into the imaginative light by novelists.[21]

17   'The Journal and Letters of Lt. Ralph Clark 1787–1792', *SETIS database*, ed. Paul G. Fidlon and R. J. Ryan <http://purl.library.usyd.edu.au/setis/id/clajour> accessed 10 July 2016.

18   Keneally, *The Playmaker*, xi.

19   Peter Quartermaine, *Thomas Keneally: 'The Bookmaker: The Playmaker'*, Modern Fiction Series (London: Hodder & Stoughton, 1991).

20   Ruth Brown, 'From Keneally to Wertenbaker: Sanitizing the System', in Ian Duffield and James Bradley, eds, *Representing convicts: new perspectives on convict forced labour migration* (London and Washington: Leicester University Press, 1997), 83.

21   Brown, 'From Keneally to Wertenbaker: Sanitizing the System', 78.

A noteworthy historical discrepancy lies in Keneally's portrayal of Ralph Clark as a genteel, even-handed theatre-maker and leader of the new nation, which contradicts the representation of the historical Ralph Clark, who recorded in his journal frequent complaints against 'the damned bitches of convict women' and 'damned whores', later re-printed in Robert Hughes' *The Fatal Shore: A History of the Transportation of Convicts to Australia, 1787–1868*.[22] Ruth Brown observes how, for artistic reasons, Keneally creates historical possibilities for Ralph Clark that depart from the historical journals in order to generate a 'perception of the Australian nation as potentially unified and self-regulating', and which accord with the novel's publication one year before the Australian Bicentenary.[23] The portrayal of Ralph Clark as genteel is also, as Brown suggests, unlikely to offend Australian feminists who, in Keneally's words, 'had a field day' with the misogynistic view of women the historical Ralph Clark exhibited in his historical journals.[24] Brown expresses concern at Keneally's willingness to change or over-simplify the 'facts' of history in order to appeal to the political climate in which he was writing, suggesting that readers are likely to believe it all because of its convincing performance of authority, and to look no further than the novel for the facts of history.[25] Keneally's performance of authority in the novel offers little self-reflexivity or doubt about the 'knowability' of history in its roseate version of Ralph Clark and the settlement constructed to suit the political climate of the day until the epilogue. Readers may be led to believe, through the convincing authoritative tone in the novel and in the Author's Note, that Keneally's claims about the colony are derived more carefully from existing historical sources than they are, and, as such, readers may not be cued to consider history's inevitable gaps and unrecorded stories from the past. However, Keneally lifts the veil of his authoritative performance in the epilogue when he changes the tone of his narration and suggests there are certain limitations in working from historical records, alluding to the possibilities afforded by the genre

---

22   Hughes qtd in Brown, 'From Keneally to Wertenbaker: Sanitizing the System', 81.
23   Brown, 'From Keneally to Wertenbaker: Sanitizing the System', 80.
24   Keneally qtd in Brown, 'From Keneally to Wertenbaker: Sanitizing the System', 80.
25   Brown, 'From Keneally to Wertenbaker: Sanitizing the System', 81.

of fiction. *The Playmaker* ends with a reference to the potentially bright futures of Mary Brenham and Alicia, Ralph Clark's and Mary Brenham's 'new-world' daughter, who do not, according to Keneally and the online SETIS database,[26] appear in known historical accounts. Keneally writes: 'Of them fiction could make much, though history says nothing.'[27]

Keneally has made significant changes in dramatizing and re-framing the convict experience from his first novel on the colony, *Bring Larks and Heroes* (1967), to his seventeenth novel, *The Playmaker* (1987), reflecting changes in Australian society and in Keneally's sense of where he fits in within it. Both *Bring Larks and Heroes* and *The Playmaker* use melodramatic conventions to describe colonial life in Australia, yet *Bring Larks and Heroes* has overtones of desperation and tragedy while *The Playmaker* shines a brighter light on the settlement and celebrates the potential for the colonial officials and convicts to create a new society. In *Bring Larks and Heroes* (1967), based on Keneally's earlier play *Halloran's Little Boat* (1966), the new colony is a place from which characters are desperate to escape and where food is scarce and punishments are harsh. Convict Quinn, sent to the colony with ten months left to serve on a seven-year sentence, is doomed to serve indefinitely because there are no records that support his claims to freedom. In *Bring Larks and Heroes*, Keneally focuses on injustices, the brutality of beating and suffering, and class conflicts from the Old World that persist in the New World. A man is charged with rape even though Corporal Halloran tells the Major that the man is a eunuch. Because the Major is hungry for a scapegoat, the eunuch hangs.[28] The novel begins with the secret marriage of Halloran and Ann, and ends with their deaths. Keneally creates classic melodramatic dichotomies of villains who wield power over helpless innocents.

Compared to its use in *Bring Larks and Heroes*, however, the melodramatic mode in *The Playmaker* is often playful, and focuses on hope

26 'The Journal and Letters of Lt. Ralph Clark 1787–1792', *SETIS database*, ed. Paul G. Fidlon and R. J. Ryan <http://purl.library.usyd.edu.au/setis/id/clajour> accessed 10 July 2016.

27 Keneally, *The Playmaker*, 364.

28 Keneally, *Bring Larks and Heroes* (London: Cassell, 1967), 84.

rather than tragedy. Melodrama and comedy are frames through which Keneally selectively celebrates the creativity of the colonial settlers in *The Playmaker* and withholds the direst consequences. An unofficial marriage union between Lieutenant Ralph Clark and the convict Mary Brenham is a cause for happiness and Clark's death in the epilogue is eased with the birth of their daughter. Even in explicitly violent scenes of hangings and beatings, the narrative does not linger on the suffering bodies but shifts to the reactions of the witnesses.

In an interview, Keneally spoke about the sense of alienation and dis-connection he created in *Bring Larks and Heroes* that echoed 'the cultural alienation that a lot of Australians felt' in the 1960s.[29] He described a move-ment from 'alienation' to 'affirmation' between the 1960s and the 1990s in his own sense of belonging to Australia.[30] With *The Playmaker*, Keneally approaches the past with greater confidence and pride, although his choices in this novel to portray colonization in such bright tones led Peter Pierce, who mostly champions Keneally's work in *Australian Melodramas*, to call Keneally a 'wholesale revisionist' with his 'sunnier version of national history'.[31] Keneally's re-framing of the colonial experience in *The Playmaker* is reflective of a particularly conservative late 1980s' white consciousness.

In 1988, the Australian Bicentenary was celebrated with an outpouring of novels, plays, and books, along with productions, projects, exhibits, and events by 'more than 6500 artists' for 'approximately 5.3 million' spectators to celebrate the country's history.[32] Controversy surrounded the year-long event and divided Australians, some of whom felt the artistic and cultural celebrations marked the anniversary of the nation's beginning without due acknowledgement of the colonization of indigenous Australians. The

29   Keneally qtd in Peter Pierce, *Australian Melodramas: Thomas Keneally's Fiction*, 29.
30   Pierce, *Australian Melodramas: Thomas Keneally's Fiction*, 29.
31   Pierce, *Australian Melodramas: Thomas Keneally's Fiction*, 29.
32   Peter qtd in Joanne Tompkins, 'Celebrate 1988? Australian Drama in the Bicentennial year', in George Shaw, ed., *1988 and All That: New Views of Australia's Past* (St Lucia: University of Queensland Press, 1988), 103 and George Shaw's 'Bicentennial Writing: Revealing Ash in the Australian Soul' in the same book for more on the Australian Bicentenary Celebrations.

Australian Bicentennial Authority (ABA) was criticized for avoiding issues of indigenous welfare and inequality and glossing over the contributions of women in history and elements in Australian history that did not contribute toward the 'Anglo-centric, male-oriented [...] myths of Australia'.[33] George Shaw wrote, 'Not knowing how to handle Australia's convict origins, or its racism, or its working-class origins, or its socialist-utopianism, or the record of conflict between settler and Aborigine, [the ABA] ignored them.'[34]

The Playmaker can be classified within a category of Bicentenary projects that focuses on the achievements of white colonials and elides significant and formative moments in the nation's colonization of indigenous people. However, the innovations of melodramatic form in Keneally's novel may distinguish it as presenting a new way to interpret some elusive possibilities of representing history. Its dramatic mode offers readers a glimpse into the author's search for a fictive frame that suggests the possibility of alternate perspectives and enactments of history – actions behind the 'scenes' – that are not explored in many historical fictions, while also suggesting some ambivalent melodramatic tensions in the colonial nation's beginnings. *The Playmaker*, in emphasizing how performative interpretations may vary according to their audience, director's vision, players, locale, and other factors, intimates that the nation's history could also be written, staged, directed, and presented in more ways than it has been in this particular rendition.

A theatrical adaptation of *The Playmaker* called *Our Country's Good*, by Timberlake Wertenbaker, was written and staged in 1988 with a focus on the productive creativity of the penal colony.[35] It was developed through interviews with contemporary prisoners and has looser ties to historical journals than does Keneally's novel. American-British playwright Timberlake Wertenbaker wrote *Our Country's Good* for the Royal Court Writers series in London and focused on the power of theatre to unify and liberate the

---

33   Tompkins, 'Celebrate 1988? Australian Drama in the Bicentennial year', 103.
34   Shaw qtd in Tompkins, 'Celebrate 1988? Australian Drama in the Bicentennial year', 104.
35   Timberlake Wertenbaker, *Our Country's Good* [1988], The Royal Court Writer's Series (London: Methuen Drama, 1991).

founders and convict colonials of a new land. Ruth Brown notes that in this theatrical adaptation of *The Playmaker*, indigenous characters 'recede [further] into the background'.[36] According to workshop notes and interviews with playwright Timberlake Wertenbaker and director Max Stafford-Clark, modern-day prisoners were interviewed for Wertenbaker's script which had been commissioned as a Joint Stock production – where improvisation and discussion are part of the devising process – and the prisoners' experiences guided much of the developmental focus of the play resulting in a less historically accurate version that resonated with contemporary prisoners.[37] Historical research from colonial diaries and Robert Hughes's non-fictional *The Fatal Shore* on life in the NSW prison colony were interpreted in light of the contemporary prisoners' modern-day experiences of what theatre meant to them while they were incarcerated.[38] *Our Country's Good* was a box-office success in the Royal Court Theatre in London in 1988 and was later revived by inmates in the Blundeston prison in Lowestoft, England in 1989, marking a symbolic return to the story's penal colony origins. *Our Country's Good* later played on Broadway in 1991.

Keneally's Melodramatic Mode in *The Playmaker*

In *The Melodramatic Imagination*, Peter Brooks draws connections between how Keneally and Honoré de Balzac both use melodrama in their novels 'as a mode of conception and expression' and 'as a certain fictional system for making sense of experience'.[39] Balzac drew on a 'variety of theatrical substrata' including a repertory of gestures, expressions, and tropes in order to create a set of representations already informed by the theatre with

36   Brown, 'From Keneally to Wertenbaker: Sanitizing the System', 82.
37   Brown, 'From Keneally to Wertenbaker: Sanitizing the System', 82.
38   Brown, 'From Keneally to Wertenbaker: Sanitizing the System', 82.
39   Peter Brooks, *The Melodramatic Imagination: Balzac, Henry James, Melodrama, and the Mode of Excess*, xiii.

recognizable meanings.[40] Keneally incorporates similar melodramatic conventions in *The Playmaker*, emphasizing gestures and grand expressions, and lingering on courtroom dramas, theatrical interruptions, and moral confrontations between good and evil and Christianity and paganism. Keneally explores the profound shifts in the lives of the late eighteenth-century convicts and colonial officials and the Manichean battles within and amongst colonial officers who adapt their morals within a transitioning society. Characters, inspired by historical people, such as Reverend Dick Johnson, a missionary, and Harry Brewer, a reformed convict turned Provost Marshal who takes a New World wife, struggle in melodramatic fashion to clarify their moral codes.

Eric Bentley suggests in *The Life of the Drama*, that melodrama belongs to the 'phase of a child's life where he creates magic worlds'.[41] Keneally develops a similar idea in *The Playmaker* in suggesting that Lieutenant Ralph Clark, through his play and melodramatic perspectives on society, possesses a sense of optimism and possibility for his country like that of a creative child. Although Keneally, in his epilogue, claims that melodrama is out of fashion, he draws on it often, in scenes where Ralph Clark mistakes Mary Brenham's identity, which heightens his sexual excitement in pursuing her,[42] when Duckling poisons Goose,[43] and in Harry Lovell's and James Freeman's last minute reprieve from hanging.[44] These melodramatic scenes emphasize the highly dramatized environment as a new society is created. The epilogue reads:

> In recounting the further destinies of our playmaker and our players in that third world of the past, one is aware of the dangers posed by melodrama. Antibiotics and plumbing have made melodrama laughable to the modern reader. It is only in our own third world, where in the one phase of time lovers are sundered, clans consumed and infants perish without once saying, 'Mother', that melodrama causes tears still to flow.[45]

40 Brooks, *The Melodramatic Imagination: Balzac, Henry James, Melodrama, and the Mode of Excess*, 148.
41 Eric Bentley, *The Life of the Drama* (London: Methuen, 1965), 217.
42 Keneally, *The Playmaker*, 317.
43 Keneally, *The Playmaker*, 355.
44 Keneally, *The Playmaker*, 122.
45 Keneally, *The Playmaker*, 359–60.

In *The Melodramatic Imagination*, Brooks champions the humanity and democracy of melodrama which 'makes its representations clear' to all those who view it[46] and sees melodrama as an ideal form in an increasingly secular world. He argues that melodrama 'comes into being in a world where the traditional imperatives of truth and ethics have been violently thrown into question'.[47] In *Australian Melodramas*, Peter Pierce holds a similar view as he examines melodrama in Australian novels: 'Melodrama is the art of a world where Christian beliefs have lost their firm hold over many of the professedly faithful'.[48]

Keneally depicts in *The Playmaker* a world in which theatre offers a secular alternative to religion. Through melodramatic frames, Ralph Clark reveals that no common faith unites the disparate population of the colony; the only thing that comes close to doing so is theatre. Reverend Dick Johnson exhorts Ralph Clark to choose Christianity over his sacrilegious play. Ralph Clark, who sees the faith and hope that the play brings his convicts, and enjoys his own God-like role as director, responds by saying, 'I must choose to be theatrical.'[49] As Ralph Clark proceeds with the play, the limitations of Christianity are explored. Ghosts, conventional in Victorian melodramas, return dramatically from the dead to haunt the colony, and the Reverend is unable to exorcize Handy Baker's spirit from Harry Brewer's hut. Keneally's use of melodrama exploits the cracks where a traditional Christian framework fails to explain the increasingly secular world. As Ralph Clark sees how the play has the power 'to summon people',[50] he begins to believe in the possibility of theatre as salvation and a means of unifying the colony.

Another element in Keneally's dramatic mode in *The Playmaker* is comedy. From Robert Sideway's over-acting to Meg Long's appreciative

---

46   Brooks, *The Melodramatic Imagination: Balzac, Henry James, Melodrama, and the Mode of Excess*, 15.
47   Brooks, *The Melodramatic Imagination: Balzac, Henry James, Melodrama, and the Mode of Excess*, 16.
48   Pierce, *Australian Melodramas: Thomas Keneally's Fiction*, 168.
49   Keneally, *The Playmaker*, 87.
50   Keneally, *The Playmaker*, 344.

farting from the wings, Keneally's description of the first reading of the Farquhar play is comedic on the scale of Shakespeare's mechanicals in *A Midsummer Night's Dream*. Comedy extends beyond the rehearsals with mistaken identities and humour being used to level classes between Harry Brewer and Goose.[51] Comedy in the novel helps to capture the sense of joy and creative discovery that characters experience in playing new roles on and off the stage.

Audience and Performativity in *The Playmaker*

Keneally's opening pages of *The Playmaker* – an advertisement, programme, and cast list – address readers as part of an inner audience of convicts and colonials who will view the first European play in the New World. These items present readers with an opportunity to examine their positioning before a historical representation rendered in fiction, to consider with which characters they are asked to align their sympathies, and to bring reflexivity to the act of 'watching' a recreation of a production from the past. The explicit invitation to join a theatrical audience of *The Recruiting Officer* calls attention to larger questions readers of *The Playmaker* may consider in the way in which we respond, either as passive spectators or as inquiring interpreters, in response to representations of history in any work of fiction.

In *The Playmaker*, Keneally constructs a sense of performativity in the colony with a range of off-stage dramatic performances at court trials, public hangings, and the staged capture of indigenous people. Convict Tom Barrett is described as giving 'the prescribed lag performance' in his trial and hanging,[52] while Ketch, the ex-convict, 'performs his public function' in his newly appointed role as colony executioner.[53] Keneally describes a range

---

51   Keneally, *The Playmaker*, 294.
52   Keneally, *The Playmaker*, 123.
53   Keneally, *The Playmaker*, 132.

of melodramatic performances that can be anticipated in an Australian penal colony where, as Veronica Kelly points out, the 'colonial stage was a primary site of [...] discursive contests',[54] although some of these rather tragic scenes are portrayed with a comic undertone in *The Playmaker*. Keneally describes, for example, Arabanoo's initial capture as a comedic performance watched by a few audiences, and shows Ralph Clark to be a woefully inept interpreter of Arabanoo and his situation.

When Arabanoo is captured by a small group of colonial officials, Lieutenant Ralph Clark and some higher-ranking officers watch indigenous women watching the event.[55] Both audiences watching are subject to the further removed audience of a reader who processes the receptions of the inner characters through a contemporary perspective. Arabanoo is dragged ashore while a female convict makes 'a speech of mock praise of the native's manhood' to the amusement of the white characters.[56] When Arabanoo is returned 'tethered' and 'manacled' to Sydney Cove, Keneally's omniscient narrator through Ralph Clark's perspective describes the event as 'something of a raw comedy'.[57] It is ambiguous whether or not Keneally is aiming for comic relief at Ralph Clark's light-hearted take on the scene of capture or rather to show distance between how the scene was perceived by Ralph Clark as opposed to how it might be interpreted by readers 200 years later. Perhaps Keneally intends both aims here. The reader is positioned to observe how Ralph Clark interprets the scene and to reconcile the split gaze of the character's interpretation within the reader's own interpretation of the larger picture, regardless of whether or not the reader is also amused or dismayed by what Ralph Clark sees.

Joanne Tompkins' discussion of the split gaze of the audience in postcolonial metatheatre can be applied to the situation of multiple audiences in *The Playmaker*. In 'Spectacular Resistance', Tompkins observes that a split gaze is created between an audience watching a play and an audience watching a play-within-a-play and has particular significance in a

---

54   Kelly, 'Melodrama, an Australian pantomime, and the theatrical constructions of colonial history', 61.
55   Keneally, *The Playmaker*, 164.
56   Keneally, *The Playmaker*, 169.
57   Keneally, *The Playmaker*, 169.

postcolonial context.[58] Tompkins' examples of postcolonial plays that feature metatheatre include Winston Ntshona's *The Island*, Louis Nowra's
The Golden Age, Wole Soyinka's *Death and the King's Horseman*, Derek
Walcott's *Pantomime*, and Monique Mojica's *Princess Pocahontas and the
blue spots*. When the audience of a theatrical play watches the actors on
stage watching the action, Tompkins argues, 'the audience's gaze is split and,
paradoxically, multiplied, to further foreground the action of re-visioning'
and that these plays 'offer possible ways to re-read metatheatrical moments
as locations of deliberate dis-location of colonial power'.[59]

Novels also use the potential of the audience's split and magnified
gaze, as in Arabanoo's capture scene in Keneally's *The Playmaker*, when a
reader's interpretive vision is split between the characters who are being
watched and the other characters who interpret what happens as a kind of
performance. Tompkins argues that in postcolonial metatheatrical plays,
the sites of split vision represent the 'location[s] of difference, ambivalence
and resistance in metatheatre'.[60] In *The Playmaker*, the dramatic mode in
scenes between colonial and indigenous characters portrays the characters
in the novel becoming witnesses to and interpreters of history, and provide
a vantage point for readers to witness and interpret the narrative frames
within their own particular contemporary context.

The Empty Stage and Imperial History

The empty stage in *The Playmaker* is used as an allegory for the New South
Wales colony to explore how colonial officials viewed their land as *terra
nullius* upon which history was staged.[61] On the eve of the play, Ralph

---

58   Tompkins, 'Spectacular Resistance': Metatheatre in Post-Colonial Drama', 42–51.
59   Tompkins, 'Spectacular Resistance': Metatheatre in Post-Colonial Drama', 45.
60   Tompkins, 'Spectacular Resistance': Metatheatre in Post-Colonial Drama', 45.
61   *Terra nullius* refers to the concept that land was considered ethically empty if the
      people who occupied it were not considered to be 'civilized' by the people who

Clark stands on the makeshift stage and feels a sense of reaching back in time to the rehearsals, and forward to the performance, in the same instant. Keneally writes: 'Everything was unlit, yet the stage seemed to him [...] to be still radiant with the latent energy of that afternoon's costumed enactment. Echoes not of past but of coming laughter filled the space.'[62] As Ralph Clark's anticipation for the performance mounts, he feels the potentiality of what will come growing stronger than his memory of what has been. An erasure of the past occurs as Ralph Clark's anticipation for the future increases. Keneally's theatrical allegory of the empty stage suggests how the colonial officials viewed the Sydney Cove colony as a space of erasure with a potentiality so keenly anticipated as to convince them that its entire previous history was wiped clean.

The disavowal of indigenous culture and society enabled the colonial officials to clear the stage, so to speak, and begin a re-staging of history. Keneally suggests in *The Playmaker* that the idea of the virgin stage was irresistible to his characters and to Ralph Clark in particular. Ralph Clark touts the production as 'the very first presentation of this or any other play ever performed on this new penal planet, which so far as anyone knew had gone from the beginning of time till now absolutely play-less and theatre-less.'[63] By proclaiming the land of the oldest known society in the world to be 'absolutely play-less and theatre-less', the novel exposes how Ralph Clark negates all indigenous theatre that transpired before him. In the epilogue, Keneally mentions indigenous theatre that pre-dates the Farquhar play, stating that the beginning of European theatre in the colony 'would consume in the end the different and serious theatre of the tribes of the hinterland'.[64] This reference is, however, withheld until the novel's end, and symbolizes how the colonial officials perceived the colony as an empty stage for their

---

colonized it. This legal fiction was challenged and overturned in 1992 in the landmark Mabo vs Queensland land rights case. See Harry Gibbs' 'Foreword' in Stephenson and Ratnapala, *Mabo: A Judicial Revolution* (University of Queensland Press, 1993).

62   Keneally, *The Playmaker*, 339.
63   Keneally, *The Playmaker*, 19.
64   Keneally, *The Playmaker*, 359.

purposes and relegated indigenous people to the sidelines of the theatrical production and the colony itself.

Some of Australia's most well-known historians, including Manning Clark, have used a dramatic mode to describe the First Fleet and the colonization of Australia in historical narratives. Paul Carter, in *The Road to Botany Bay*, designates this kind of historical writing, the staging of history, as 'imperial'.[65] Carter posits two modes of recording history – imperial (that which is factual, already completed, and staged for an unseen spectator) and spatial (that which is in process, admits uncertainty, and takes account of materials such as journal fragments and unfinished maps). When Captain Cook first arrived in what would become Australia, Carter argues that he perceived a space, not a place, yet in his writings, 'the spatial event [was] replaced by a historical stage'.[66] Carter suggests that historians viewed and portrayed Australia as 'a stage where history occurred', where history was 'a theatrical performance'.[67] Australia's most prolific historian, Manning Clark, presents history in this way, as a drama unfolding, in his multi-volume, *A History of Australia*. Clark uses the 'convention of the all-seeing spectator' in his descriptions of the first colony as though he was watching a performance in progress:

> Some cleared ground for the different encampments; some pitched tents; some landed the stores; a party of convicts erected the portable house brought from England for the Governor on the east side of the cove.[68]

Manning Clark represents history with an emphasis on theatrical re-enactment and provides clearly prescribed stage directions for each character. His dramatized mode, in Carter's view, conveys the historic scene as if the full potentiality and destiny of the moment as an ordered and dramatic event was evident at the time of its occurrence.[69] One of the key characteristics in Manning Clark's and other historians' imperial dramatic accounts is a sense

65   Carter, *The Road to Botany Bay*, xiv.
66   Carter, *The Road to Botany Bay*, xiv.
67   Carter, *The Road to Botany Bay*, xiv.
68   Carter, *The Road to Botany Bay*, xiv.
69   Carter, *The Road to Botany Bay*, xiv.

of destiny and the desire to create heroes for the nation: 'Imperial history's mythic lineage of heroes is the consequence of its theatrical assumption that, in reality, historical individuals are actors, fulfilling a higher destiny.'[70]

Keneally's *The Playmaker* integrates aspects of what Carter calls 'imperial history' in its narration of history through a dramatic mode. Keneally, like Manning Clark, was also influenced by the early journals of the First Fleet chroniclers and drew on them for inspiration for his research.[71] In *The Playmaker*, Ralph Clark and other colonial characters perceive scenes theatrically, suggesting that the nation's future is destined to unfold with the same certainty as a drama unfolds onstage each night on what appears to be an empty stage. However, Keneally differs from the imperial dramatic mode of Australian historians in his concern with and focus on rehearsals, which comprises much of the novel. In that sense, Keneally exchanges the certainty of destiny for the possibility of potential, uncertain futures. The novel suggests that roles are rehearsed until they become naturalized. In *The Playmaker*, Keneally emphasizes the rehearsals, role-playing and 'work-shopping' of the nation.

The Playmaker depicts a number of convicts that envision new roles for themselves in society. When Duckling, a prostitute, poisons Goose, her madam, during the performance of the play, the novel explores the dramatic tensions that come when characters take on more powerful positions in society. Amstead, an old convict, is stationed alone on a vegetable island as a night watchman and his growing sense of entitlement can be seen in the easy way he chastises Ralph Clark for his infrequent visits. Amstead on his island becomes an allegory for the colonial officers on theirs who rehearse new roles as rulers.

Certain class distinctions and boundaries fade in *The Playmaker* and are expressed through dramatic gestures of physicality. Ralph Clark observes the power that Arabanoo, dying, wields over the governor, who nurses him

---

70   Carter, *The Road to Botany Bay*, xvii.
71   Keneally acknowledges the following sources in the Author's Note of *The Playmaker*:
      The Journal and Letters of Lieutenant Ralph Clark, David Collins' *An Account of the
      English Colony in New South Wales*, and *The Crimes of the First Fleet Convicts and
      Sydney Cove, 1788–1790*.

lovingly: 'There was something shamefully servile about [the governor]. His posture was for a second so like that of a lover leaning over a lover that Ralph [...] saw the oarsmen smirk.'[72] Keneally describes the governor's physical gestures as they might be described in stage directions in a play. He suggests the imaginative and speculative possibility of a homosexual love between the Governor and Arabanoo that, if it were true (and there is little to suggest more than a passing affection between them recorded in journal entries in the SETIS database[73]), would certainly have been omitted from historical accounts at the time. In *The Melodramatic Imagination*, Peter Brooks argues that melodrama in modern literature can offer a means of 'utter[ing] the unspeakable' and suggests the body as it is described becomes a signifier of meanings that words cannot easily express.[74] The scene in which Arabanoo lies dying with the Governor by his side, where body language and physicality is highlighted, may signal other possibilities of censored stories that hegemonic historical representations are likely to leave unexplored but are prompted by such melodramatic representations in fiction about history.

The especial contribution of Keneally's *The Playmaker* is not in its debatable historical authenticity or the performance of historical authenticity by the author but rather in its innovative use of the melodramatic and dramatic modes to focus on the creative spirit of colonial Australians. It stages a version of imperial history in a novel underscored with comedy and re-visited with optimistic eyes around the time of Australia's Bicentenary. *The Playmaker*, while situated firmly within a white, patriarchal, conservative perspective, dramatizes aspects of history and conflicts in early colonial society with performative possibilities, exploring highly expressive emotions, the rehearsing of nationhood and the theatrical sensation where readers see through more than one perspective at a time, which encourages

---

72   Keneally, *The Playmaker*, 223.
73   'The Journal and Letters of Lt. Ralph Clark 1787–1792', *SETIS database*, ed. Paul G. Fidlon and R. J. Ryan <http://purl.library.usyd.edu.au/setis/id/clajour> accessed 10 July 2016.
74   Brooks, *The Melodramatic Imagination: Balzac, Henry James, Melodrama, and the Mode of Excess*, 4.

a reflective and potentially expansive mode of perceiving historically based narratives in fiction.

Glissando: A Melodrama

David Musgrave's *Glissando: A Melodrama* (2010), published twenty-three years after *The Playmaker*, uses melodrama and satire to critically examine a fictive but familiar Australian past. While Keneally's *The Playmaker*, written just before the Bicentenary celebrations, presented an optimistic and somewhat paternalistic view of the past of late eighteenth-century white colonial officials and colonial life in NSW, Musgrave's *Glissando* arrived at a political juncture in 2010 where it was unlikely that an uncritical position toward the mistreatment of indigenous people or a gentrified portrait of First Fleet officers in a novel would be as favourably received. *Glissando* was published more than two decades after the historical Australian Bicentenary protest march in 1988 where more than 40,000 people challenged society's definition of Australia Day in terms of recognizing indigenous people as the original inhabitants and survivors of colonization. Significant land claims had been made in between the publications of the two novels, particularly with the Mabo decision in 1992 that ruled Australia was never *terra nullius* or empty land, and key cultural gains were made during this time with the Stolen Children Report published in 1997, and Prime Minister Kevin Rudd's apology to the Stolen Generations for abuse suffered by indigenous Australian children put in institutions and missionary homes between 1930 and 1970. In literature, postcolonial concerns and subjectivity took on increasing importance in this period as more affective approaches to historical representation in the arts continue to flourish, as explored in Ross Gibson's 'Palpable History'[75] and Della Pollock's 'Performative Writing'.[76]

75   Gibson, 'Palpable History', 179–86.
76   Pollock, 'Performing Writing', 73–103.

Glissando: A Melodrama, the first novel written by David Musgrave, a Sydney-based poet, academic, and founder of independent poetry press Puncher and Wattman, employs melodrama and satire to examine key themes from Australian history in a form that challenges easy categorization and calls attention to the limits of genre and the possibilities that come from combining disparate modes. Musgrave incorporates melodramatic content and themes from Australian history in *Glissando* – sensationalist, improbable, and tragic – to explore the founding motifs of orphans growing up in a new land; to remember the dispossession, mistreatment, and murder of indigenous people; and to illuminate possibilities for a novel that engages with history and gains its power from a range of affective modes of aesthetic representation.

Glissando begins as an Australian *Bildungsroman* set at the beginning of the twentieth century with the picaresque adventures of protagonist Archie Fliess, an orphan who is cared for by Madame Octave, who runs an avant-garde theatre company in New South Wales. It is satiric in the vein of Laurence Sterne's *Tristam Shandy* or Jonathan Swift's *Gulliver's Travels*, and one of its targets is the small-minded and inward-looking men in New South Wales who work as theatre critics for Williamson's National Theatre and are at war with the new experimental union theatres. Archie Fliess searches through the journals of his mad explorer grandfather to discover that Wilheim Fliess has designed and left behind three ancestral homes, each one more improbable than the next, to Archie and his brother Reggie, who has been traumatized by a near-drowning accident and turned into a musical prodigy. Archie is abducted early on in the novel by theatre ruffians who want to steal the deed to the National Theatre, which Archie's grandfather, according to legend, won in a bet, and which is in Archie's possession. Archie escapes and is cared for by Warrum and Weeyah, two Worratha men, who have been asked to take care of the Glissando property until its owner can be found and which time, the owner and the Worratha men, will then jointly own the property. It is a story of love and loss, dispossession, and a search for identity in a dizzying heterogeneous text that exposes the inevitable limitations of any one mode of representation used to capture a sense of a nation's past and philosophical origins in fiction.

Glissando received high critical acclaim and was shortlisted for the Prime Minister's Literary Award and the UTS Glenda Adams Award for New Writing. One reviewer astutely places the style of Musgrave's novel as 'sitting somewhere between Baz Luhrmann and Samuel Beckett', yet claims that *Glissando* is 'an insight into how well a melodrama can suit a character who prefers to avoid narrating sincere emotions' (*Australian Literary Review*).[77] While I agree with the first part of the review, I disagree with the latter which holds too narrow a view of the genre of melodrama in the suggestion that melodrama is at odds with sincere emotions. Rather, it is more accurate to suggest that Archie in *Glissando* explores a heightening and intensification of emotions through stylized melodramatic conventions. While melodrama typically includes improbable events and sensationalism, the emotions driving the plots and situations are deep-rooted in sincere emotions and desires. Melodrama in *Glissando* defines a mode through which readers can look closely at the representation of the extremities and excesses of emotions, the tension between tragedy and a desire to return to innocence, and the attempt turn gestures and silences into compelling narrative. These wide-ranging components of the melodramatic form inform the novel and provide resonance as deep-running emotions drive the characters to search for their origins, establish new homes and come to terms with their places in Australia.

Glissando: A Melodrama is a highly musical work, as the prefix 'melo' (the Greek word for 'song') in the novel's subtitle suggests, and melancholic tones underscore the narrative at key points and accompany profound questions surrounding colonial conflict and the rise and fall of Archie's life with haunting persistence. Music is, and historically has been, a central element of melodrama. Abrams observes, in *A Glossary of Literary Terms*, that the term 'melodrama' was originally applied to all musical plays, including opera.[78] In early nineteenth-century London, music as an accompaniment in plays 'to strengthen the emotional content of the scenes' and also

---

77   Qtd in *Glissando Reviews*, Sleepers Publishing <http://sleeperspublishing.com/2011/product-1/> accessed 10 August 2016.

78   M. H. Abrams, *A Glossary of Literary Terms*, 7th edn (Boston: Heinle & Heinle, 1999), 110.

to 'circumvent' the Licensing Act of 1737–1843 which restricted spoken dramas to the patent theatres on Drury Lane and in Covent Garden but permitted 'musical entertainments' to be produced elsewhere.[79] Music is used as a trope in *Glissando* to acknowledge the power of performative modes; to evoke and organize memories from the past, creating an experience of reading that calls upon more than the logical parts of our minds which receive and process facts and descriptions about the past. Music, even transliterated as it is in *Glissando* to text on the page, calls upon other sensory perceptions within the body and can create affective and resounding connections with the text for readers who may recall hearing a *glissade* on a piano, a rising blur of notes playing as the hand glides up or down the keyboard in a flourish, when it is described in the novel to denote the minor tones of the characters' lives, the construction of the house Glissando, or the finale of the narrator's last days. Musgrave, who has played and composed music since childhood, suggests music is a 'kind of master trope in the book for how art can shape our lives, for good and for ill'.[80] Through Reggie's transliterated music that evokes the reverberating tones of a piano's *glissade*; through the melodrama of lost parents, tragic loves, and unjust murders in a settler-invader culture; and through lengthy satirical episodes, Musgrave alternates between modes in search of resonant methods to create his wide-reaching novel on Australian ideals, identity, and an imagined life at the beginning of the twentieth century. In *Glissando*, melodramatic content is paired with satire, in contradistinction to Keneally's pairing of melodrama in *The Playmaker* with comedy, to shed light on the illusions that Australians create about themselves and are slow to examine.

The model of satire that most closely matches the form used in *Glissando* is Menippean satire, which Musgrave studied in the 1990s at Sydney University with the late Professor Bill Maidment. Musgrave's

---

79   Abrams, *A Glossary of Literary Terms*, 110.
80   Richard Bilkey, 'Interview: David Musgrave on Glissando', *Bookseller +Publisher* <http://www.fancygoods.com.au/booksellerpublisher-magazine/2010/04/09/ interview-david-musgrave-on-%E2%80%98glissando%E2%80%99-sleepers-publishi ng/> accessed 9 April 2010.

interest in Menippean satire led to his PhD dissertation on the topic and, later, to his book *Grotesque Anatomies: Menippean Satire since the Renaissance* (2014). Menippean satire is characterized by a lengthy attack on certain mental attitudes rather than on specific individuals using extraordinary situations used to 'test philosophical ideas and theories'.[81] While Menippean satire is difficult to define due to its 'tendency to puncture generic boundaries and to fuse with other forms, such as the Renaissance anatomy, or the novel',[82] Menippean satire can be broadly characterized by its heterogeneity of form,[83] encyclopaedic scope,[84] extended philosophical target[85] and intellectual exuberance.[86] In the Middle Ages, Menippean satire targeted philosophy, religion, and 'other powerful ideologies', 'tending towards encyclopaedism and concerned with the impossibility of a single world view being adequate to explain the world'.[87] Paul Salzman calls Menippean satire 'a rather ill-defined genre' that combines 'a mix of allegory, picaresque narrative and satirical commentary'.[88] Menippean satire was most popularly theorized by Northrop Frye who emphasized its close ties to Renaissance anatomy, and by Mikhail Bakhtin, who aligned it with the idea of the carnivalesque and its potentiality of subversive alterity.[89] For Howard Wisebrot, Menippean satire is 'a form that uses at least two other genres, languages, cultures or changes of voice to oppose a dangerous, false, or specious threatening orthodoxy'.[90] Menippean satire does not usually sustain the length of the novel but can 'infect the novel' in a Derridean-like

81   David Musgrave, *Grotesque Anatomies: Menippean Satire since the Renaissance* (Cambridge: Cambridge Scholars Publishers, 2014), vi.

82   Musgrave, *Grotesque Anatomies: Menippean Satire since the Renaissance*, ix.

83   Musgrave, *Grotesque Anatomies: Menippean Satire since the Renaissance*, 21.

84   Musgrave, *Grotesque Anatomies: Menippean Satire since the Renaissance*, 23.

85   Musgrave, *Grotesque Anatomies: Menippean Satire since the Renaissance*, 23.

86   Musgrave, *Grotesque Anatomies: Menippean Satire since the Renaissance*, 9.

87   Musgrave, *Grotesque Anatomies: Menippean Satire since the Renaissance*, viii.

88   Paul Salzman, 'Narrative Contexts for Bacon's New Atlantis', in Bronwen Price, ed., *Francis Bacon's New Atlantis* (New York: Manchester University Press, 2002), 39.

89   Musgrave, *Grotesque Anatomies: Menippean Satire since the Renaissance*, 11.

90   Wisebrot qtd in Musgrave, *Grotesque Anatomies: Menippean Satire since the Renaissance*, 17.

contamination of genres[91] or appear 'by incursion' as a 'brief guerrilla attack that emphasizes the danger in the text and then departs'.[92]

Not restricted to one particular era, Menippean satire has roots in antiquity, proliferated in the Renaissance, and has made a comeback in contemporary times in postmodern novels such as *Glissando*, Salman Rushdie's *Midnight Children*, and novels by Angela Carter, Thomas Pynchon and others.[93] In an interview, Musgrave explains how he was drawn to the way Laurence Sterne in *Tristram Shandy* was 'parodying encyclopaedic knowledge, and making fun of the attempt to make representation complete and total'.[94] Musgrave's *Glissando* satirizes the possibility of a single totalizing representation of an understanding of history and sends this possibility up through camp exaggeration and an overall search through theatre, music, nature, and architecture for organizing principles that can assist in forming compelling ways of understanding the world even if they inevitably come up short. In *Glissando*, Musgrave exhibits qualities from his own definition of Menippean satire from *Grotesque Anatomies* with structural heterogeneity in diverse forms and genres (Wilheim's journal, newspaper clippings, a theatrical script, lengthy satirical episodes and melodrama) and in the vast thematic variances of the novel where vulgarity, grotesquery, eccentricity, and the absurd sit alongside melodramatic extremes of salvation and mourning. Chapters 18 to 20, in particular, satirize the gluttonous and grotesque Basil Pilbeam for his over-blown sense of importance as a theatre critic and his band of sycophants who transport him in a car that transforms into a palanquin in spectacular melodramatic fashion. The conversation at the feast for Pilbeam is rendered in an extended theatrical script within the novel.[95] Readers imagine the staging around the provided dialogue as the characters develop ridiculous and obscene gastronomic theories to better the world and their rising places in it. The satire

---

91 Musgrave, *Grotesque Anatomies: Menippean Satire since the Renaissance*, 21.

92 Wisebrot qtd in Musgrave, *Grotesque Anatomies: Menippean Satire since the Renaissance*, 17.

93 Musgrave, *Grotesque Anatomies: Menippean Satire since the Renaissance*, vi–vii.

94 Richard Bilkey, 'Interview: David Musgrave on Glissando', n.p.

95 Musgrave, *Glissando: A Melodrama*, 300–30.

signals a marked departure from serious engagement with melancholy or tragedy. It is over-the-top and likely to be read with delight, groans, and ironic scrutiny. Pilbeam and his cronies are represented with heightened theatricality; they are conscious of being watched and enjoy the roles they play. Musgrave uses this episode to expose, through an exaggerated satirical and dramatic lens, the shortcomings and vanities often associated with a stereotypical 'big fish in a small pond' Australian identity.

The Pilbeam satire focuses on a war between the National Theatre and an experimental avant-garde theatrical group rather than on Australia's role in the First World War. The novel's focus on a war between modes of artistic representation in *Glissando* serves a few purposes: it suggests, with irreverence, that the theatre as a means of exploring and re-visiting the past has some value that has been overlooked, but, more so, that the critics at war possess a comically short-sighted perspective of the bigger picture beyond their immediate interests, and the satire 'reveal[s]' the caricatured characters for 'the philistines [Australians] so often are'.[96] Directly after the Menippean satiric episode of Basil Pilbeam, Archie narrates how he loses his greatest love, Nicola, to one of the theatre critics and discovers that Mme Octave and his brother Reggie have died at sea. *Glissando* offers its most outrageous satire just before relaying Archie's most despairing tragedy of losing his family. The laughs set readers up for a greater fall as the style shifts briskly from Menippean satire to melodramatic sorrow.

Glissando makes only one oblique reference to the First World War at the novel's end in a witty scene when a writer named Patrick approaches Archie to read his grandfather's journal that he had heard about while he was in Intelligence in Alexandria during the war.[97] The writer is clearly intended to be Patrick White, depicted with asthma, a Mediterranean-looking partner named Maloney (instead of Manoly) and a non-descript last name Archie can't remember, 'Grey, I thought it was, or Brown',[98] who comes to Archie for historical inspiration to write his great Australian explorer novel. Archie's awareness of the writer who later becomes a Nobel Prize winner is

96   Williamson, 'A Spiritual Superiority: Glissando Review', n.p.
97   Musgrave, *Glissando: A Melodrama*, 371–6.
98   Musgrave, *Glissando: A Melodrama*, 376.

so laughably dim that he dismisses 'Patrick Brown and his book' as an artistic effort that must not have gotten off the ground as Archie can't find it at the news agent's shop.[99] Musgrave's allusions to Patrick White's *Voss* (1957) a vast philosophical novel of an historical German naturalist who disappeared in the Outback in the 1840s, creates a link between *Voss* and *Glissando*, two novels that employ non-realistic modes to imagine Australian minds and psychologies as the nation was colonized and developed.

With an understanding of how the Menippean satire operates in *Glissando*, let us return to melodrama, the other predominant genre in the novel, and examine why it is such an apt and culturally relevant means through which to represent Australian historical memory. One of Musgrave's most compelling uses of melodrama in *Glissando* is concerned with the desirable but impossible recovery of innocence, both Archie's and that of the nation responsible for the dispossession and mistreatment of indigenous people. There is an inherent tension in the melodramatic genre between the desire to return to innocence and the knowledge that innocence is unattainable. The irreconcilable desire to return to innocence is deep-rooted in the psyche of Australian settlers and their descendants and manifests itself in many narratives of colonial and postcolonial writing. In 'Making Stories', Jerome Bruner suggests non-realistic frames in fiction can create realities so compelling 'that they shape our experience not only of the worlds the fiction portrays but of the real world' and prompt readers to recognize and grow from their loss of innocence.[100]

Great fiction proceeds by making the familiar and the ordinary strange again – as the Russian formalists used to put it, by 'alienating' the reader from the tyranny of the compellingly familiar. It offers alternative worlds that put the actual one in a new light. It explores human plights through the prism of imagination. At its best and most powerful, fiction, like the fateful apple in the Garden of Eden, is the end of innocence.[101]

---

99   Musgrave, *Glissando: A Melodrama*, 376.
100 Jerome Bruner, *Making Stories: Law, Literature, Life* (Boston: Harvard University Press, 2002), 9.
101 Bruner, *Making Stories: Law, Literature, Life*, 9–10.

In *Glissando*, the end of innocence for Archie comes with the melodramatic realization that he played a role in the tragic killing of either Warrum or Weeyah, who were both living on the land near Glissando and were shot at by police for trespassing. Archie possesses his grandfather's letter that assigns custody of the land to the Worratha people. Had he left the letter with Warrum or Weeyah, it might have saved them.[102] Archie writes, 'it became clear to me that my unwitting complicity in the whole tragic scene was what I should rightly have feared'.[103] He reads in a newspaper clipping of the injuries sustained by the 'brave Sergeant McKessar' in the struggle and discovers that the Worratha children living there were taken from their families by the Aborigines Protection Board and sent to foster homes. One of the unnamed black men was shot twice in the chest and died instantly while another died later in custody.[104] The surviving victim of the shooting faced trial 'on charges of trespass and assault'.[105] This tragic scene leaves Archie mournful, reflective, and angry at himself for the death of his friends and at 'the brutality with which they had been pushed aside and their lives savaged by the law'.[106] Here Musgrave delivers melodrama of situation, deep emotion, and the loss of innocence. There are no histrionics in this representation, nor sensationalistic solutions; rather, this moment of melancholic melodrama engenders pathos for the victims, heightened emotion, polarization of good and evil and Archie's feelings of futile regret and mourning at the unjust tragedy of colonialization in Australia.

While this particular incident of the police shooting the Worratha people and taking their children away is fictional, it is derived from historical fact and comes from a historical context based on lawfully enforced injustice for indigenous people in Australia. The melodrama pulls at the reader of *Glissando* to feel the weight and sorrow of tragic fates and lost innocence through recognizable conventions of the melodramatic genre. This melodramatic mode of engaging with history in fiction is in line with

---

102   Musgrave, *Glissando: A Melodrama*, 157.
103   Musgrave, *Glissando: A Melodrama*, 156.
104   Musgrave, *Glissando: A Melodrama*, 158.
105   Musgrave, *Glissando: A Melodrama*, 158.
106   Musgrave, *Glissando: A Melodrama*, 159.

Gibson's proposal in 'Palpable History' for creating a mode of historiography that appeals to the senses and generates 'felt convictions' rather than 'an argument' or a 'particular semantic *meaning*'.[107] In narratives of Australian history, there are many instances where historical textual evidence is sparse, one-sided or lacking in conviction once transcribed. In answer to this, Gibson proposes:

> We need non-textual (but designed and structured) patterns of propositions about the past, propositions that register in the nervous system, that register as pulses, flows, rhythms and lapses. And we need to propose these patterns in such a way that the perceiver gets convinced 'in the bones' rather than in the portions of our sensibility that manage linguistic, textual argument.[108]

Gibson does not suggest that more conventional, discursive history has no use; rather that it, along with 'imaginative speculation', is partially useful and likely productive if used together.[109] Melodrama in *Glissando*, and particularly in the scene of the killings by police, provides a frame through which an affective response may reverberate within a reader by means of its emotional resonance rather than its factual accuracy. The heightened tragedy, Archie's despair at having not taken action, the polarization of good and evil – all of these recognizable melodramatic conventions from the theatre – may serve to create a memorable theatrical portrait or provide a flash of embodied sensation that might live on in a reader's memory.

Gibson cites Australian historian Greg Dening who says 'that the most important historical work happens when scholars apply imagination to evidence'.[110] Imagination here for Musgrave is not pure invention but a means of finding a way to 'grasp the forces that have pushed out of the past and are shaping the world now'.[111] Gibson, in his writing about his own installation *Street X-Rays*, describes a 'palpable' feeling that arises from certain modes of historiography that appeals to the senses that leads

---

107   Gibson, 'Palpable History', 179.
108   Gibson, 'Palpable History', 179.
109   Gibson, 'Palpable History', 185.
110   Gibson, 'Palpable History', 185.
111   Gibson, 'Palpable History', 179.

to an '*awareness*' of history rather than '*knowledge*'.[112] This kind of embodied knowing, Gibson suggests, 'makes you think about the presence of the past in ordinary time, and in you, and in the larger world which holds you and reacts to you'.[113] Musgrave's *Glissando* looks to the past not for a pure access to the historical facts there, but to trace through emotional and psychological connections that suggest a path toward who Australians have become. Musgrave represents a stylized version of the past in *Glissando* that is marked by postcolonial concerns and postmodern sensibilities. This mode of representation echoes Frederic Jameson's view that readers can only ever view the past through our own contemporary frames of reference as we live in a 'perpetual present' even as we examine history.[114]

Melodramatic conventions in *Glissando* are used to draw attention to the silences, gestures, and gaps in historical records, and to the irretrievable past that Musgrave imagines and transposes to fiction. In 'Cinematic Uses of the Past', Marcia Landy maintains that 'one of the major characteristics of melodrama is its tendency towards muteness, its ability to remind us of the limits of the spoken word and hence of the constraints of official representation'.[115] In *Glissando*, after Reggie recovers from his near-drowning, he becomes gifted at music and almost entirely stops communicating through words. He translates his impatience and anger into 'dark counter-melodies in the symphonies of his day-to-day life', and Archie discovers 'the enormous range across which humans connect with each other: the language of the face, the timbre of voices and the elegant soliloquies of hands'.[116] Archie writes, 'Even without speaking, I understood Reggie with greater directness than the others.'[117] Musgrave's recourse to Reggie's silence and gestures, which are characteristic of the melodramatic form, serve as reminders for readers of the greater embodied stories that elude

112   Gibson, 'Palpable History', 182.
113   Gibson, 'Palpable History', 182–3.
114   Jameson, 'Postmodernism and Consumer Society', 28.
115   Marcia Landy, *Cinematic Uses of the Past* (Minneapolis: University of Minnesota Press, 1996), 21.
116   Musgrave, *Glissando: A Melodrama*, 181.
117   Musgrave, *Glissando: A Melodrama*, 181.

transcription in historical records and some realistic modes of historical fiction. Archie's grandfather, Wilheim Fliess, also believed that non-textual ways of telling stories were vital and wrote in his journal, 'words are not so much unreliable as simply not of the right order'.[118] The final section of the book, The Theatre of Memory, begins with Archie's revelations about how hard it is to tell his story in words: 'Any story, stretched out for long enough, reveals the silence at its heart'.[119] *Glissando* concludes with Archie's desire to construct a Theatre of Memory, like Robert Fludd's mnemonic system based on an Elizabethan public theatre that offers a metaphoric space for preserving memories. Archie writes about the lives he has remembered and the lives lived before, 'and beyond that there is the world waiting to be remembered into being yet again'.[120]

Musgrave's *Glissando* employs music, melodrama, and Menippean satire in the task of making affective, satirical, and compelling connections between readers and the text in its multi-pronged effort to imagine the history of Australia 'into being yet again'.[121] The novel presents a variety of innovative and stylized genres that are used to develop the art of memory in fiction. *Glissando* acknowledges the limitations of historical representation in fiction, showing traits of postcolonial self-reflexivity, in its exaggerated Menippean satirical episodes that illuminate certain Australian hypocrisies and shortcomings. It engages with melodramatic revelations, emotional depths and excesses, and stylized conventions that signal a loss of innocence and tensions between hope and despair that Musgrave suggests are central to the Australian context at the beginning of the twentieth century. Musgrave finds ways to harness the power of classic forms of satire and melodrama from earlier times and contemporize them with postmodern self-reflexivity and a critical awareness of postcolonial issues.

Both Keneally's *The Playmaker* and Musgrave's *Glissando* use melodrama and dramatic modes in fiction as representational devices for creating performative, reflexive, and emotionally heightened versions of Australia's

118 Musgrave, *Glissando: A Melodrama*, 134.
119 Musgrave, *Glissando: A Melodrama*, 355.
120 Musgrave, *Glissando: A Melodrama*, 390.
121 Musgrave, *Glissando: A Melodrama*, 390.

past about a secular world in transition. Keneally's use of melodrama in *The Playmaker* displays a selectively optimistic and conservative view of Australia's colonial past that gives an indication of Keneally's late 1980s' view on the eve of Australia's Bicentenary. The dramatic mode in the novel draws attention to larger issues of how early colonials staged their histories on what they believed was an empty stage and how central were the activities of role-playing and rehearsing a new nation. The novel introduces interpretive roles for readers who are positioned before performative accounts of history in fiction. Lieutenant Ralph Clark is dramatized as a genteel and rather innocent official who facilitates harmonic connections and growth in the colony through the play which operates, much like Shakespeare's 'theatrum mundi' or 'all the world's a stage' concept, as a metaphor for society. Keneally brings to life a version of history constructed to appeal to his established readership despite certain departures from historical evidence, and develops a character that lays a claim to higher fidelity to historical sources than finally conceded by Keneally in the epilogue. Musgrave's *Glissando* examines the idea of innocence and culpability for Australian settlers and their descendants with more scrutiny and an awareness of postcolonial contexts, and in this novel the form of melodrama is attended by Menippean satire rather than the gentler art of comedy. Melodrama in *Glissando* exposes the lost innocence of Archie after he fails to save Warrum and Weeyah and reflects a more sombre view of Australian postcolonialism published in 2010. It sounds a call for a range of vital performative forms to invigorate the exploration of the past in fiction. Both novels develop dramatic modes that appeal to the emotions and enact possibilities of un-scripted and potentially un-scriptable stories and declare the fiction writer's challenge in constructing history and the need to experiment with innovative aesthetic forms.

CHAPTER 2

Performing Identity in Tomson Highway's *Kiss of the Fur Queen*

Cree Canadian playwright, composer, and writer Tomson Highway transposes storytelling traditions, classical piano, and theatre into his first novel, *Kiss of the Fur Queen* (1998). In this semi-autobiographical novel of two Cree brothers, Jeremiah and Gabriel Okimasis, Highway creates a sense of vitality and the living moment to express the brothers' journeys of survival and decolonization through storytelling and the performative arts. Highway's incorporation of performances and performative modes embodies a distinctive energy and force that is derived from storytelling and a combination of mythologies from Cree and Western cultures that have informed Highway's identity.[1] The overall structure of the novel is performative, in that the content of each of the six parts reflects the particular mood and style of a selected term from classical music, and the novel contains storytelling traditions and other dramatic performances where characters develop and reflect on their cultural identities. These range from an indigenous soap opera, roleplaying in church, historical re-enactments in high school, and a mixed-cast Gilbert and Sullivan school production, to large-scale theatrical and musical productions. Highway explores, through performative content and structures, how the two brothers develop strategies for decolonization and construct cultural identities as Cree and Canadian after being taken away as children to live in a residential school in Winnipeg in the 1950s and surviving sexual abuse from priests who were in charge of their wellbeing.

---

1   Highway's critical analysis, *Comparing Mythologies* (Ottawa: University of Ottawa Press, 2003), addresses the ways in which contemporary Canadian culture and his own identity is shaped by a mixture of indigenous and Western mythologies.

The critical success of Highway's most well-known plays, *The Rez Sisters* (1986) and *Dry Lips Oughta Move to Kapuskasing* (1989), has led to Highway's status as one of Canada's leading playwrights.[2] Highway wrote the third play in the Rez cycle called *Rose* (2003). Other works include *Ernestine Shuswap Gets her Trout* (2005), a play about a group of First Nations People in British Columbia expecting a visit from the prime minister; a one-woman musical called 'The (Post) Mistress: a One-Woman Musical' (2013); three children's books written in both English and Cree, a libretto to the first Cree opera and a musical cabaret for young audiences in English, French, and Cree.[3] Highway knows a number of languages (Cree, Dene, English, French, and Spanish) and trained as a concert pianist; *Kiss of the Fur Queen* demonstrates his search for a mode of performative storytelling that comes from the complex convergence of his cultures and traditions. Highway was born near Maria Lake in Manitoba in 1951, and his first language was Cree.[4] He lived with his parents and eleven siblings until he was sent to a residential school at the age of six where he was forced to speak English. He later graduated from the University of Western Ontario as an English major and today holds ten honorary doctorates from Canadian universities. Highway worked as the artistic director of the Native Earth Performing Arts Inc. and for the Native People's Resource Centre (1975–1978) before becoming a playwright and

2   Thomson Highway's awards include the Winner of the Dora Mavor Moore Award for *Dry Lips Oughta Move to Kapuskasing* (1989), Nominee for the Governor General's Literary Award for *Dry Lips Oughta Move to Kapuskasing* (1989), Nominee for the Governor General's Literary Award for *The Rez Sisters* (1988) and Winner of the Dora Mavor Moore Award for *The Rez Sisters* (1986). Both of these plays won the Dora Mavor Moore Awards for Best New Play, and the Floyd S. Chalmers Awards for Best Canadian Play, and were nominated for Governor-General's Awards. *Dry Lips* was the first Canadian play in Canadian theatre history to be mounted in a full production with an extended run at Toronto's Royal Alexandra Theatre (1990) <http://www.tomsonhighway.com/biography.html> accessed 4 January 2016.
3   Highway's critical works include *Comparing Mythologies* (Ottawa: University of Ottawa Press, 2003) and *From Oral to Written: A Celebration of Native Canadian Literature, 1980–2010* (Vancouver: Talonbooks, 2017).
4   Biographical details here from <http://www.tomsonhighway.com/biography.html> accessed 4 January 2016.

author. The main characters in his novel, Jeremiah and Gabriel, share key features with Highway himself and his brother, Rene, now deceased, who was a professional dancer. Like the Highway brothers, the Okimasis brothers explore artistic media, including music, dance, and drama, to find appropriate storytelling genres in which to perform their histories and experiences.

There are a number of reasons why indigenous oral narratives and performative modes work effectively and evocatively in this novel to convey the historical realities of indigenous characters in Canada. In the preface to *Kiss of the Fur Queen*, Highway suggests, in an allusion to Aristotle's words from *Poetics*, that a storyteller provides a potentially fuller picture than a historian. He writes: 'The difference between the historian and poet/storyteller is that where the historian relates what happened, the storyteller tells us how it might have come about.'[5] Russell Bishop suggests 'that storytelling is a useful and culturally appropriate way of representing the "diversities of truth" within which the story teller rather than the researcher retains control'.[6] In 'The Nêhiyawak Nation through Âcimowina', Paulina Johnson looks closely at the Nêhiyawak or Plains Cree people of western Canada, who have 'long practiced âcimowina, oral narratives, and these stories are embedded with teachings and lessons that are pertinent to Nêhiyawak being'.[7] While Highway's characters in the novel are Woods Cree rather than Plains Cree, indicated by the dialect spoken in the novel,[8] Johnson offers a significant insight into the way history is viewed and transmitted in Cree culture. Drawing on sources from Cree historians Winona Wheeler[9]

5   Highway's notion echoes Aristotle's belief in *Poetics* that the difference between history and poetry is that 'one relates what has happened, the other what may happen' (x).
6   Linda Tuhiwai Smith, *Decolonizing Mythologies: Research and Indigenous Peoples* (London: Zed Books, 1999), 145.
7   Paulina Johnson, 'The Nêhiyawak Nation through Âcimowina: Experiencing Plains Cree Knowledge through Oral Narratives', *Totem: The University of Western Ontario Journal of Anthropology* 23/1 (2015), 72.
8   Van Essen, 'nehiyawaskiy (Cree Land) and Canada: Location, Language, and Borders in Tomson Highway's *Kiss of the Fur Queen*', 106.
9   Winona Wheeler, 'Cree Intellectual Traditions in History', in Ute Lische and David T. McNab, eds, *Walking a Tightrope: Aboriginal People and their Representations* (Waterloo: Wilfrid Laurier University Press, 2010), 189–213.

and Neal McLeod,[10] Johnson points out that the Western idea of history is not universal with its elitist, colonial, 'document-driven approaches'.[11] In Cree culture, 'the primary and secondary source material comes from living individuals who cannot be called historians'[12] as 'there is no word for 'history' in the Western sense'.[13] Instead of constructing history in the form of conventional academic texts, indigenous people have tradition-ally passed on beliefs and values through oral narratives that overlap upon one another, offering 'new insights and valuable information on historical events'.[14] Johnson describes the Cree perception that oral narratives are deadened when they are written down: 'Devaluing oral history and writ-ing it down causes the moment in time to become no longer alive, when in Cree belief it was êpimatciw akitêmaka, something that has spirit, and something that can give life'.[15] Highway's attempts to preserve the spirit of oral storytelling in *Kiss of the Fur Queen* works to defy the fixity of text and capture a sense of the living practice of oral narratives. Even though the novel fixes the stories and other performances in particular incarnations in text, the novel's emphasis on live storytelling and other performances point out how vital they are in live form in Cree culture for developing cultural memory, identity, and a world view. Johnson writes, 'The ability to tell Indigenous pasts is not only a healing process for Indigenous peo-ples; it is also a form of decolonization of the colonial practices that have merged themselves into our lives year after year.'[16]

Kiss of the Fur Queen emphasizes survival and strength as it engages strategies of decolonization and empowerment through storytelling and other artistic performances mediated through text. Highway's writing has

---

10   Neal McLeod, *Cree Narrative Memory: From Treaties to Contemporary Times* (Saskatoon: Purich Publishing Limited, 2007).

11   Johnson, 'The Nêhiyawak Nation through Âcimowina', 78.

12   Johnson, 'The Nêhiyawak Nation through Âcimowina', 72.

13   Shawn Wilson, *Research is Ceremony: Indigenous Research Methods* (Black Point, NS: Fernwood 2008).

14   Johnson, 'The Nêhiyawak Nation through Âcimowina', 77.

15   Johnson, 'The Nêhiyawak Nation through Âcimowina', 79. See also Wheeler, 'Reflections on the Social Relations of Indigenous Oral Histories', 196.

16   Johnson, 'The Nêhiyawak Nation through Âcimowina', 71.

emerged out of an earlier context of indigenous writing characterized by loss, disempowerment, and subjugation. After Mohawk poet E. Pauline Johnson's first book of poetry in 1895, which was 'heavily edited', and the publication of only a few other texts, Penny Petrone notes nearly six decades of almost no publishing by indigenous writers in Canada between 1914 and 1969 when generations of children were taken from their parents and placed in residential schools.[17] While non-indigenous writers in Canada were struggling to find a voice or as Dennis Lee says, a cadence,[18] through which to express their new land in either of the country's two founding languages that carried values and ways of seeing imported from European countries, indigenous writers faced additional and more complex challenges, as Highway describes, writing from the 'invaded' position rather than the 'settler' position.[19] Unlike 'settlers' writing back to empire and searching for a voice that spoke of their postcolonial identities in a new land, indigenous people experienced a more fraught and oftentimes traumatic task as writers because of institutionalized and informal racism, inequality, domination, and, in many cases, being forced to use English which carried 'a world view very different from and even hostile to, their own'.[20] Jeanette Armstrong writes, 'Indigenous peoples in North America were rendered powerless and subjugated to totalitarian domination by foreign peoples.'[21] Additional considerations that faced, and continue to face, some indigenous writers include making the cultural decision of whether or not to put oral stories in print and the practical factors of a limited readership if choosing to publish in an indigenous language and not in English.

17 Penny Petrone, *Native Literature in Canada: From the Oral Tradition to the Present* (Toronto: Oxford University Press, 1990), 95.

18 Dennis Lee, 'Cadence, Country, Silence: Writing in Colonial Space', *Boundary 2: A Journal of Postmodern Literature and Culture* 3/1 (Autumn 1974), 151–68.

19 Tomson Highway, 'An Interview with Tomson Highway', by Barbra Nahwegahbow, *A Voice for First Nations* 1/4 (1991), 17.

20 Highway and Nahgewahbow, 'An Interview with Tomson Highway', 17.

21 Jeanette Armstrong, 'The Disempowerment of First North American Native Peoples and Empowerment Through Their Writing', in Daniel David Moses and Terry Goldie, eds, *An Anthology of Canadian Native Literature in English* (Toronto: Oxford University Press, 1991), 209.

A period of protest literature by indigenous writers began in 1969 in Canada with seminal texts including Harold Cardinal's *The Unjust Society* (1969), Maria Campbell's autobiographical *Halfbreed* (1973), and Howard Adams' *Prisoner of Grass* (1975). During the late 1970s and early 1980s, autobiographical works emerged and particularly the stories of indigenous women, with Beatrice Culleton's *In Search of April Raintree* (1983), Jeanette Armstrong's *Slash* (1985), and Lee Maracle's *I Am Woman* (1988). There was an expansion in the field of drama with Thomson Highway's *The Rez Sisters* (1986), *Dry Lips Oughta Move to Kapuskasing* (1989), and Daniel David Moses' *Coyote City* (1988). A number of anthologies of indigenous writing were published during the 1980s and early 1990s, along with a wave of literary analyses by indigenous writers.[22]

While Highway takes 'some liberty' with 'the chronology of certain historical events' in *Kiss of the Fur Queen*,[23] he looks closely at a range of significant issues pertaining to Canadian and First Nations history, such as the separation of indigenous children from their families, sexual and emotional abuse in residential missionary schools, and the rape and murder of an indigenous woman from The Pas, Manitoba. Highway integrates performative and storytelling modes which challenge more traditional modes of writing history in fiction. Elizabeth Theobald suggests theatre is 'the predominant expressive vehicle' for indigenous writers in Canada because it is a 'logical extension of traditional storytelling'.[24] She suggests storytelling is 'about taking your audience on a journey through the use of your voice, your body, and the spoken word. And going from that onto the stage is just the next logical progression.'[25] Highway's storytellers use dance, music, theatre, mythology, and television, to connect with inner audiences, and

---

22   For an overview of the historical context of indigenous writing in Canada, including a distinction between the challenges facing immigrants and indigenous writers, see Tamara Palmer Seiler's 'Multi-vocality and national literature: Toward a post-colonial and multicultural aesthetic', *Journal of Canadian Studies* 31/3 (Autumn 1996), 148–65.

23   Highway, *Kiss of the Fur Queen*, iii.

24   Elizabeth Theobold, 'Storytelling to Stage: the Growth of Native Theatre in Canada', *The Drama Review* 41/3 (Autumn 1997), 140–53.

25   Theobold, 'Storytelling to Stage: the Growth of Native Theatre in Canada', 140.

subsequently readers, with varying degrees of intimacy, and create holistic versions of history where the spirit of the event is represented rather than the more conventional historical details of time, event, and place. Highway's move to fiction from the theatre brings with it some advantages as well as new challenges in capturing and sharing Cree oral traditions and other performances with a sense of a living spirit of connection and discovery. While a novel can be shared with fewer expenses than a dramatic production, novels are written and read in isolation and do not usually generate a sense of community or connectivity, as live plays, storytelling, and other performances do. The visual and aural qualities of live theatre, which are immediate and often electrically charged, are nearly impossible to replicate in novels. Yet, one of the benefits of Highway's engagement with dramatic structures and performative modes in *Kiss of the Fur Queen* is his generation of a sense of a 'living moment' and of connections with readers.

Storytelling and Music: Performative Structures of the Novel

Highway's cultural roots were determined by Cree and urban North American influences. Anne Nothof observes that in Highway's plays there is no essential concept of 'pure' culture but hybridizations of Cree and North American worlds.[26] In his writing, Highway updates Cree mythology to a modern urban context. Highway explains in an interview, 'I grew up with myths; they're the core of our identity as a people. But I'm urban by choice, so I translate that mythology into contemporary terms. The trickster now takes strolls down Yonge Street and goes into bars.'[27] Even as he contemporizes myths, Highway maintains that he is indebted to 'the storytellers

---

26   Anne Nothof, 'Cultural Collision and Magical Transformation: The Plays of Tomson Highway', *Studies in Canadian Literature* 20/2 (1995), 36.

27   Highway qtd in Ray Conlogue, 'Another Triumph for Tomson Highway', *Globe and Mail* (10 February 1989), A 18.

of [his] people, the myth-makers, the weavers of dreams'.[28] He writes, 'For it is on their shoulders that we, the current and upcoming generations of native writers, stand. Without them, we would have no way of telling our stories and, ultimately, no stories to tell.'[29]

At a few points in *Kiss of the Fur Queen*, Highway describes how ancestors pass down stories. Jeremiah's father appears, just after his death, before Jeremiah in the early morning hours and re-tells the story of the *Son of Ayash* so that Jeremiah can re-create the legend as a play.[30] At the Wasaychigan Hill Pow Wow, Jeremiah and Gabriel watch Amanda Clear Sky's grandmother, Ann-Adele Ghostrider, tell the story of Chachagathoo, while her 'face kept melting and regenerating, melting and regenerating, the eyes and mouths of a thousand women'.[31] Indigenous storytellers in the novel are not portrayed singly, but in a community of tellers.

Highway creates storytellers who participate with their listeners in the creation and passing on of stories. In Cree storytelling, as illustrated in *Kiss of the Fur Queen*, each story grows from the collective memory of everyone who has told it and it keeps changing as it is told and re-told. The characters in *Kiss of the Fur Queen* relish the embellishment of stories. Little Seagull Ovary tells Jeremiah's sister Chichilia how her baby brother was delivered to the earth:

> This was the tale of newborn babies falling from beyond the stars, rousing cantankerous, hibernating bears, magnanimous lyric-poet rabbits, and such [...]. Chichilia giggled as the midwife embellished the ancient yarn as only her very advanced age earned her the right to do.[32]

Stories change with each telling over time unlike static stories in a book. Gabriel, named Ooneemameetoo at birth, claims to remember the story of his arrival himself, while Jeremiah, born Champion, insists that he was the one who first told his brother his birth story. The narrative discloses:

28   Highway, *Kiss of the Fur Queen*, iii.
29   Highway, *Kiss of the Fur Queen*, iii.
30   Highway, *Kiss of the Fur Queen*, 275
31   Highway, *Kiss of the Fur Queen*, 245
32   Highway, *Kiss of the Fur Queen*, 32.

> In truth it was Kookoos Cook, sitting on the pew with Champion on his lap, who would never tire of telling his nephews the yarn, which, as the years progressed, became ever more outrageous, exaggerated, as is the Cree way of telling stories, of making myth.[33]

Barbara Godard observes that a number of formal devices in storytelling, such as those she cites from Bauman, 'figurative language, parallelism, special formulae, appeal to tradition and a disclaimer of performance', 'have the power to engage the audience's participation' and bind 'its members to the performer as co-participants in an event'.[34] *Kiss of the Fur Queen* provides the opportunity for Chichilia and the reader to engage in the story of Gabriel's birth and baptism in its evolving versions through multiple tellers. Little Seagull Ovary, the midwife who was baptized Peroxide Lacroix, chooses the name Ooneemameetoo, meaning Dancer, for the baby who made the stars dance before his birth. Van Essen points out the delight Cree speakers may derive from the stories and jokes embedded in some of the character's names and nicknames which create another method of decolonizing resistance and empowerment for Cree-speaking readers who are included in 'an insider readership of Cree speakers'.[35]

In addition to Cree storytelling, concepts from European classical music structure the novel. *Kiss of the Fur Queen* is divided into six parts, and each part is sub-titled with an Italian musical term that corresponds thematically with the content of the section. Part One (Chapters 1–4) is sub-titled *Allegro ma non troppo*, meaning quick and cheerful but not too fast. In these chapters, Highway establishes the life of the young family with the brothers where Champion, later called Jeremiah, saves his little brother from the caribou. Part Two (Chapters 5–11) is sub-titled *Andante cantabile*, which means moderate tempo in a singing style and follows the childhood of the brothers. Jeremiah goes to residential school and Gabriel

33 Highway, *Kiss of the Fur Queen*, 38.
34 Barbara Godard, 'Listening for the Silence: Native Women's Traditional Narratives', in Thomas L. King, Cheryl Calver and Helen Hoy, eds, *The Native in Literature: Canadian and Comparative Contexts* (Toronto: ECW Press, 1987), 137.
35 Van Essen, 'nêhiyawaskiy (Cree Land) and Canada: Location, Language, and Borders in Tomson Highway's *Kiss of the Fur Queen*', 106.

joins him there where the young boys are forced to speak English and are sexually abused by the priests. The sub-title of Part Three (Chapters 12–22) is *Allegretto grazioso* – slower than allegro, and graceful, like an elegiac, mourning song. This section explores Jeremiah's experiences at high school, his loneliness, and the beginning of his alcohol addiction. Part Four (Chapters 23–33) is sub-titled *Molto agitato*, which means very agitated with excitement. This section discusses the homecomings of Jeremiah and Gabriel each summer and the cultural rift between the boys and their parents and community. Part Five (Chapters 34–40) is sub-titled *Adagio expressivo*, which means slowly and expressively with feeling. The section describes Jeremiah's desolation, William William's death, Jeremiah's social work in the community, and how the brothers help one another. The sub-title for Part Six (Chapters 41–9), *Presto con fuoco*, means very quick with fire or passion. This section describes the artistic creations and collaborations of Jeremiah and Gabriel as they move beyond abuse into various passionate performances.

Certain phrases recur and function like musical refrains throughout the novel: 'campfire smoke, pine needles, of reindeer moss after rain', 'make me bleed, father, make me bleed', and 'Weeks'chiloowew!'[36] Highway uses musical terms to show the passing of time: 'Jeremiah's 16th notes lift him through the landscapes of his youth and end up, six years later, fluttering bird-like to a landing in Winnipeg.'[37] Music is important thematically as well as structurally as Jeremiah's classical European training distances him from the music that is popular in his community back home. Jeremiah's and Amanda's friends and family feel alienated by Jeremiah's impromptu performance of Chopin. One listener shouts, 'That there is whiteman music',[38] and demands honkytonk music for dancing instead. In his professional debut concert, Jeremiah bridges the gap by interpreting the passions

---

36   Highway glosses this term as 'the wind's a-changing! with childish pronunciation (a cry of joy, of boundless elation, as nonsensical yet as expressive of a point as 'heavens to Betsy!')' in *Kiss of the Fur Queen*, 310.

37   Highway, *Kiss of the Fur Queen*, 96.

38   Highway, *Kiss of the Fur Queen*, 255.

of the north into a classical piece, but eventually he is unable to sustain the diametric pulls of the cultural divide and ends up abandoning the piano.

The novel, with its integration of different performative modes, is an example of what Mikhail Bakhtin would call a hybrid. By hybrid, Bakhtin means 'the mixing, within a single concrete utterance, of two or more different linguistic consciousnesses, often widely separated in time and social space.'[39] While Bakhtin suggests that all novels are hybrids containing a range of linguistic codes, he argues that an 'intentional and conscious hybrid' incorporates two or more linguistic and stylistic discourses 'artistically organized' in a single form.[40] Cree storytelling and classical piano are just two of the performative modes that Highway combines in addition to other modes mediated for the text, such as theatre, televised dramas, and dance. Highway creates tension by juxtaposing Cree storytelling with the musical structuring of the chapters and the hybrid structure embodies the divisive splitting that Jeremiah experiences as a young boy taken from his family.

Command Performances of Language

In *Kiss of the Fur Queen*, Jeremiah and Gabriel grow up amidst more than one linguistic discourse. They speak Woods Cree as their mother tongue and are forced to speak English at residential school before they can understand what they are being made to say. The discourse in the novel incorporates what Bakhtin defines as 'heteroglossia' where more than one linguistic system is at work to express multiple ideologies and the distinct world views of characters.[41] In the novel, Highway engages with heteroglossia in a few ways, as he integrates some unglossed Cree phrases to develop connections with Cree-speaking readers in some places and includes some Cree phrases

39 Mikhail Bakhtin, *The Dialogic Imagination*, ed. Michael Holquist, trans. Caryl Emerson and Michael Holquist (Austin: University of Texas Press, 1981), 429.
40 Bakhtin, *The Dialogic Imagination*, 366.
41 Bakhtin, *The Dialogic Imagination*, 324.

that can be translated through the glossary by non-Cree-speaking readers in others. When Jeremiah and Gabriel are first forced to speak English and stumble through the Hail Mary prayer looking for recognizable morsels in the language, Highway demonstrates the foreign and impenetrable qualities of English as it was used as a controlling and colonizing device carrying with it an entirely different world view than the boys' own.[42] Gabriel's rendition of 'Hail Mary' operates on more than one level simultaneously: 'Hello merry, mutter of cod, play for ussinees, now anat tee ower of ower beth, aw, men.'[43] In Bakhtinian terms, this dialogism is an example of 'a double-voiced discourse' where one phrase delivers two meanings at the same time as it expresses 'the direct intention of the character who is speaking' and 'the authorial intentions but in a refracted way'.[44] As Gabriel substitutes the Cree word 'ussinees', which means 'pebble' in Cree, in the prayer for 'us sinners', Gabriel wonders, 'what need did this mutter of cod have of a pebble?'[45] As readers first scan the sentence, they share a moment of disorientation with the boys as English is represented even to English-speakers as a foreign language and then, as certain words in the prayer become recognizable and laden with double meanings, readers may smile at the boys' innocent interpretation of the prayer. However, non-Cree-speaking readers are likely to miss yet another layer of meaning. Van Essen reveals that Cree-speakers not only understand 'usinees' to mean 'little rocks' or 'pebbles' but also 'testicles' which foreshadows Gabriel's sexual abuse by Father Lafleur with a layered reference encoded in Cree.[46] This layer of understanding, which is only accessed through a knowledge of Cree as it is not glossed, reverses a traditionally dominant anglophone position as 'English-speakers become outsiders while Cree-speakers become insiders'.[47]

---

42   Highway, *Kiss of the Fur Queen*, 63.
43   Highway, *Kiss of the Fur Queen*, 71.
44   Bakhtin, *The Dialogic Imagination*, 324.
45   Highway, *Kiss of the Fur Queen*, 71.
46   Van Essen, 'nêhiyawaskiy (Cree Land) and Canada: Location, Language, and Borders in Tomson Highway's *Kiss of the Fur Queen*', 112.
47   Van Essen, 'nêhiyawaskiy (Cree Land) and Canada: Location, Language, and Borders in Tomson Highway's *Kiss of the Fur Queen*', 116.

Highway's characters speak a 'double-voiced discourse'[48] that is common among indigenous writers who have been forced to speak or write in English. Highway writes *Kiss of the Fur Queen* predominantly in English but also uses 'Creenglish' – a mix of Cree and English – and glosses only some of the Cree phrases within it which, as Van Essen suggests, 'unsettles the Anglophone readership'.[49] For some indigenous writers, the English language represents the loss of an indigenous language and a disconnection to culture and family, yet it remains the most viable possibility for publishing. Indigenous writers use a range of strategies to incorporate elements of indigenous languages into English and to create a sense of oral narrative. Basil H. Johnston believes language and culture are inseparable and it is impossible to know the culture without speaking an indigenous language.[50] Alternatively, Maria Campbell maintains that a writer can suggest nuances of an indigenous language, even if s/he doesn't speak one, in English.[51] To this purpose, Campbell writes in a dialect English that captures the sense of Mitchif, her first language. She does not write in Mitchif, she asserts, because it is not taught and its readership is limited.[52] Thomas King uses the term 'interfusional' to describe writing by indigenous authors which combines the oral and the written,[53] as found in the stories of Okanagan storyteller Harry Robinson, transcribed by Wendy Wickwire, in *Write*

48 Bakhtin, *The Dialogic Imagination*, 324.
49 Van Essen, 'nêhiyawaskiy (Cree Land) and Canada: Location, Language, and Borders in Tomson Highway's *Kiss of the Fur Queen*', 110.
50 Basil H. Johnston, 'Is That All There Is? Tribal Literature', in Daniel David Moses and Terry Goldie, eds, *An Anthology of Canadian Native Literature in English* [1991] (Toronto: Oxford University Press, 1998), 106.
51 Maria Campbell qtd in Harmut Lutz, *Contemporary Challenges: Conversations with Canadian Native Writers* (Saskatoon: Fifth House Publishing, 1991), 56.
52 Campbell qtd in Lutz, *Contemporary Challenges: Conversations with Canadian Native Writers*, 56.
53 Thomas King, 'Godzilla vs Post-colonial', *World Literature Written in English* 30/2 (1990), 10–16. King explores four models of Indigenous writing: tribal, interfusional, polemical, and associational.

It on Your Heart: The Epic World of an Okanagan Storyteller.[54] Robinson learned many of his stories from his grandmother in Okanagan, and he modulated Okanagan structures, rhythms, and expressions into English as he told them to Wickwire.

Making the decision to publish at all raises difficult issues for some indigenous writers because of certain cultural beliefs and traditions. In the preface to *An Anthology of Canadian Native Literature*, Daniel David Moses discusses the sense of alienation that occurs when written ideas become, as a result of publishing, separated from the author. Moses says the writing of ideas was first used as 'a storage medium' and now believes people have 'become oppressed by it'.[55] Moses emphasizes that a number of indigenous people work with words and do not publish. For some indigenous people, he says, 'If the material is working orally within the community, that's enough.'[56] However, the fact that Moses' words reach us through a written medium highlights the inherent paradox. In order for the stories to reach a large audience, publishing is likely. In addition to exposing aspects of indigenous culture that may be considered sensitive or sacred in a very public way, publishing imposes a fixity on the stories that is incompatible with the spontaneity and flexibility of oral storytelling.[57] Highway's performative dramatic mode, though written, gestures toward the oral and connective components of his cultural storytelling.

54   Harry Robinson, *Write It On Your Heart: The Epic World of an Okanagan Storyteller*, ed. Wendy Wickwire (Vancouver: Talonbooks/Theytus, 1989), 13.
55   Daniel David Moses and Terry Goldie, *An Anthology of Canadian Native Literature in English* [1991] (Toronto: Oxford University Press, 1998), xxv.
56   Moses and Goldie, *An Anthology of Canadian Native Literature in English*, xxvi.
57   See Maria Campbell and Linda Griffiths, *The Book of Jessica: A Theatrical Transformation* (Toronto: The Coach House Press, 1989), on the difficulties in representing sensitive aspects of indigenous spirituality in public pieces of theatre or literature.

Rehearsing New Roles

Kiss of the Fur Queen highlights the process of rehearsing and constructing new roles in theatre and in society. At the end of the novel, Jeremiah finds fulfilment through his work as a playwright. Re-writing his cultural history is the first step, but locating it in the body – his own and the bodies of the other performers – is even more satisfying than the writing itself. When Jeremiah rehearses an early version of *Son of Ayash* with Gabriel and Amanda Clear Sky, Amanda criticizes the script for coming too much from Jeremiah's head and not from the heart or the body.[58] She says: 'These lines, they're so ... they're unplayable. I can't do a thing with them.'[59] Gabriel points to his forehead and groin and explains: 'It's all head, Jeremiah, all head and no gut. Watch.'[60] Gabriel leads the actors in a physical improvisation to bring the actors' bodies into the legend. Jeremiah hardly recognizes his script as, 'one by one, the company fell in with the chant, a dance, a Cree rite of sacrifice, swirling like blood around the altar and bouncing off the bass of the piano like, yes, magic'.[61] After the actors 'workshop' the script with music and dance, they release it from its static textual confines and open it up to a more embodied form.

This scene provides an example of how a dramatic mode in a novel can bring about a sense of an embodied enactment within the confines of text. Jeremiah's script fails initially because it does not bring a sense of physicality or the body into the story. Without any sense of the physical, the story is thin, reiterative, and largely irrelevant to the actors, let alone to the audience who will later see the production. Readers witness Gabriel and the company improvise and re-imagine the story with their bodies. The enactment allows the story to live again in a present moment. In some more conventional novels on indigenous people, discourse on the

---

58 A production of *Son of Ayash*, written by Jim Morris, was performed in Toronto by Native Earth Performing Arts in 2008.
59 Highway, *Kiss of the Fur Queen*, 279.
60 Highway, *Kiss of the Fur Queen*, 280.
61 Highway, *Kiss of the Fur Queen*, 280.

body and on the body's role in expressing its history is neglected. Here, the dramatic mode centres the body in the telling of a story which carries cultural significance to the brothers. The brothers' creative efforts hark back to Abraham's dying words from the *Son of Ayash:* 'My son, [...] with these magic weapons, make a new world.'[62] While the magic weapons in the legend were a spear, an axe, and a fox's pelt, Jeremiah and Gabriel use theatre, music, language, and dance as the magic weapons which connect the players to their cultural heritage.[63]

In *Iskwewak Ka' Ki Yaw Ni Wahkomakanak: Neither Indian Princesses nor Easy Squaws*, Janice Acoose describes how Louis Riel, leader of the Métis, prophesied just before he was executed in 1885 that his people would rise up a hundred years later, and 'artists, musicians, dancers, writers, and other visionaries would lead the way to a cultural renaissance.'[64] Highway's novel illustrates how artistic leaders invigorate and regenerate cultural stories.

One of Jeremiah's primary concerns is to make his culture relevant for future generations of Cree people. He sees *Son of Ayash* as the '[c]losest thing the Cree have to their own Ulysses' and adds his own 'modern twist[s]' so that the urban Cree children he teaches, his *Muskoosisuk* or 'little bears', can see reflections of themselves in the world.[65] Interestingly, in the same year *Kiss of the Fur Queen* was published, Highway wrote his first children's picture book, *Caribou Song*, which tells the story of two brothers who survive being trapped by a herd of caribou. One page is in English, the next page is in Cree, and English and Cree alternate throughout the book. Highway's search for inventive storytelling forms in drama, fiction, children's literature, opera, and musicals, and highlights his commitment to and interest in oral traditions and a living indigenous language.

62   Highway, *Kiss of the Fur Queen*, 267.
63   Highway, *Kiss of the Fur Queen*, 302.
64   Janice Acoose, *Iskwewak Ka' Ki Yaw Ni Wahkomakanak: Neither Indian Princesses nor Easy Squaws* (Toronto: Women's Press, 1995), 115–17.
65   Highway, *Kiss of the Fur Queen*, 277–8.

Brown Skin, White Masks

Highway's characters, while growing up, see no positive reflections of themselves in Western urban society or in the arts. He uses a dramatic mode in *Kiss of the Fur Queen* to re-work stereotypes and create positive and subversive images of indigenous artists. Readers are cast in various audiences at different points in the novel and witness how racial and cultural stereotypes are created by dominant classes as a means of seizing and maintaining power and providing an 'other' to hold against their own self-affirming identity constructions. We also see how Cree characters reject and manipulate these stereotypes as a strategy of resistance, empowerment, and survival.

At residential school, Jeremiah searches for an image of himself in the giant chart depicting God, Satan, and the realms of Heaven and Hell. Heaven was full of blond men with wings and harps, and there were no brown people, or accordions.[66] Only when Jeremiah looks down in the realms of Hell does he see 'dark-skinned people' sitting and 'skinny, slimy creatures with blackish-brownish scaly skin, long, pointy tails, and horns on their heads'.[67] He exclaims, 'Aha! This is where the Indians are, [...] relieved that they were accounted for on this great chart.'[68] In *Prison of Grass: Canada from a Native Point of View*, Harold Adams describes a scenario similar to the one experienced by Jeremiah: 'As soon as native children enter school they are surrounded with white-supremacist ideas and stories.'[69] Adams argues that children 'cannot avoid seeing the cultural images and symbols of white supremacy, because they are everywhere in society, especially in movies, television, comic books, and textbooks'.[70]

66   Highway, *Kiss of the Fur Queen*, 59.
67   Highway, *Kiss of the Fur Queen*, 60.
68   Highway, *Kiss of the Fur Queen*, 60.
69   Harold Adams, *Prison of Grass: Canada from a Native Point of View* (Saskatoon: Fifth House, 1989), 14.
70   Adams, *Prison of Grass: Canada from a Native Point of View*, 14.

Janice Acoose recalls a similar bombardment in residential school where she was taught to 'reject [her] cultures, languages, history, and ancestors'.[71] She writes:

> I also wasn't aware how those seemingly innocent stories from our primary readers about Dick, Jane, Spot and Puff served an ideological system much different to my own. As I grew older, however, I began to wonder why I could never find reflections of my wonderfully alive and continually busy home life in those early books used in school.[72]

As a result of the ideological forces of Canada she calls 'weccp' ('white-eurocanadian-christian-patriarchal'),[73] Acoose internalized her differences as inferiorities. She believed 'the easy squaw, Indian-whore, dirty Indian, and drunken Indian stereotypes' that had been thrust upon her.[74] Acoose refers to Ngugi wa Thiong'o's *Writers in Politics* in which Ngugi describes the negative impact 'distorted images' have on colonized people in literature.[75] Ngugi sees literature as a particularly oppressive and insidious form of colonization because it 'works through influencing emotions, the imagination, the consciousness of a people'.[76] As ruling classes create gratifying images of themselves, they often construct distorted reflections of colonized people to serve their own ideological purposes. Some distortions, such as the ones discussed by Ngugi, are overtly derogatory, while others, such as the valorization of 'native' purity and nobility, reflect the projection of idealized qualities that non-indigenous people may find themselves lacking or desiring. As Terry Goldie says, building on Olivier Richon's observations of Orientalism in art and Bill Pearson's analysis of

71   Janice Acoose, 'Post Halfbreed: Indigenous Writers as Authors of Their Own Realities', *Looking at the Words of Our People: First Nations Analysis of Literature* (Penticton: Theytus Books, 1993), 27–44.

72   Acoose, 'Post Halfbreed: Indigenous Writers as Authors of Their Own Realities', 20.

73   Acoose, 'Post Halfbreed: Indigenous Writers as Authors of Their Own Realities', 20.

74   Acoose, 'Post Halfbreed: Indigenous Writers as Authors of Their Own Realities', 29.

75   Ngugi qtd in Acoose, 'Post Halfbreed: Indigenous Writers as Authors of Their Own Realities', 15.

76   Ngugi wa Thiong'o, *Writers in Politics* (London: Heinemann Educational Books, 1981), 50.

the image of the Maori by pakeha (white) writers, 'imperialist discourse valorizes the colonized according to its needs for reflection'.[77]

In *Kiss of the Fur Queen*, Jeremiah and Gabriel learn to internalize their differences in a predominantly white high school in Winnipeg. Over time, they come to imagine themselves as white and it is only when Amanda Clear Sky joins their school that Jeremiah is confronted with the perception of how others actually view him:

> Jeremiah was put on his guard: was it because this young – and undeniably Indian – girl confronted him with his own Indianness, which his weekly bus sightings of the drunks on North Main Street had driven him to deny so utterly that he went for weeks believing his own skin to be white as parchment?[78]

In *Black Skin, White Masks*, Franz Fanon analyses the denigration that occurs when one is taught by the ruling powers to hate oneself. While Fanon's theory developed from his experience growing up as a black man in Martinique, *Black Skin, White Masks* provides a useful example for understanding some aspects of performative identity that can be applied to a Canadian-indigenous context as the brothers internalize and perform 'white' identities in Highway's novel. Jeremiah and Gabriel are taught by society to 'act white' as they learn to simultaneously reject their language and culture. Fanon describes this condition as a dead end and suggests the only choice for people in this situation is to 'turn white or disappear'.[79] For Jeremiah, internalizing self-hatred and inferiority under a white mask is the most damaging role he plays. Later on, Amanda Clear Sky teaches Jeremiah and the class about Wounded Knee, the Cherokee Trail of Tears and the effects of smallpox blankets on indigenous people which are not mentioned in the history textbooks at school.[80] She encourages the Okimasis brothers not to be passive recipients of stereotypes and to reject the farce of their

---

77   Terry Goldie, *Fear and Temptation: The Image of the Indigene in Canadian, Australian and New Zealand Literatures* (Kingston: McGill-Queen's University Press, 1989), 12.

78   Highway, *Kiss of the Fur Queen*, 123.

79   Frantz Fanon, *Black Skin, White Masks*, trans. Charles Lam Markmann (London: Paladin, 1970), 100.

80   Highway, *Kiss of the Fur Queen*, 147.

'white' identities. Amanda dares the brothers to remove their white masks and urges them to re-claim their souls through performative modes.

In *The Wretched of the Earth*, Fanon describes three stages of development in the imaginative work of colonized writers. In the first stage, writers 'produce [...] work to be read exclusively by the oppressor'.[81] In the second stage, writers produce work to be read by their own people. In the third stage, which Fanon proposed but never saw actualized, writers create a national literature which would call to arms 'the whole people to fight for their existence as a nation'.[82] Writers in the third stage would update 'the stories, epics, and songs of the people' in order to 'modernize the kinds of struggle which the stories evoke[d]'.[83] Fanon saw the updated stories as powerful tools that would first draw in and then mobilize the public. He wrote: 'Every time the storyteller relates a fresh episode to his public, he presides over a real invocation'.[84]

Fanon believed that compelling forms of dramatic expression could rally a community to act and 'make unreal and unacceptable the contemplative attitude, or the acceptance of defeat'.[85] Unlike Bertolt Brecht, who believed that an excess of dramatic feeling, or a catharsis in an audience, pre-empted political action, Fanon believed the stirring nature of drama and the shared dramatic histories and legends would arouse and essentially rehearse the necessary emotions in the audience members which would ideally lead to revolutionary changes. While Fanon's idea of a 'whole people' coming together is too simplified in the context of diverse indigenous cultures uniting as 'one nation' in a multi-cultural and postcolonial society, his theory interestingly values drama and storytelling as part of a significant political stage in the creative development of colonized cultures. His idea of the invocation underscores the way in which a story, or perhaps even

81   Frantz Fanon, *The Wretched of the Earth*, pref. Jean-Paul Sartre, trans. Constance Farrington (Harmondsworth: Penguin Books, 1967), 240.
82   Fanon, *The Wretched of the Earth*, 240.
83   Fanon, *The Wretched of the Earth*, 240.
84   Fanon, *The Wretched of the Earth*, 241.
85   Fanon, *The Wretched of the Earth*, 243.

a dramatic mode in fiction, summons an audience to visit active versions of history.

While Jeremiah is a performer in *Kiss of the Fur Queen*, he is also an audience member who watches the Ojibway pow wow with scepticism and self-hatred. Catholicism has taught Jeremiah to view indigenous religion as devil-worship. He recoils when he sees indigenous men at the pow wow in traditional dancing regalia and finds something 'pagan', 'primitive' and 'satanic' about it (162). Jeremiah has been taught to view his Cree roots as what Fanon calls 'a sort of quintessence of evil' or 'colonial disease'.[86] According to Fanon,

> Every effort is made to bring the colonized person to admit the inferiority of his culture which has been transformed into instinctive patterns of behaviour, to recognize the unreality of his nation, and, in the last extreme, the confused and imperfect character of his own biological structure.[87]

After stumbling upon the scene at the Winnipeg Indian Friendship Centre where everyone else participates, Jeremiah is an audience of one. He differentiates between 'Indians civilized enough for jeans and other human dress such as T-shirts' and the 'clutch of feather-tufted dancers' in the centre of the action.[88] In Jeremiah's view, the dancers parody embarrassing stereotypes: 'Had he just walked into a Buffalo Bill Wild West extravaganza? A John Wayne movie? Where were the horses, the tired pioneers, the circle of dusty chuckwagons?'[89] He laughs at Amanda Clear Sky dressed up like Princess Pocahontas in her 'get-up' and says, 'Disney Indians, [...] Hollywood Indians dress like that'.[90] Jeremiah is engulfed in pervasive stereotypes from Hollywood Westerns and Disney animations and sees the representations around him as inauthentic copies of white stereotypical ideas of Indians.

---

86   Fanon, *The Wretched of the Earth*, 41.
87   Fanon, *The Wretched of the Earth*, 236.
88   Highway, *Kiss of the Fur Queen*, 171.
89   Highway, *Kiss of the Fur Queen*, 171.
90   Highway, *Kiss of the Fur Queen*, 173.

While Gabriel joins the round dance, Jeremiah remains as an onlooker:
'Jeremiah merely scratched his balls, for, after ten years of southern Manitoba
pow wows – scraping drunks off the street and taking them there by the van
load – they still made him feel like a German tourist.'[91] Jeremiah is finally
drawn in when he hears Ann-Adele Ghostrider tell an Ojibway version
of the story of Chachagathoo that unsettles what he has been taught to
believe by his priest growing up.

Jeremiah was taught by his mother, of Cree descent in Northern
Manitoba, that Chachagathoo had *machipoowamoowin* or 'bad dreaming
power'.[92] Their Cree priest made Chachagathoo out to be a Satanic witch
but Ann-Adele Ghostrider, who is Ojibway, instead praised Chachagathoo
for exorcising the Weetigo out of a man who was possessed. Highway
describes the Weetigo as a 'cannibal creature that devours human flesh;
an anti-hero figure used to explain what evil is'.[93] The brothers learn that
Ann-Adele Ghostrider's Ojibway people were not against Chachagathoo,
as the Northern Manitoba Cree were taught to be by the Church, but,
rather they admired her spirit and *mithoopoowamoowin* or 'good dreaming power'.[94] 'Your parents' generation? In the north? Lied to and lied to
and lied to!' Ann-Adele Ghostrider exclaims.[95] This is a turning point for
Jeremiah who begins to examine the motives of the Church and starts to
see spiritual enrichment in Cree culture where he previously saw stereotypes. Highway writes:

> The drums had stopped, but eight hours of their nonstop presence had implanted
> their blood-like pulse in the marrow, and the brothers Okimasis spent that evening –
> and the night, the weeks that followed – drifting in a dream-like euphoria. Poowow,
> to dream, poowamoowin, the act of dreaming.[96]

91 Highway, *Kiss of the Fur Queen*, 242.
92 Highway, *Kiss of the Fur Queen*, 197.
93 Duncan McKeough, 'The Storyteller: Tomson Highway', *Info Culture Magazine*:
    Special Coverage <http://www.infoculture.cbc.ca/archives/special_coverage/spec
    ial_coverage_tomsonhighway.html> accessed 18 May 2008.
94 Highway, *Kiss of the Fur Queen*, 247.
95 Highway, *Kiss of the Fur Queen*, 247.
96 Highway, *Kiss of the Fur Queen*, 245.

Re-utilization of Stereotypes

Highway re-works stereotypes of indigenous identities in urban Canadian society. One of its strategies is to hail the Okimasis brothers into being in a way that is similar to Louis Althusser's theory of interpellation in 'Ideology and Ideological State Apparatuses'.[97] Althusser demonstrates how an individual recognizes himself or herself as a subject within the ideology of society. He uses an example of a policeman who shouts, 'Hey, you!' at someone on the street. This is called 'hailing'. Most likely, someone will turn around and submit himself or herself as the subject called. The reaction is the process by which we voluntarily acknowledge ourselves to be subjects within the dominant ideology of society (in this example, within the ideology of law and order). Althusser uses 'interpellation' to dispel the humanist concept of a coherent, unified identity by illustrating how an individual continually constructs an identity through a network of discursive and social structures.

When Gabriel refers to himself as a Cree Nijinsky, in effect he hails himself within an existing white ideology where indigenous people are not typically regarded as world-renowned artistic legends. The novel hails the brothers before the reader and inner audiences into a variety of performative roles, including Cree Adonis, Cree Scholar, and Cree Dionysus. The adjectival use of Cree is ambiguously complex. While new conceptions of artistic identities for Jeremiah and Gabriel are forged through the bridged identities – Cree this, Cree that – Highway uses the modifier 'Cree' ironically to emphasize how audiences view the boys first as 'Indians', no matter what further distinctions they may achieve. Yet there is a certain gleeful celebration detectable in each one of Highway's Cree descriptors; an irrepressible and parodic energy erupts in each indigenous comparison to the 'incomparable' white European ideal. The adjectival modifier has a distancing effect on the reader. Each time the term is used, the reader is jolted out

97   Louis Althusser, 'Ideology and Ideological State Apparatuses: Notes Toward an Investigation', *Lenin and Philosophy, and Other Essays*, trans. Ben Brewster (New York: Monthly Review Press), 123–73.

of the story and prompted to perceive the character from the perspective
of dominant white majority. The term urges readers to consider, repeat-
edly, and with some humour, racial inequality for indigenous people and
performers, and the energy of resistance and empowerment, as the brothers express their passions.

When the Okimasis brothers participate in the high school production
of *The Gondoliers*, the novel describes how Gabriel's brown skin pre-occupies
the white audience and prevents spectators from becoming involved in
the play itself. Jeremiah plays piano, and when one of the actors falls ill,
Gabriel takes on the lead role of Giuseppe Palmieri.[98] Highway describes
Gabriel as the audience members see him: 'an Indian-Italian gondolier,
Cree-Spanish prince'.[99] He writes:

> There were two facts of indisputable and universal clarity: first, the pianist in the
> orchestra was as Indian as Sitting Bull and, second, one of the gondoliers-cum-
> princes, as identical as Tweedledum and Tweedledee, was white as nougat, the other
> brown as cocoa.[100]

The musical is continually upstaged by the colour-blind casting of the
indigenous brothers. The audience is captivated by the 'Indian' playing the
Italian gondolier, which they 'never imagined', and by 'the Indian pianist',
which they found 'curious, even thought-provoking'.[101] Audience members
at the production within the novel perceive at least two layers of illusion in
the performance onstage. They see a character playing a role, but foremost,
they see their conception of an 'Indian' playing an Italian. Through a literary
version of metatheatre, a reader's interpretive vision is, in Joanne Tompkins'
terms, 'split' and 'paradoxically, multiplied'[102] between the audience who
is challenged by what it sees and the players who bring on the challenge.

98   Highway, *Kiss of the Fur Queen*, 157.
99   Highway, *Kiss of the Fur Queen*, 157.
100   Highway, *Kiss of the Fur Queen*, 155.
101   Highway, *Kiss of the Fur Queen*, 157.
102   Joanne Tompkins, '"Spectacular Resistance": Metatheatre in Post-Colonial Drama', 45.

Highway writes that Gabriel 'instinctively [...] knew that he was doing something revolutionary, perhaps historical, definitely head-turning'.[103]

Highway made revolutionary and historical contributions in writing some of the first and most powerful plays for indigenous characters in Canadian theatre history. Before Highway's *The Rez Sisters* in 1986, most plays with indigenous characters were written by whites and featured a range of stereotypes. Early Canadian dramas, such as *Ponteach: A Tragedy* (1766) and *Tecumseh* (1886), perpetuated the idea of the noble savage in the 'Indian heroic tragedy'.[104] George Ryga's *The Ecstasy of Rita Joe* (1967) confronted the social problems faced by indigenous people in Canada with a sympathetic yet stereotypical view and Métis Maria Campbell developed a play called *Jessica* (1989) with non-indigenous actor Linda Griffiths, based on Campbell's autobiography *Halfbreed* (1973). However, for Campbell, this was a fractious process which led to her decision not to work on a collaborative writing project with a non-indigenous writer again: 'It's been very painful. There was no respect for the place that I came from. You don't go walking into somebody's personal places and pick through their stuff and decide what you're going to walk off with!'[105] Campbell's and Griffith's play, *Jessica*, was published along with a commentary about the process of its creation in *The Book of Jessica*. During the 1970s and 1980s, a number of indigenous theatre companies formed, including the Association for Native Development in the Performing and Visual Arts in Toronto, the Native Theatre School, and the Native Earth Performing Arts (1982). In 1984, the De-Ba-Jeh-Mu-Jig Theatre Group was formed on Manitoulin Island, and it was for this group that Highway wrote his first play, *The Rez Sisters*.

Kiss of the Fur Queen illustrates the ways in which stereotypes created by dominant forces begin to be unsettled and subverted by indigenous

103 Highway, *Kiss of the Fur Queen*, 155.
104 Terry Goldie, 'Indigenous Stages: the Indigene in Canadian, New Zealand and Australian Drama', in Thomas King, Cheryl Calver and Helen Hoy, eds, *The Native in Literature* (Toronto: ECW Press, 1987), 7.
105 Campbell qtd in Lutz, *Contemporary Challenges: Conversations with Canadian Native Writers*, 56.

characters through strategies of appropriation and re-appropriation.[106] In 'Signs Taken for Wonders', Homi Bhabha describes hybridity as a 'strategic reversal of the process of domination through [...] the production of discriminatory identities that secure the '"pure" and original identity of authority'.[107] Highway describes Amanda Clear Sky at the pow wow inviting Jeremiah to dance in stereotypical terms that quickly become subverted: 'With a saucy grin, the dusky Indian maid held out a slender hand, "Wanna dance?"'.[108] The 'dusky Indian maid' in the narration is subverted and re-appropriated as Amanda performs a modernized and urban interpretation of the stereotype. She does not acquiesce silently or bewitch Gabriel through modest wiles; she grabs his hands, yells, 'Come on, come on, come on, come on', and drags him kicking and screaming onto the dance floor.[109] Highway places Amanda in the role of aggressor and Jeremiah in the role of feminized 'maid' in a more empowered and updated encounter, and the concept of the 'Indian maid' is exposed for the stereotypes it carries within it.

In another example, Highway exploits the stereotype of the 'ever wily Indian' in Gabriel's seduction of Father Vincent Connolly. When the priest tells Gabriel the rectory is occupied, 'the ever wily Cree boldly offered him tea at his residence'.[110] Here, the 'ever wily Indian' uses all his skills of cunning to plan a sexual rendez-vous with a priest. Gabriel enacts a new version of the stereotype, where the 'ever wily Indian' is out to seduce, rather than scheme against, his victim. The scene subverts the stereotypical captor/victim dynamic that is conventionally represented between whites and indigenous people in history. In both of the previous examples of re-utilizing stereotypes, Highway performs Bhabha's idea of hybridity: he 'unsettles the mimetic or narcissistic demands of colonial power but

---

106   Similar parodies of stereotypes of indigenous people are explored in Monique Mojika, *Princess Pocahontas and the Blue Spots: Two plays* (Toronto: Women's Press, 1991).

107   Homi K. Bhabha, 'Signs taken for wonders: questions of ambivalence and authority under a tree outside Delhi, May 1817', *Critical Inquiry* 12/1 (Autumn 1985), 154.

108   Highway, *Kiss of the Fur Queen*, 173.

109   Highway, *Kiss of the Fur Queen*, 173.

110   Highway, *Kiss of the Fur Queen*, 185.

re-implicates its identifications in strategies of subversion that turn the gaze of the discriminated back upon the eye of power'.[111] By role-playing new versions of the old stereotypes that served the needs of non-indigenous people in history, Highway begins to change the representation of the dynamic of power between white and indigenous characters.

Representing Violence in Highway's Writing: Mythology and Comic Shades

While Highway portrays violence in his novel, including graphic and tragic accounts of rape, sexual assault, and murder, the undertone of his writing is not one of despair, but, rather, growth and humour. His main characters generally move beyond violence and abuse in their lives, as with Jeremiah and Gabriel, although this is not always the case. In *Dry Lips Oughta Move to Kapuskasing*, Highway describes the brutal rape and murder of a young indigenous girl, Zhaboonigan, by a gang of white boys. In *Kiss of the Fur Queen*, Highway describes similar violent rapes against three indigenous women perpetrated by white men using a screw driver and a broken bottle. These attacks allude to the historical case of Helen Betty Osborne, in which a young indigenous girl was raped and brutally beaten by four men in a car on 13 November 1971 in La Pas, Manitoba.[112] One report indicated 'a screw driver was at least one weapon used' in the sexual attack.[113] The report concluded 'that Helen Betty Osborne fell victim to vicious stereotypes born of ignorance and aggression' when she was picked up by four drunken men who showed no regard for her humanity.[114]

---

111   Bhabha, 'Signs taken for wonders: questions of ambivalence and authority under a tree outside Delhi, May 1817', 154.
112   Acoose, *Iskwewak Ka' Ki Yaw Ni Wahkomakanak*, 69.
113   Acoose, *Iskwewak Ka' Ki Yaw Ni Wahkomakana*, 69.
114   Acoose, *Iskwewak Ka' Ki Yaw Ni Wahkomakana*, 69.

The third female rape victim in *Kiss of the Fur Queen*, referred to as the Madonna of North Main, is pregnant when she gets into the car with the four drunken men. She, unlike the first two victims, is not later found dead. Jeremiah sees her, or a vision of her, at the Hell Hotel after he wins the trophy for the piano competition. She is 'mountainous' and '27 months pregnant' and tells Jeremiah: 'You make me so proud to be a fuckin' Indian, you know that?' (216). She transcends her role as a victim and appears before Jeremiah in a vision of robust fertility and survival. Highway presents a mythological vision of the mountainous Madonna of North Main that inspires Jeremiah into his own artistic fertility. The young, enormously pregnant, and fiercely proud woman presents a contrast to the other two female victims who died in the ditch and the alley. The Madonna of North Main symbolizes Gerald Vizenor's term of 'Native survivance' as she personifies 'an active sense of presence' which performs 'the continuance of native stories' and rejects 'dominance, tragedy and victimry'.[115] Highway's use of myth in the vision of the Madonna of North Main emphasizes the vital role mythology plays in Cree narratives. In *Comparing Mythologies*, Highway defines 'three distinct terms' for the concept of narrative in Cree:

> The first term is *achimoowin*, which means 'to tell a story' or 'to tell the truth.' The second is *kithaskiwin*, which means 'to tell a lie,' meaning 'to weave a web of fiction,' as it were. And the third, which lies at a point exactly halfway between these first two is *achithoogeewin*, which means 'to mythologize.' Meaning that the visionaries of my people, the thinkers who gave birth and shape to the Cree language as we know it today, chose the exact halfway point between truth and lie, non-fiction and fiction, to situate mythology.[116]

Highway explains how mythologies form narratives that are central to the development and shaping of all societies and 'Cree mythology' or 'Cree *achithoogeewin*' instruct Cree people in 'distinct ways of thinking, of relating to our planet, of relating to our universe, of relating to our bodies and

---

115   Gerald Vizenor, *Manifest Manners: Postindian Warriors of Survivance* (Lincoln: University of Nebraska Press, 1994), vii.
116   Highway, *Comparing Mythologies*, 21–2.

ourselves, of relating to the very environment in which, and because of which, we live, breathe, and walk'.[117]

Highway uses comic elements in some of his most serious scenes. The comedy is wry and, at times, quite painful, and prevents readers from falling into despair along with the characters by bringing them back to an immediate, and oftentimes, ironic, present. In *Dry Lips*, the Marilyn Monroe poster farts just after Dickie Bird shoots himself in the head. In *Kiss of the Fur Queen*, the scene in which Father Lafleur sexually abuses young Jeremiah and ejaculates over him directly precedes the scene where adult Jeremiah plays a rousing rendition of 'O Come all ye faithful' on the organ as he recalls the abuse.[118] In a Brechtian way, Highway's tragic-comic mode prevents readers from becoming emotionally overcome by the stories of abuse which might promote and perpetuate the idea that indigenous people are victims. Brecht believed that catharsis aroused by sentimental empathy in the theatre prevented critical thinking and political action. While Highway's characterizations are more emotionally realized than Brecht's are, Highway, like Brecht, does not allow readers to wallow in sorrow or become overcome in a cathartic release. Highway frames sombre moments with humour, allowing readers to perceive emotional scenes and then recover from them with a tragic-comic jolt. The humour in the narrative reflects a spirit of vitality that is represented in Highway's plays and valued in indigenous cultures. In an interview with Duncan McKeough, Highway says:

> We can only think of ourselves as victims for so long. You know we faced the fact that we have been victims. We close that chapter, we deal with it. We air out that chamber of horrors and it's water under the bridge. We move on. And that's another reason why I wrote the novel.[119]

From within and outside indigenous cultures, indigenous writers face expectations of how indigenous characters should be represented. Highway has been criticized for creating characters who are urban, Western-educated,

---

117 Highway, *Comparing Mythologies*, 28.
118 Highway, *Kiss of the Fur Queen*, 81.
119 Duncan McKeough, 'The Storyteller: Tomson Highway', 1.

and isolated from indigenous communities. Rolland Nadjiwon argues that Highway sees progress as moving toward and privileging European ideals, as opposed to living on the reservation.[120] Yet, Nadjiwon's definition of what is 'authentically' indigenous does not accommodate a range of contemporary identities of indigenous people who may not live in a community of other indigenous people or know an indigenous language, yet still identify as indigenous. In 'The Myth of Authenticity', Gareth Griffiths describes how a thirst for 'aboriginal authenticity' can be counter-productive: 'In such a fetishized use of the inscription of the authentic a further and subtler example of control emerges, one which in this use may function just as negatively in its impact on the effective empowerment of [...] aboriginal voices.'[121] Highway draws from contrasting backdrops of the reservation and the city-scape in his performative novel of the Okimasis brothers who define their own urban, artistic indigenous identities.

Like Highway, Métis writer Marilyn Dumont explores how indigenous writers are affected by people's expectations of what is authentically indigenous. While she identifies common elements that appear often in indigenous literature – a connectedness to the environment, an awareness of messages from the animal and spirit world, a strong sense of community – she argues that the 'authenticity' comes by virtue of the writer's identity and identification as indigenous, which is presented as rather a check-list of indigenous content. She says:

> If you are old, you are supposed to write legends [...]. If you are young, you are expected to relate stories about foster homes, street life and loss of culture and if you are in the middle, you are supposed to write about alcoholism or residential school. And somehow throughout this, you are to infuse everything you write with symbols of the native worldview, that is: the circle, mother earth, the number four or the trickster figure.[122]

---

120   Rolland Nadjiwon, 'Harvesting the Colonies', *ASAIL Notes* 13/31 (1996), 8.
121   Gareth Griffiths, 'The Myth of Authenticity', in Bill Ashcroft, Gareth Griffiths and Helen Tiffin, eds, *The Post-Colonial Studies Reader* (London: Routledge, 1995), 241.
122   Marilyn Dumont, 'Popular Images of Nativeness', *Looking at the Words of Our People: First Nations Analysis of Literature* (Penticton: Theytus Books, 1993), 47.

Dumont writes that indigenous people are scrutinized by both non-indigenous and indigenous people for being 'too Indian or not Indian enough'.[123] With growing numbers of indigenous people living in urban centres, writers, including Highway and Dumont, challenge the image of the rural and traditional indigenous person that is perpetuated by the hegemonic and indigenous cultures. Dumont contends there is no one static concept of what is indigenous, and argues that 'monolithic, singular images of "Nativeness" [...] are popularly seductive but ultimately oppressive'.[124]

Trickster Extraordinaire: Maggie Sees

Highway suggests the Trickster is 'as pivotal and important a figure in our world as Christ is in the realm of Christian mythology'.[125] He describes the 'many guises and names' that the Trickster goes by: 'Weesageechak' in Cree, 'Nanabush' in Ojibway, 'Raven' in others, 'Coyote' in still others. The Trickster has a fluid, rather than a fixed, gender and appears in both masculine and feminine guises.[126] Highway defines the Trickster as 'essentially a comic, clownish character' who 'straddles the consciousness of man and that of God, the Great Spirit'.[127] The Trickster returns to the brothers periodically in the character of Maggie Sees.

Miss Maggie Sees is a shape-shifter and consummate performer. She materializes to Jeremiah, after his father's death, as a showgirl who also is a fox. Maggie Sees, which translates to *fox* in Cree (*maggeesees*) is the

123   Dumont, 'Popular Images of Nativeness', *Looking at the Words of Our People: First Nations Analysis of Literature*, 49.
124   Dumont, 'Popular Images of Nativeness', *Looking at the Words of Our People: First Nations Analysis of Literature*, 48.
125   Tomson Highway, *Dry Lips Oughta Move to Kapuskasing* (Saskatoon: Fifth House, 1989), 12.
126   Highway, *Dry Lips Oughta Move to Kapuskasing*, 12.
127   Highway, *Dry Lips Oughta Move to Kapuskasing*, 12.

antithesis of the conventional Christian God. She is a *seer*, as her name
Sees suggests. She appears in white chiffon, with a bushy tail, gobs of eye
shadow, 'missile-like tits' and 'ice-blond meringue hair'.[128] When Jeremiah
demands to know who she is, she says:

> Honeypot, if I were you, I'd watch my tongue. Cuz you're talkin' to Miss Maggie Sees.
> Miss Maggie-Weesageechak-Nanabush-Coyote-Raven-Glooscap-oh-you-should-
> hear-the-things-they-call-me-honeypot-Sees, weaver of dreams, sparker of magic,
> showgirl from hell. [...] Show me the bastard who come up with the notion that
> who's running the goddamn show is some grumpy, embittered, sexually frustrated
> old fart with a long white beard hiding like a gutless coward behind some puffed-up
> cloud and I'll slice his goddamn balls off.[129]

Miss Maggie Sees' direct, assertive diatribe hits Jeremiah in the guts.
Highway highlights the performative qualities of Maggie Sees by portraying her in language and imagery from the theatrical stage. She functions
in the way a Chorus or narrator figure does, although she does not hesitate
to don a costume and enter the main action of the stage. She can become
invisible when she wants to be, and only reveals herself to characters at
her own discretion.

Maggie Sees is a sexy, irreverent, and formidable Trickster. She is
contemporary and all-knowing but not moralizing. Maggie Sees makes a
number of appearances to Jeremiah and Gabriel as a spiritual guide. She
comforts them in dreams after they are sexually abused in residential school
and she accompanies Ann-Adele Ghostrider in the form of a white ermine
cape in the hospital when Gabriel is dying.[130] When Gabriel dies, she comes
to Jeremiah as the fox in the stole of the winner of the Fur Queen pageant,
and winks to comfort him.[131] Maggie Sees' performances as a Trickster
cue Gabriel to consider elements of Catholicism that are theatrical: the
ornate vestal garments, the rituals of song, the incense and bells. Once
Gabriel realizes that certain aspects of Catholicism are performative, the

---

128   Highway, *Kiss of the Fur Queen*, 231.
129   Highway, *Kiss of the Fur Queen*, 233–4.
130   Highway, *Kiss of the Fur Queen*, 299.
131   Highway, *Kiss of the Fur Queen*, 306.

religion becomes de-mystified for him, and he begins to question it and, at the same time, explore North American Indian religion.[132] Maggie Sees encourages Jeremiah to discover and perform his identity in the arts along with Amanda Clear Sky and Gabriel who pursue roles in television and dance, respectively.

Maggie Sees' performance is linked to the sounds of the natural world. Highway writes, 'as the Cree chanteuse parted lips for her opening note, the fog swept back in. All Jeremiah was left with was the sound of the north wind, slow, persistent, moaning, the most beautiful song he had ever heard.'[133] Highway describes the natural world performing through techniques of anthropomorphism and suggests an awareness of a series of natural performances in a way that colonial powers do not seem to hear them. Nature plays a predominant role in the novel, as Highway suggests it plays in indigenous culture. Characters argue with 'the fierce north wind', a young pine tree gives directions, and Abraham recalls 'how the northern lights had whispered truth into his dreams.'[134]

Enacting History

Highway's *Kiss of the Fur Queen* performs hope and history, mythology and survival for two Cree brothers who tell their life stories and develop their identities through Cree storytelling and various artistic performances. Highway engages dramatic structures and performative modes from indigenous and non-indigenous cultures in the text, which symbolize the very hybridized structure of Jeremiah's complex and combined cultural identity. In *Comparing Mythologies*, John Moss attends to the nuances of colonial domination and indigenous survival and identity-formation when he writes,

132   Highway, *Kiss of the Fur Queen*, 183.
133   Highway, *Kiss of the Fur Queen*, 234.
134   Highway, *Kiss of the Fur Queen*, 104.

Highway 'is not Cree-Canadian or Canadian-Cree; he is Cree and he is Canadian.'[135]

Highway's novel encourages readers to think closely about the use of mythology in significant cultural narratives, Cree and Western, and the performances of stereotypes for the harm they do and the potential subversive energy created when they are unsettled. The novel examines the artistic and political context of indigenous artists surviving systemic abuse that is seldom explored in history books or in historically based fiction. *Kiss of the Fur Queen* offers what Rachid Behghiti calls 'a counter-movement' that disrupts 'Canada's historiography of exclusion'[136] in its form and in its content, and the novel explores how art is integral to life in indigenous cultures rather than an imitation of it as it is often perceived in non-indigenous cultures.[137] The novel empowers Cree-speaking readers who may recognize stories within Cree names and places and find humour and a feeling of community in the words that are not glossed from particular Cree dialects, and it may inspire non-Cree readers to learn more about the language and culture. *Kiss of the Fur Queen* offers a range of performances – dramatic, linguistic, musical, and more – for readers to interpret and essentially celebrate the life stories of Jeremiah and Gabriel, and make the moments of their lives as present and impressionable in the readers' minds as they would be onstage.

135   John Moss, 'The Opposite of Prayer: An Introduction to Tomson Highway',
       Comparing Mythologies, Charles R. Bronfman Lecture in Canadian Studies (Ottawa:
       University of Ottawa Press, 2002), 15.
136   Belghiti, 'Choreography, Sexuality, and the Indigenous Body in Tomson Highway's
       Kiss of the Fur Queen', 3.
137   Belghiti, 'Choreography, Sexuality, and the Indigenous Body in Tomson Highway's
       Kiss of the Fur Queen', 7.

CHAPTER 3

Performing the Nation in Peter Carey's *Illywhacker*

Peter Carey's *Illywhacker*, winner of several prestigious literary honours,[1] examines the performative aspects of national identities and cultural stereotypes in twentieth-century Australia through the theatrical first-person narration of travelling showman Herbert Badgery. The picaresque narrator engages readers in an imaginative historical account of Australia from 1919 to 2025, into a dystopic future. Written in 1985, when postcolonialism and postmodernism informed much literature in Australia and worldwide, Carey creates a performative novel that delivers an unusual historiography told by an untrustworthy but engaging narrator. Badgery portrays Australia as a nation searching for an identity beyond that of a colonial outpost of Britain or an exploited trade partner of the USA, while coming to terms with its exploitation of its own inhabitants and, more specifically, the indigenous people who live there. *Illywhacker* has inspired a range of critical analyses examining its postcolonial and postmodern approaches,[2] magic realism and the picaresque.[3] This chapter addresses the performative and

1   *Illywhacker* won the Victorian Premier's Literary Award (1986), The Age Book of the Year (1985), the Book Council Award (1985), the Ditmar Award for Best Australian Science Fiction Novel (1986) and the Vance Palmer Prize for Fiction (1986). It was short-listed for the Booker Prize (1985) and the World Fantasy Award for Best Novel (1986).
2   To examine postcolonial and postmodern approaches in *Illywhacker*, see Paul Kane's 'Post-colonial/Postmodern; Australian Literature and Peter Carey', *World Literature Today* 67/3 (1993), 519–22.
3   For a focus on magic realism and performative historiography in *Illywhacker*, see Richard Todd's 'Narrative Trickery and Performative Historiography: Fictional Representation of National Identity in Graham Swift, Peter Carey, and Mordecai Richler', in Wendy B. Faris and Lois Parkinson Zamora, eds, *Magic Realism: Theory, History, Community* (Durham: Duke University Press, 2012). For more on the

theatrical showmanship of Carey and of Badgery, the titular illywhacker, a
'professional trickster' or 'spieler',[4] who champions the underdog, exposes
pretences and gets his corner of the world on the map as the novel asks
readers to examine the false masks and provincial mindsets that Carey
suggests limit some Australians in this portrait. *Illywhacker* explores the
beginnings of trade relations between Australia and America in the twentieth century and the posturing that characters from both countries employ
for strategic gain.

Peter Carey, world-renowned author and two-time Booker Prize
winner,[5] was born in Bacchus Marsh, Victoria, Australia in 1943 and has
lived in New York since 1990. Educated at Geelong Grammar school,
Carey studied science at university for a year before working in advertising
and beginning his self-directed literary education. He published a short
story collection, *The Fat Man in History* (1974), and since then has written thirteen novels, two additional short story collections, imaginative
non-fiction – *30 Days in Sydney: A Wildly Distorted Account* (2001) and
Wrong About Japan (2005) – a children's book, screen-plays, essays, and
more. His prolific writing career has received international acclaim; one
reviewer calls him 'mesmerizing and incomparable'[6] and another wrote in
a review of Carey's Booker Prize-winning novel *Oscar and Lucinda* (1988),
'Genius is a devalued, overworked word, but make no mistake about it, in
that department Peter Carey has been richly blessed.'[7] John Updike praises
Carey for using his expatriate perspective 'to contemplate and reshape some
notable legends of his homeland'.[8]

---

variety of critical approaches to *Illywhacker* and Carey's other works, see Andreas
Gaile, *Fabulating Beauty: Perspectives on the Fiction of Peter Carey*, Cross/Culture
78 (Amsterdam: Rodopi, 2005).

4   Carey, *Illywhacker*, 9.
5   Carey won the Booker Prize for *Oscar and Lucinda* (1988) and *True History of the
     Kelly Gang* (2001).
6   Philip Hensher, 'Review of My Life as a Fake', *The Times*, 20 September 2001.
7   'Review of Oscar and Lucinda', *Punch* <http://petercareybooks.com/all-titles/oscar-
     and-lucinda/reviews/> accessed 12 November 2016.
8   Updike qtd in Mary Ellen Snodgrass, *Peter Carey: A Literary Companion* (Jefferson,
     NC: McFarland & Company, 2010), 5.

Dominant and recurring themes in Carey's writing are metaphorical imprisonment and the search for a national identity. Carey observes that his books from 1979 to the 1990s have a 'lot to do with entrapment and metamorphosis'.[9] These themes are central in *The Fat Man in History* (1979), *The Tax Inspector* (1991), and *The Unusual Life of Tristan Smith* (1994), which examines life in the theatre for a misfit who longs for acceptance and hides beneath a mask that is both limiting and liberating.

A central concern in Carey's oeuvre is the re-working of history and historiography as demonstrated both in the verbose and performative *Illywhacker* (1985), exploring the lives of showman Badgery, his family and first-generation immigrants to Australia, and in *True History of the Kelly Gang* (2001), winner of the Man Booker Prize and selling over 2 million copies, in which Carey channels the voice of Ned Kelly, Australian outlaw and national icon, in an extended letter to Kelly's fictitious daughter. More recently, Carey has worked with the theme of fraud in *My Life as a Fake* (2003) and *Theft* (2006) and investigated the underbelly of democracy in America with *His Illegal Self* (2008), *Parrot and Olivier in America* (2009) and *Amnesia* (2012). What is noteworthy about Carey's work through the decades is the originality of the forms of his novels and the great range of central allegorical images, ventriloquized voices, and unconventional historiographies found therein.

Some of the performative and theatrical qualities created in Carey's work come through first-person narrators and an understanding of how action and character drive scenes. In an interview, Carey observes that the experience of adapting *Bliss* for film and co-writing the screenplay of *Until the End of the World* impacted positively upon his writing: 'My fiction is now far more informed by an understanding of dramatic art.'[10] He elaborates, 'Soon after [writing the screenplays], when I was writing *Tristan Smith*, which is set in the theatre, I began to think more about how you

---

9   Carey qtd in Lisa Meyer and Peter Carey, 'An Interview with Peter Carey', *Chicago Review* 43/2 (Spring 1997), 83.

10   Peter Carey qtd in Radhika Jones, 'Peter Carey, The Art of Fiction No.188', *Paris Review* 177 (Summer 2006) <http://www.theparisreview.org/interviews/5641/the-art-of-fiction-no-188-peter-carey> accessed 8 May 2016.

make a scene work through action. You start to conceive of dialogue as the disturbance on the surface that occurs as the result of tectonic shifts beneath.'[11]

Carey's *Illywhacker* portrays nationalism in Australia as a theatrical construct that is rehearsed and sustained through convincing performances by members of the hegemonic majority who shape their Australian identities from British and American models. *Illywhacker* exposes theatrical underpinnings of postcolonial identity politics in Australian culture: how Australian-born characters emulate the British, how first-generation Chinese-Australian immigrants exploit racial stereotypes as 'camouflage', as Homi Bhabha describes,[12] and how Australian stereotypes are manufactured for export to American and Japanese investors. The final image of the novel transpires inside a strange museum-type tourist attraction called the 'Best Pet Shop in the World' where human beings are imprisoned in actual cages that symbolize rigid Australian stereotypes.

In *Illywhacker*, Herbert Badgery is a captivating but unreliable narrator who tells readers that lies are central to the Australian identity. *Illywhacker* alludes to a range of liars from Badgery himself to the writers behind the notorious Ern Malley literary hoax and suggests that tall tales have a significant history in Australia. The modernist poems of the fictitious poet Ern Malley were published and celebrated in the 1940s until it was revealed that they were created by James McAuley and Harold Stewart as a prank and submitted to Max Harris' journal *Angry Penguins* under an invented name to expose the pretentions of modernist poetry. Carey alludes to this hoax in *Illywhacker* by calling Badgery's publication, *Malley's Urn*.[13] Carey's later novel *My Life as a Fake* (2003) also explores the famous literary scandal which has been credited with negatively impacting the development of a literary audience for modernist writing.[14]

---

11   Jones, 'Peter Carey, The Art of Fiction No.188', n.p.
12   Homi K. Bhabha, *Nation and Narration* (London: Routledge, 1990), 131.
13   Peter Carey, *Illywhacker*, 587.
14   Bill Ashcroft, 'Reading Carey Reading Malley', *Australian Literary Studies* 21/4 (2004), 28–39 <http://search.informit.com.au/documentSummary;dn=9000521 36593731;res=IELAPA> accessed 8 May 2016.

Carey's *Illywhacker* examines how a young postcolonial nation tells its story in fiction when it does not have centuries of literature to build upon. In an interview, Carey suggests that the absence of a comprehensive literary history presents liberating opportunities for authors: 'You have a sense – and I'm sure it's true of Canadian as well as Australian literature – that you can do anything. The page is still blank. We really can make ourselves up.'[15] Carey carries the motif of invention into his exploration of national identity and the storyteller's role in *Illywhacker*. One of the epigraphs to *Illywhacker* is Mark Twain's observation that Australian history reads 'like the most beautiful lies; and all of a fresh new sort, no mouldy old stale ones. It is full of surprises and adventures, the incongruities, and contradictions, and incredibilities; but they are all true, they all happened.'[16] From the outset, readers are advised that it is useless to try, as Badgery says, 'to pull apart the strands of lies and truth', and it is best instead to 'relax and enjoy the show'.[17]

Despite the invitation to relax, however, a passive spectator is not what *Illywhacker* demands or creates. Carey, through Badgery, positions readers as spectators within the narrative through direct addresses and implores them to take action as they witness the events of history. Readers are positioned as witnesses to a number of scenes while they are also shown the processes behind the scenes as though they are simultaneously backstage and in various audiences. Badgery presents a 'history-in-the-making' of Australia in the twentieth century as he dramatizes moments of historical and political significance in his life. From an under-privileged class, Badgery dramatizes his life as a kind of everyman's history, albeit a rather remarkable one, rather than a polished performance. Badgery describes metatheatrical scenes and ad-hoc theatre and recounts tales of his travelling theatre company that performed in local venues before ordinary people in the 1930s. Badgery champions the life of the everyman enthusiastically

15 Eleanor Wachtel, '"We Really Can Make Ourselves Up": An Interview with Peter Carey', *Australian and New Zealand Studies in Canada* 9 (1993), 104.
16 Mark Twain qtd in Carey, *Illywhacker*, 7.
17 Carey, *Illywhacker*, 11.

despite his rather unconvincing claims that he would prefer to tell another more 'significant' story:[18]

> I would rather fill my history with great men and women, philosophers, scientists, intellectuals, artists, but I confess myself incapable of so vast a lie. I am stuck with Badgery & Goldstein (theatricals) wandering through the 1930s like flies on the face of a great painting.[19]

Badgery enacts scenes from his life theatrically in the narrative. He makes the reader conscious of his own gaze on himself and on the scenes he re-creates. Like a voyeur, he allows the reader to peer into private exchanges, such as the one between his future wife, Phoebe, and her teacher, Annette Davidson, who was hired to give Phoebe history lessons when she was young and ended up being her lover: 'Some history. There they are now. Their conversation is as clear as crystal. I simply have to reach out and take it.'[20] Badgery varies the critical distance between readers and the scenes they view as a film director might, at times pulling back to a wider focus, and other times offering readers what seems to be a close-up. Badgery cautions readers how the story needs to unfold dramatically, with attention to pace and perspective: 'You do not, not ever, leap straight to the main performance.'[21]

Badgery represents a confrontation with railway police and communist bagmen in language from the theatre: 'I was, by then, an accomplished Thespian; I understood the value of silence on a stage, how it can be used to induce suspense, and then hysteria.'[22] He stands up to the head policeman and pretends to be a 'Wobbly' spokesman, an International Worker of the World, to defend the bagmen who, he argues, should not be penalized for riding the trains without paying as they search for work in a depressed economy. Badgery's metatheatrical reflections on his own performance as defender create a distanced, yet present mode of reviewing and exploring the tensions of the 1930s and political roles performed on informal stages.

18   Carey, *Illywhacker*, 326.
19   Carey, *Illywhacker*, 326.
20   Carey, *Illywhacker*, 15.
21   Carey, *Illywhacker*, 533–4.
22   Carey, *Illywhacker*, 339.

Badgery's performance with an Industrial Worker of the World (a.k.a, a 'wobbly') at the railway can be understood through the theatrical framework developed by Marxist director Augusto Boal who developed the concept of invisible theatre as part of his Theatre of the Oppressed, where actors engage with people who are not performers and are unaware that they are involved in a form of protest theatre intended to bring attention to social issues and oppression in everyday life.[23] In invisible theatre, actors carry out their roles and involve the people around them in an improvised scene that usually highlights issues of class and capitalism. In 'Theatre as Discourse', Boal provides an example of an actor/diner who offers labour instead of money to pay his bill in a restaurant and then rallies the waiter, who does not know he is a part of a dramatic scene, to join him in fighting the capitalist system that oppresses them both.[24] Invisible theatre is a strategy Carey adapts into the novel in the railway scene where Badgery involves a number of unwitting participants in his theatrical rebellion against authority for social justice for the underclass.

Readers observe Badgery stage and re-stage scenes from his past in *Illywhacker*, providing commentaries to his dramatizations. While Badgery rehearses a range of personae and a loose affiliation with the Marxist party, he ultimately reveals that he is loyal to himself alone. Joanne Tompkins suggests that metatheatre in postcolonial plays 'is often a self-conscious method of re-negotiating, re-working – not just re-playing – the past and the present.'[25] In a similar way, metatheatre, when presented in some novels, provides critical distance for reflection, analysis, and dissent. Metatheatre in fiction offers Badgery, and by extension, readers, a representation of Badgery's life that illuminates both possible and improbable versions of historical events. Through metatheatrical commentary and the benefits of retrospection, Badgery applauds and critiques his performances of

23 Augusto Boal, 'Theatre as Discourse', in Michael Huxley and Noel Witts, eds, *The Twentieth-Century Performance Reader* (London: Routledge, 1996), 87.

24 Boal, 'Theatre as Discourse', 88.

25 Joanne Tompkins, '"Spectacular Resistance": Metatheatre in Post-Colonial Drama', 42.

personal rebellion against state authority, creating distance for the reader
to watch him watching his successes and failures.

The Theatrical Picaresque and an Australian Local Theatre

While some critics have categorized *Illywhacker* as picaresque, the theatrical aspects of the picaresque genre in relation to this novel have yet
to be examined in detail. M. D. Fletcher discusses the parodic nature of
the picaresque form in *Illywhacker*,[26] while Sue Ryan describes the novel
as a 'flawed picaresque', in part due to its narrator who learns over the
course of the novel, unlike the conventional picaresque hero who remains
unchanged.[27] Blaber and Gilman note that picaresque writing is popular
in postcolonial countries, where marginalized picaros write back to their
dominant cultures and metonymic connections between the life of the
picaro and the life of the nation are made.[28] Historically, the picaresque
tradition arose in a time of social transformation in Spain in the sixteenth
and seventeenth centuries as the middle class increased and the aristocracy
waned.[29] The picaresque novel is episodic and features a narrator who comes
from low means and is alienated in some way from mainstream society.
Often orphaned or without parents, the picaro (usually male) ekes out a

---

26   M. D. Fletcher, 'Australian Political Identity: Aboriginal and Otherwise. Carey/
     Malouf/Watson', unpublished conference paper from 42nd APSA conference at
     Australian National University, 3–6 October 2000, 13 <http://www.apsa2000.anu.
     edu.au/confpapers/fletcher.rtf> accessed 20 January 2006.
27   Sue Ryan, 'Metafiction in Illywhacker: Peter Carey's Renovated Picaresque Novel',
     Commonwealth: Essays and Studies 14/1 (Autumn 1991), 37.
28   Ronald Blaber and Marvin Gilman, *Roguery: The Picaresque Tradition in Australian,
     Canadian and Indian Fiction* (Springwood, NSW: Butterfly, 1990), 21.
29   Blaber and Gilman, *Roguery: The Picaresque Tradition in Australian, Canadian and
     Indian Fiction*, 15.

living through a series of schemes, yet generally does not reform or learn much from his experiences.[30]

While the term picaresque is applied to novels customarily, it has historical connections to theatre and to a theatrical mode of organization and presentation. Helen H. Reed describes how Cervantes brought his picaros to the stage in a number of his plays and used theatre as a central organizing framework in his picaresque narratives.[31] She suggests that the term 'picaresque novel' is modern and implies 'a greater consensus' of generic boundaries than would have existed in Cervantes's day when the picaresque rubric might have been extended to drama.[32] Typically, picaros are actors or performance artists of some kind who employ disguises, create illusions in attempts to exercise power over others, and eventually turn to writing or relating the narratives of their own lives. In some picaresque texts, Reed suggests, the picaro's closest attempts at self-discovery come through his recurrent performances and sense of the stage as a microcosm of the world.[33]

In Cervantes' novels and plays, Reed identifies metatheatrical patterns of dialogue and description, scene changes, and spectacular renderings of events.[34] In Cervantes' picaresque writing, picaros temporarily take over the narrator's role and tell their stories to a friend or a double, creating narrative distance between the teller, the listener, and the tale.[35] In some other picaresque texts, there is neither friend nor double, just the reader who serves as the designated listener, as in *Illywhacker*. In both kinds of picaresque writing, a metatheatrical awareness surrounds the relationship between the picaro, who stages the story, and the reader, who either

---

30   In *Roguery: The Picaresque Tradition in Australian, Canadian and Indian Fiction*, Blaber and Gilman provide a comprehensive analysis of the picaresque genre and its evolution, considering the groundwork by Ulrich Wicks, Claudio Guillén, Richard Bjornson, Frank Kearful, and Walter Reed (9–32).

31   Helen H. Reed, 'Theatricality in the Picaresque of Cervantes', *Cervantes: Bulletin of the Cervantes Society of America* 7/2 (1987), 72.

32   Reed, 'Theatricality in the Picaresque of Cervantes', 71–2.

33   Reed, 'Theatricality in the Picaresque of Cervantes', 76.

34   Reed, 'Theatricality in the Picaresque of Cervantes', 72.

35   Reed, 'Theatricality in the Picaresque of Cervantes', 75.

observes a character playing a listener, or is implicated in the listener's role, himself or herself.

Metatheatrical narration is used in *Illywhacker* when its picaro, Badgery, stages a scene for the reader in which a younger version of himself performs before a commentating older version of himself. This staging encourages a complex interpretation from readers who watch the initial scene, Badgery's revised version of it, and the space between the two narrations. Blaber and Gilman call this technique 'dual narration', expanding upon Ulrich Wicks' observation that the first-person narrative voice is made up of an experiencing 'I' and a narrating 'I', and demonstrates a split in the picaro's identity.[36] Such a split, common on stage when two actors play a single character at two or more different stages, such as in Michel Tremblay's *Albertine in Five Times*,[37] occurs in *Illywhacker* when Badgery describes how he sees himself viewing Phoebe for the first time, as though he is a character separate from himself in time and space: 'Herbert Badgery stood there staring at her. I can see him. He is almost as much a stranger to me as he is to her.'[38] The split between the experiencing 'I' and the narrating 'I' divides the reader's gaze and draws attention to the physical and theatrical aspects of Badgery's tale.

On a fundamental level, the picaro is a performer who is involved in dramatic adventures and in the theatrical process of relating his exploits. Theatricality is a way of participating in and perceiving the world, and offers Badgery the chance to play roles that would normally be inaccessible to him because of his low or marginalized status in society. Badgery is not a disembodied voice that takes over the narrative from time to time but a visceral and physically present storyteller who acts out against the establishment through ruses, tricks, and performances. His digressive references to his flatulence, incontinence, psoriasis, and growing breasts create a clear image of his material presence in the reader's mind. Badgery interrupts his own stories with an impressive range of bodily functions – from ripping

36   Blaber and Gilman, *Roguery: The Picaresque Tradition in Australian, Canadian and Indian Fiction*, 23–4.
37   Michel Tremblay, *Albertine in Five Times: A play* (Vancouver: Talonbooks, 1986).
38   Carey, *Illywhacker*, 26.

farts on the first page to nursing his grandson on the last – that creates an exaggerated and theatrical awareness of his body as he tells his tales. His transgressive body is in tune with his moral ambivalence as he ventures outside the hegemonic norms of his world and the narrative norms of decency, streaking headlong into the realm of Bakhtin's 'grotesque realism'.[39]

In *Rabelais and his World*, Bakhtin describes 'material bodily principles' of excess in Rabelais' *Gargantua and Pantagruel*.[40] The narrative's focus on grotesque realism, exaggerated physicality, and excesses of eating, drinking, defecating, and sex, provides comedic release from an authoritarian society. The laughter that comes from such physical humour serves to 'relativise and degrade the official' while questioning the norms of society and the hierarchical.[41] Such exaggerated physicality in *Illywhacker*, where Badgery exposes his intimate bodily processes and sexual perversions (including having sex with his mother-in-law), exhibits Rabelaisian qualities, and evokes the subversive and base humour of the early Roman and Commedia dell'Arte theatre where exaggerated phalluses are worn on the outside and servants typically triumph over their masters in a reversed social world.

Another prominent picaresque characteristic in the novel is its emphasis on material specificity. *Illywhacker* stages bodies in 'actual' locales, such as the Ford Plant in Geelong, the Post Office in Buninyong, and Punt Road in Melbourne, and interrupts the tale to dramatize the setting convincingly for readers so that they may envision their place in it alongside the characters. Badgery asks readers: 'Have you ever seen the Punt Road hill where it comes down past Domain Street towards the Yarra? By God, it's steep!'[42] A named place carries the connotative power of intimacy even if the reader is unfamiliar with the particular locale. Something authentic and tangible about material specificity fosters connections between characters and readers who may recognize a particular town or pub, or substitute

---

39   Mikhail M. Bakhtin, *Rabelais and his World*, trans. Helene Iswolsky (Cambridge, Mass: M. I. T. Press, 1968), 18.

40   Bakhtin, *Rabelais and his World*, 18.

41   Blaber and Gilman, *Roguery: The Picaresque Tradition in Australian, Canadian and Indian Fiction*, 12.

42   Carey, *Illywhacker*, 26.

simulacra for the named places in their minds. Frank Kearful ascribes the strength of the picaresque novel to its situated Spanish historical and social contexts and traces a 'devolution' of the novel as it moved from Spain to Germany and France and disintegrated into other weakened and derivative genres.[43] Carey writes Badgery's particularized and theatrical world into existence and mythologizes his vision of Australia, town by town, pub by pub, into fiction. Through the litany of local names and places, the novel generates a sense of a community with the reader who re-visits or comes to know Badgery's world intimately. Badgery and his partner, Leah Goldstein, scrape out a living through vaudevillian shows and shady scams which involve Badgery's children, performing in actual warehouses and factories that stand today.[44]

A similar focus on situated locales and recognizable characters can be seen in mid-twentieth-century Australian plays where playwrights dramatize visionaries, bushrangers, adventurers, and larrikins, and use colloquial language to create a sense of Australian culture that is distinct from the British culture and values that dominated the stage from colonization until the mid-twentieth century.[45] Paul McGillick refers to Jack Hibberd's plays from the 1970s as 'communally creative act[s]' in which the audience supplied the 'cultural context', and argues that without the situated-ness and the audience's interaction, 'the dramatic event [would lack] authenticity'.[46] Bob Ellis, co-author of *The Legend of King O'Malley*, argues that local theatre

43   Frank J. Kearful, 'Spanish Rogues and English Foundlings: On the Disintegration of Picaresque', *Genre* 4 (1971), 384.
44   Dorothy Hewett researches a number of contemporary theatres in Australia that began in warehouses and factories and other non-purpose-built venues. Contemporary Australian companies such as La Mama, Nimrod and the Pram Factory began in warehouses and factories. See Dorothy Hewett, 'Shirts, Prams and Tomato Sauce', *Meanjin* 35/3 (1976), 316–23.
45   These plays include *Flash Jim Vaux* (1972) by Ron Blair, *The Legend of King O'Malley* (1970) by Bob Boddy and Michael Ellis, *The Chapel Perilous* (1971) by Dorothy Hewett, and *A Toast to Melba* (1976) by Jack Hibberd. See Hewett, 'Shirts, Prams and Tomato Sauce', 312–23.
46   Paul McGillick, *Jack Hibberd: Australian Playwright Series* (Amsterdam: Rodopi, 1988), 58.

can 'only work within the context of the small, open and claustrophobically close-up arenas where it was born'.[47] Like Hibberd and Ellis, Carey values local stories and characters, and maintains that 'literature grows out of place'.[48] Carey's dramatic mode generates a sense of the interaction between players and the local audience in the early days of Australian theatre and the camaraderie of irreverence that arose from that exchange. Theatre was not detached and sophisticated but rough and ready, and a part of the audience's world. Audiences were hungry for reflections of themselves and who they might like to be; Carey incorporates this desire for local reflection into *Illywhacker* and in his other works set in Australia and in America.

Imagining National Identity

In *Imagined Communities*, Benedict Anderson suggests that the novel is one of a few key factors that unite the consciousnesses of people in a nation into an imagined community.[49] Anderson attributes the development of the imagined community, in part, to the rise of print-capitalism in the form of novels and daily newspapers which flourished in Europe in the eighteenth century and provided an experience of simultaneity that had not existed before.[50] These developments provided opportunities for people to 'think about themselves, and to relate themselves to others, in profoundly new ways'.[51] Anderson demonstrates how novelists from different countries construct imaginary communities in the minds of their readers by referring

---

47 McGillick, *Jack Hibberd: Australian Playwright Series*, 110.

48 Wachtel, "'We Really Can Make Ourselves Up": An Interview with Peter Carey', 105.

49 Benedict Anderson, *Imagined Communities: Reflections on the Origin and Spread of Nationalism* [1983] (London: Verso, 1991), 25.

50 Anderson, *Imagined Communities: Reflections on the Origin and Spread of Nationalism*, 25.

51 Anderson, *Imagined Communities: Reflections on the Origin and Spread of Nationalism*, 36.

to calendrical time, a familiar landscape, and a solitary hero who journeys within a detailed 'socioscape'.[52] The novels show characters in a single nation leading simultaneous yet unconnected lives. Anderson suggests the novel is a 'precise analogue of the idea of the nation, which also is conceived as a solid community moving steadily down (or up) history'.[53] One technique that Anderson suggests is effective in creating a sense of a national collective is the repetition of the construction '*our* young man', as used in the novel *Semarang Hitam* by Indonesian writer Mas Marco Kartodikromo.[54] The pronoun 'our', in the minds of Marco's readers, assembles an imagined collective of Indonesians who support and follow the protagonist through an imagined nation. As Anderson puts it, 'Marco's "our young man" [...] means a young man who belongs to the collective body of readers of Indonesia, and thus, implicitly, an embryonic Indonesian "imagined community".'[55]

In *Illywhacker*, Badgery constructs a particular imagined community of Australians who are his co-patriots and his audience members. Through a narrative that comments on its own theatricality, Badgery performs for an imagined readership that is familiar with his self-reflexive critique of national identity. His 'audience' which is constructed to be sympathetic, patriotic, and sophisticated, inspires him to create and critique new performances of nationalism which fit the chameleon-like nation Badgery portrays Australia to be in the mid-1980s. The novel's frequent recourse to performance and a dramatic mode shows its desire to create a sense of a forum or a public collective between members in an imagined community. This sensation of connection is felt more tangibly in the theatre where the interior world of characters is played out in the communal world of the

52   Benedict Anderson refers in *Imagined Communities* to *Noli Me Tangere* (1887) by Filipino writer José Rizal, *El Periquillo Sarniento* (1816) by Mexican writer José Joaquín Fernandez de Lizardi, and *Semarang Hitam* (1924) by Indonesian writer Mas Marco Kartodikromo, 32.

53   Anderson, *Imagined Communities: Reflections on the Origin and Spread of Nationalism*, 26.

54   Anderson, *Imagined Communities: Reflections on the Origin and Spread of Nationalism*, 32.

55   Anderson, *Imagined Communities: Reflections on the Origin and Spread of Nationalism*, 32.

audience, and spectators encounter the performance in real space, real time, and in the presence of other people watching it happen. *Illywhacker* draws on dramatic conventions from the theatre to animate its imagined reading community and to infuse it with the energy of a living, public collective.

In *Thought and Change*, Ernest Gellner writes: 'Nationalism is not the awakening of nations to self-consciousness; it *invents* nations where they do not exist.'[56] Anderson, in *Imagined Communities*, agrees with Gellner's premise but portrays the invention of nationalism as 'imaginative' and 'creative',[57] while Gellner associates it with 'fabrication' and 'falsity'.[58] Anderson suggests that Gellner implies that 'nationalism *masquerades* under false pretences'[59] when he refers to small groups within nations, which are more unified than nations are, for example, through cultural-linguistic similarities, and suggests they are 'truer' communities than nations.[60] Anderson reminds readers that any group that is too large to meet in one place is an imaginary community, cultural groups included. While a comparative study on theories of nationalism is beyond the scope of this project, I would like to highlight how Anderson, and to a lesser extent Gellner, use language commonly associated with theatre and performance – for example, imagination, masquerade, and falsity – in describing the invention and development of nations. Extending from Gellner's and Anderson's terminology, the invention of nationalism can be seen as a theatrical process that is achieved and sustained through convincing performances by members of the hegemonic majority, and such performative aspects are emphasized in Carey's novel. Of course, it is simplistic to state that it is *solely* a theatrical process, which is not my intention here. I would like to suggest, however, that notions of

56 Ernest Gellner, *Thought and Change* (London: Weidenfeld and Nicolson, 1964), 168.
57 Anderson, *Imagined Communities: Reflections on the Origin and Spread of Nationalism*, 6.
58 Gellner, *Thought and Change*, 148.
59 Anderson, *Imagined Communities: Reflections on the Origin and Spread of Nationalism*, 6.
60 Gellner, *Thought and Change*, 169.

guise, imagination, performance, and character development are central to the invention of nationalism and national identity.

Illywhacker presents an idea of nationalism that accommodates Gellner's view, that the invention of nationalism involves falsity and pretence, and also Anderson's perspective, that the process requires imagining and creation. The novel suggests that nationalism and, by extension, national identities are created through rehearsals and performances before audiences within and outside of the country. New conceptions of national identities emerge as the mental pictures and beliefs of the country change, yet these new conceptions struggle against the performances of the nation's hegemonic script.[61] Carey reflects that in writing *Illywhacker* he was not only defining what it meant for his characters to be Australian but announcing it to the world:

> I was trying to show what was magical and amazing about Australia and I suppose that most of it was for me, for us [Australians], but there is no doubt that I was also presenting my country to the metropolitan center. You could say *Illywhacker* was driven by the will to force the metropolitan centers to inhabit the world from our perspective. After all, we have so willingly adopted their perspective and it is perhaps time they considered ours.[62]

Role-Playing and National Performances

Badgery plays a variety of roles in *Illywhacker* including home-builder, aviator, snake charmer, lover, and old man, and he becomes attuned to the role-playing of others. The novel explores the issue of indigenous land claims through the motif of Badgery's compulsive home-building and renovating of other people's properties, which can be read as part of his performance

---

61   Carey's short story 'American Dreams' explores the idea of rehearsing and exploiting a static Australian national identity for American tourists. In Peter Carey, *Collected Stories* (London: Faber, 1995), 171–82.

62   Nathanael O'Reilly, 'The Voice of the Teller: A Conversation with Peter Carey', *Antipodes* (December 2002), 166.

as a settler Australian who feels compelled to make a real home in a land that has been seized from its indigenous people. In *Fear and Temptation*, Terry Goldie defines indigenization as the process that occurs when a settler moves to a new place and recognizes an Other there as having 'greater roots in the place'.[63] The settler begins a process of attempting to become more native to the place than the perceived Other. *Illywhacker* portrays Badgery's indigenization as a performance Badgery designs to convince himself, and others, of his material and symbolic ties to the land. Carey implies that the stereotypical Australian dream to own a home is met by the possibility that a home built on indigenous land may never feel like a home.

The motif of building houses surfaces several times in the novel as Badgery builds shanties and lean-tos and renovates other people's businesses (Shirl's milk bar, Charles' pet emporium). Many buildings in the novel are represented as illusory and temporary, like props or set-pieces on a stage and, in Badgery's words, are 'full of trickery and deception'.[64] Badgery demonstrates how the city of Sydney impersonates sophisticated European cities. As though it were a theatrical set, Badgery warns: 'If you push up against it too hard you will find yourself leaning against empty air.'[65] He points to the insubstantial nature of the city and comments, 'I would not be surprised to wake one morning and find the whole thing gone, with only the grinning façade of Luna Park rising from the blue shimmer of eucalyptus bush.'[66] Badgery and his grandson, Hissao, who later becomes an architect, sketch buildings that are inferior copies of other places, 'buildings that lied about their height, their age, and most particularly their location. There was not one that did not pretend itself huddled in some European capital with weak sun in summer and ice in winter'.[67] Even the buildings are impostors in the new land, theatrical sets that seem ready to be taken down for the next production.

63   Terry Goldie, *Fear and Temptation: The Image of the Indigene in Canadian, Australian and New Zealand Literatures*, 14.
64   Carey, *Illywhacker*, 547.
65   Carey, *Illywhacker*, 547.
66   Carey, *Illywhacker*, 547.
67   Carey, *Illywhacker*, 547.

Three other significant nationalistic performances are developed in *Illywhacker* and presented through Badgery's eyes: Australia is represented in the role of a child who imitates and rejects Mother England; minority immigrants in Australia stage their marginalized statuses and perform 'disappearing acts'; and national stereotypes are designed and marketed for export.

In the novel, familial metaphors are played out on a national stage. Australia is depicted as England's child and the child of other influential nations, such as America. Australia's role as an abandoned child in *Illywhacker* follows a motif of forsaken children that also appears in Carey's novels, *Oscar and Lucinda* and *The Unusual Life of Tristan Smith*. In an interview, Carey describes Australian history as 'a history of orphans'.[68] He says: 'Australia is a country made by people who were cast-off, exiled, orphaned. We suffered for a long time from that sense of exile, our separation from the roots of our culture.'[69] In *Illywhacker*, Herbert Badgery feels an acute sense of separation from and abandonment by his parents, having lost his mother at a young age and left his father at the age of ten. He finds a father figure in Goon Tse Ying, a Chinese-Australian businessman, who cares for Badgery yet rejects him years later. History repeats itself when Badgery's son, Charles, seeks a foster mother in Leah Goldstein when his mother, Phoebe, abandons him.

Badgery finds the performances of Australians who impersonate the accents and postures of Englishmen repugnant, and he holds the poseurs responsible for preventing the country from growing up and coming into its own. When Badgery meets Cocky Abbot Jr, he is enraged at Abbot's impersonation of an 'Imaginary Englishman'.[70] He says:

> It was what happened in this country. The minute they began to make a quid they started to turn into Englishmen. Cocky Abbot was probably descended from some old cockney lag, who had arrived here talking flash language, a pickpocket, a bread-stealer, and now, a hundred years later his descendants were dressing like his gaolers and torturers, disowning the language, softening their vowels, greasing their way into

68   Carey qtd in Wachtel, '"We Really Can Make Ourselves Up": An Interview with Peter Carey', 104.
69   Carey qtd in Wachtel, '"We Really Can Make Ourselves Up": An Interview with Peter Carey', 104.
70   Carey, *Illywhacker*, 125.

> the plummy speech of the men who had ordered their ancestors lashed until the flesh had been dragged in bleeding strips from their naked backs.[71]

Carey writes that Badgery's own father had affected a posh British accent and 'never missed a chance to say "I am an Englishman" or "as an Englishman" when he was actually born in Warrnambool, Australia'.[72] Badgery emphasizes the nasal Australian diction to retaliate against the pseudo-Poms who refuse to let go of their English accents and postures. What Badgery really wants is for these men to exchange one performance for another and to develop Australian accents, postures, and characters in which they will take some pride.

Carey depicts the relationship between America and Australia in terms of a domineering father and a sycophantic child. America has the confidence which Australians lack, and it is this confidence, according to Badgery, 'not steel mills or oilwells, that is the difference between the two nations'.[73] When Charles enters into a cross-marketing campaign with Holden at his pet emporium, he does not realize that Holden, 'Australia's Own Car', is sending the profits over to the 'Yanks'.[74] Badgery asks Charles, 'why are we so easy to fool?'[75] The only answer seems to be to imitate those doing the fooling; as well as imaginary Englishmen, there are as many who imitate Americans. It pains Badgery to hear that the official who presides over his son Charles' funeral, 'had modelled his style of speaking on an American tape recording'.[76] Badgery imagines how the official would have practised 'until there was only the slightest trace of his Australian accent left'.[77] Badgery wants to believe that Australians can 'invent themselves'[78] and grow up independently without clinging to England or America. *Illywhacker* reminds readers, however, the invention of a nation comes from familiar epistemes.

71   Carey, *Illywhacker*, 126.
72   Carey, *Illywhacker*, 38.
73   Carey, *Illywhacker*, 346.
74   Carey, *Illywhacker*, 520.
75   Carey, *Illywhacker*, 519.
76   Carey, *Illywhacker*, 578.
77   Carey, *Illywhacker*, 578.
78   Carey, *Illywhacker*, 91.

As Partha Chatterjee points out in 'Whose Imagined Community?', the invention of an imagined community is not so freely 'invented' if it is based on models from Europe and the Americas.[79] The novel highlights the poses, gestures, and accents which show, through a dramatic mode, the traces of Australia's imperial models and how they condition the imaginations and behaviours of the settlers and their descendants.

Although Badgery rejects his father, his English heritage and American investors, his actual degree of independence is minimal. His business ideas do not get off the ground, he spends time in jail and ends up caged in the pet emporium on display for the public. Badgery looks to his children and grandchildren to invent new roles, independent national identities, and to reject neocolonial connections. He fantasizes that his children have extraordinary potential for the future as a result of their bizarre upbringing: 'Spawned by lies, suckled on dreams, infested with dragons, my children could never have been normal, only extraordinary.'[80] He may well be fantasizing about his country's potential, too. When both his children die before Badgery does, the 'extraordinary' task falls to his grandson, Hissao, who ends up making his fortune by capitalizing on classic Australian stereotypes that define, and arguably restrain, the nation.

Disappearing Tricks and Vanishing Acts in Multicultural Australia

When Chinese immigrants came to Australia to mine for gold in the 1850s and 1860s, they were met with xenophobia, extreme hostility, and violence.[81] Goon Tse Ying, Badgery's surrogate father figure, tells young Badgery how

79   Partha Chatterjee, 'Whose Imagined Community?', *The Nation and Its Fragments; Colonial and Postcolonial Histories* (New Jersey: Princeton University Press, 1993), 5.
80   Carey, *Illywhacker*, 359.
81   The sentiment is clear in a letter to the editor in the *Ballarat Star* about Chinese immigrants: 'If these heathens who came here to pollute our blood and debauch our young

Chinese-Australians were the target of violent race riots at Lambing Flats, and other small towns in New South Wales and Victoria, in the 1860s. In *Illywhacker*, Goon Tse Ying re-enacts a riot and shows ten-year-old Badgery how to disappear, like some Chinese miners wished they could do, in a figurative sense, in order to survive. In the novel, Badgery actually learns how to do this 'disappearing act' and performs it on a few disastrous occasions.

Goon Tse Ying wants Badgery to experience a sense of the terror that caused first-generation minorities to want to disappear in a society that is hostile towards them. Goon plays the white English Australian, and Badgery, the Chinese miner. Goon asks young Badgery how he would escape the angry mob who chased the Chinese men and burned the tents of those who hid.

> 'Do you know what to do?' He whispered.
> 'No.'
> 'You disappear,' Goon Tse Ying hissed [...]. 'Completely.'[82]

Goon performs, on Badgery, a re-enactment of the attack. He sings 'Waltzing Matilda' in a haunting falsetto,[83] parodying the rousing melody that is loved by the nation that excludes him. Goon's performance terrifies Badgery to the extent that the boy fears he will be killed.[84]

The disappearing trick that Goon Tse Ying teaches Badgery is a theatrical extension of how some Chinese Australians seemed to 'disappear' in order to survive in Australian society. The 'White Australia' policy, passed in Australia in 1901, and its effects were felt long after the policy's abolishment.[85] Despite the growth of multicultural Australia, a number of controversies, specifically the Cronulla race riots in Sydney in 2005 and

---

children are not put under severe regulations we may reckon an epidemic sooner or later that may be as deadly as leprosy' (*Ballarat Star*, 20 August 1866 <http://www.abc.net.au/federation/fedstory/ep2/ep2_culture.htm> accessed 3 July 2006).

82 Carey, *Illywhacker*, 216.
83 Carey, *Illywhacker*, 219.
84 Carey, *Illywhacker*, 219.
85 See Section 8 – The Abolition of 'White Australia' Policy on the website for the Australian Government: Department of Immigration and Multicultural and

attacks against Indian students in Melbourne and Sydney in 2009, highlight continued evidence of xenophobia and racism in a predominantly white society. In *Illywhacker*, Mr Wong's shop hides without a sign or a window: 'Behind the arch was a trellised veranda, and behind this wooden skirt, Wong, his family, and his customers hid their business from the English.'[86] Carey went on to explore this kind of disappearing act from first-generation minorities further in his novel, *The Unusual Life of Tristan Smith*: 'When I finished writing [*Tristan Smith*], I thought this has to make a lot of sense to a lot of immigrants, the sense that one's cultural self has to be denied, hidden, in order to survive. First generation immigrants tend to do a lot of that, hiding inside masks.'[87]

Of course, not all Chinese Australians disappear in the novel. Goon refuses to hide and prepares two distinct characters for the public: one that plays up his minority status and the other that imitates the dominant majority. Graham Huggan, in *The Post-Colonial Exotic*, introduces the term 'staged marginality' to describe how characters stage their minoritized background theatrically for the benefit of a dominant audience.[88] Huggan bases the term on the work of sociologist Dean MacCannell who sees modern tourism as a 'staged authenticity' in which tourists are exposed to settings or objects that have been designed to satisfy what tourists believe is authentic in foreign and exotic cultures.[89] Huggan points to Salman Rushdie's *The Satanic Verses* (1988), V. S. Naipaul's *The Enigma of Arrival* (1987), and Hanif Kureishi's *The Buddha of Suburbia* (1990) as examples of novels in which characters dramatize their own marginalized statuses for a variety of purposes, not the least to wield power, to varying degrees, over the individuals from the dominant culture watching the

---

Indigenous Affairs <http://www.immi.gov.au/facts/08abolition.htm> accessed 21 November 2016.

86   Carey, *Illywhacker*, 210.
87   Meyer, 'An Interview with Peter Carey', 78.
88   Graham Huggan, *The Post-Colonial Exotic: Marketing the Margins* (London: Routledge, 2001), xii.
89   Huggan, *The Post-Colonial Exotic: Marketing the Margins*, 87.

performances.[90] Characters that have been cast or have cast themselves as stereotypes use those roles as a cover, as Huggan suggests,[91] or, in Bhabha's words, as 'camouflage'.[92]

There is some ambivalence surrounding the double inscription of a minority status through staged marginality. As Huggan argues, and as is clearly depicted in *Illywhacker*, while an individual's performance may be empowering in its intentional mimicry, it risks reiterating confining stereotypes.[93] Goon vacillates strategically between playing 'Chinese' according to the hegemonic majority's preconceptions and imitating the hegemonic majority: 'He adopted their dress when it suited him and spoke their language without a trace of accent'.[94] He teaches young Badgery 'the different accents of [the] King's language and how to use each one'.[95] On the other hand,

> He could be loud, play the fool like old Mr Chan at his ugly daughter's pre-wedding feast, going from table to table with his brandy bottle and loudly, raucously even, assuming the role that was expected of him, so that an Englishman, not understanding, would wish to know the name of the old man who was disgracing himself in so un-Chinese a manner.[96]

Goon exploits stereotypes of the Chinaman by playing to the expectations of the English Australians. He reserves his proper English Australian impersonation for young Badgery. Although Goon plays up his performance of 'staged marginality', he believes it is important that he and other Chinese Australians learn English perfectly and mix with other English Australians so they have the opportunity of operating in more than one sphere. Goon masters both positions and enacts his subversive performance of subservience when it benefits him to do so.

---

90   Huggan, *The Post-Colonial Exotic: Marketing the Margins*, xii.
91   Huggan, *The Post-Colonial Exotic: Marketing the Margins*, 88.
92   Homi K. Bhabha, 'Of Mimicry and Man: The Ambivalence of Colonial Discourse', *The Location of Culture* (London: Routledge, 1994), 131.
93   Huggan, *The Post-Colonial Exotic: Marketing the Margins*, 103.
94   Carey, *Illywhacker*, 210.
95   Carey, *Illywhacker*, 214.
96   Carey, *Illywhacker*, 216.

In contrast to Goon's staged marginality, Eddie Wysbraum, Leah's father's close friend, performs a denial of his status as a Jew in public in his attempt to be accepted by the dominant society. He orders pork in a restaurant 'so loudly that the group at the next table [...] all giggled and began – Leah heard them – to tell a joke involving Jews and pork.'[97] Wysbraum announces how he likes 'a good piece of crackling' to the hilarity of the other diners.[98] While Wysbraum aims to be accepted through his denial of Judaism, the other diners mock him for his performance of the Jew who over-compensates in an exaggerated denial of his religion. When Leah joins the Kaletsky family for a Passover seder, she is completely unfamiliar with the food, prayers, and rituals as she has been taught nothing of Judaism by her parents. She runs from the table in tears, crying, 'I am a fraud, I am a fake, a fake, a fake. I cannot be anything.'[99] While the Kaletskys, Wysbraum, and Leah are not as visible in Australian society as is Goon Tse Ying, or as ostracized, they are outsiders and must negotiate how to play their minority roles as Jews in Australian society to their best advantage, either by embracing their cultural traditions or rejecting them, all the while considering how their performances are perceived by those with anti-Semitic assumptions.

Badgery's grandson, Hissao, performs his cultural identity in a few ways. He does not disappear in society or deny his difference overtly, but operates as a cultural chameleon, developing different public faces, costumes, gestures, and accents, to suit his environment. Unlike the early Chinese immigrants or the Jews, Hissao feels a strong sense of belonging to the country, despite his Asiatic features that mark him outwardly as a minority. Hissao's biology is ambiguous and may invoke magic realism; his features are suggested to have come either from Emma Badgery's fear of a Japanese invasion in 1943 when Hissao was born[100] or from having a

---

97   Carey, *Illywhacker*, 356.
98   Carey, *Illywhacker*, 356.
99   Carey, *Illywhacker*, 262.
100 Anthony J. Hassal, *Dancing on Hot Macadam: Peter Carey's Fiction* (St Lucia: University of Queensland Press, 1994), 111. Hassall's article explores magic realism in terms of Hissao's conception.

Japanese soldier as his biological father, although this is left unclear. Despite his biology, Hissao has an uncanny ability to change himself, as the most versatile actors do, to meet each new performance.

When Hissao first meets Leah, he enacts a parody of a Japanese wise man to put her at ease,[101] and to dissociate himself from the stereotype that he knows is a possible view of himself but one that he hopes she does not share. His performance is not successful as Leah sees a slick, smiling salesman where she had expected to see a son displaying grief for his recently deceased father. In a second, more convincing dramatic performance, Hissao manages to sell the 'Best Pet Shop in the World' to Japanese investors by transforming himself into the likeness of them. Hissao flies to Tokyo where his 'foreign face'[102] allows him to blend in. He removes the markers that make him Australian, his curly hair, baggy suit, and scruffy shoes,[103] adopts 'English suits and a wristwatch' and, with his 'foreign face', thus 'transformed himself [...]. In the corridors of Mitsubishi he was all but invisible.'[104] Hissao's attention to the performative markers of cultures allows him to operate on Australian and international stages. He is aware of the impact of his own stage presence and, like an actor, can make himself prominent or invisible within a scene, as the circumstance demands.

A Living Museum: Marketing Exportable Identities

In the final chapter, Hissao re-builds the 'Best Pet Shop in the World' and cages his family members and other Australians, including 'lifesavers, inventors, manufacturers, bushmen, [and] aboriginals' inside for the viewing public.[105] Badgery greets a throng of paying visitors that passes by his

---

101 Carey, *Illywhacker*, 583.
102 Carey, *Illywhacker*, 595.
103 Carey, *Illywhacker*, 596.
104 Carey, *Illywhacker*, 596.
105 Carey, *Illywhacker*, 599.

cage. The reader is placed not precisely among the visitors, but as a spectator watching the spectators who visit the exhibit. With metatheatrical awareness, Badgery performs for his immediate audience and for the reader who 'sees' the performance and its viewers. The combined gazes of the reader and the visitors upon Badgery and the other caged characters create a sense of a public theatrical performance in the novel. It is this final scene which prompts the reader to re-imagine the entire novel as an extended oral performance that Badgery delivers through the bars of a cage as though the reader has paused there just long enough to hear it.

The image of the caged humans goes to the heart of what Carey perceives to be the demise of the Australian national identity: that Australians deny the metaphorical prisons that they put themselves in. In an interview, Carey said his first image of the novel was its final scene: 'I began with the image of my country as a pet shop, people living in cages, being well-fed, thinking they are happy, but denying the nature of their prison.'[106] The image of the caged characters dramatizes an Australia in the mid-1980s that remains imprisoned by lingering stereotypes that are commercially viable but confining and ultimately coercive. Conversely, the Pet Shop marks an entrepreneurial spirit, albeit a dark one, that Badgery hopes will guide Hissao toward a better future for his family despite the means it takes to achieve it. Carey remarks in an interview, 'I wanted the story to be set in a period in Australian life when people had a kind of entrepreneurial optimistic nationalism.'[107]

Earlier in the novel, when Nathan Schick, an American producer, wants to promote Leah's and Badgery's vaudeville act in the United States, he tells Leah and Badgery that they must first create 'an Australian hook'[108] and 'Distinctive Australian Flavour'.[109] Schick rejects the idea of using a snake as a mascot because 'they all look the same' to Americans and he dismisses

106 Ray Willbanks, 'Peter Carey', *Speaking Volumes: Australian Writers and their Work* (Ringwood: Penguin, 1992), 49.
107 Willbanks, 'Peter Carey', 50–1.
108 Carey, *Illywhacker*, 347.
109 Carey, *Illywhacker*, 349.

emus, claiming that the Americans will mistake them for ostriches.[110] Schick sees an opportunity for exploiting the country and designs an American-friendly production of Australian culture for success overseas. He says: 'What I want is an Aussie act for the States. This is a great country, but it hasn't even started to be exploited.'[111]

In *Making It National: Nationalism and Australian Popular Culture*, Graeme Turner observes ways in which Australia constructs, performs, and exploits its image, particularly for export overseas. He explores the popularity of the stylized Aussie bloke persona by pointing to the extraordinary commercial success of Paul Hogan's *Crocodile Dundee* in the 1980s in America,[112] and the tourism ad from which Hogan's famous line, 'throw another shrimp on the barbie', became a catchphrase for Australian leisure to non-Australians everywhere, even though an Australian would never say 'shrimp' for what is known as a 'prawn'.

Most of the type-characters in the display, sheep shearers, lifesavers, bushmen, and aboriginals, are drawn from mental images of what Australia represents to the outside world and contribute to a largely masculine and rural notion of national identity. Yet some of the caged characters break this pattern and rebel against their own signs. Badgery leaves behind the classic Australian roles of illywhacker and battler to play the part of a feminized old man, and Leah denies her label of *Melbourne Jew* to anyone who will listen, exclaiming that it is a lie like the rest of the show.[113] In spite of her protests she finds that 'visitors prefer to believe the printed information' as it is, after all, 'written and signed by independent experts'.[114] Her live performance challenges the visitor's preferences for documents and 'facts' that are simpler to absorb than the reality of a more complex subject position.

In *Debutante Nation*, Susan Magarey, Sue Rowley and Susan Sheridan propose an alternative dramatization to Australia's tough, outdoorsy, true

110   Carey, *Illywhacker*, 347.
111   Carey, *Illywhacker*, 348.
112   Graeme Turner, *Making it National: Nationalism and Australian Popular Culture* (Sydney, NSW: Allen and Unwin, 1993), 6.
113   Carey, *Illywhacker*, 599.
114   Carey, *Illywhacker*, 599.

blue and, overall, masculine identity. The authors propose 'an alternate reading of the national self'[115] and dramatize a feminine identity for the country. They emphasize 'debutantes rather than bushranging desperadoes', exhibiting a 'readiness to play with the gender of nationhood [...] even cross-dressing'.[116] Graeme Turner suggests that *Debutante Nation* emphasizes 'the need for an alternative reading' of the nation by the very fact that the image 'seems, in the context of the dominant traditions in the writing of Australian history, so frivolous'.[117] The final image of Badgery nursing Hissao presents an alternate dramatization of an Australian male identity. Badgery's performance, while bizarre and unsettling, is intimate and nurturing in contrast to conventional dramatizations of Mother England, and deconstructs more traditional conceptions of Australian masculinity. The image is, notably, not for public display, but takes place privately, after midnight, in Badgery's cage.

In an article on interactive museums, Scott Magelssen describes how theatrical and interactive performances in museums have the potential to reach visitors in ways that 'shift the primary emphasis away from the document and the archive'.[118] While museums characteristically affirm and enforce state-approved notions of culture and history through exhibits, Magelssen describes how living museums can offer individuals personal claims to history through a simulation of experience. In conventional museums, 'the individual's claim to a personal history [...] is likely to be erased or absorbed into state history'.[119] While Magelssen believes 'living museums' are not as subversive or revolutionary as they may become in the future, as none of the living museums he studied had yet devised ways to allow the interaction between visitors and historical characters to be more than

115   Susan Magarey, Sue Rowley and Susan Sheridan, eds, *Debutante Nation: Feminism Contests the 1890s* (St Leonards, NSW: Allen & Unwin, 1993), xx.
116   Magarey, Rowley and Sheridan, eds, *Debutante Nation: Feminism Contests the 1890s*, 162–5.
117   Turner, *Making it National: Nationalism and Australian Popular Culture*, 7.
118   Scott Magelssen, 'Making History in the Second Person: Post-touristic Considerations for Living Historical Interpretation', *Theatre Journal* 58 (2006), 303.
119   Magelssen, 'Making History in the Second Person', 293.

superficial, explore unscripted dialogue or to let audience members play the roles of significant historical characters, he sees great potential in them so that visitors can have the experience of being co-creators rather than consumers of history.[120]

To make more genuine connections between historical characters and visitors, Magelssen proposed that living museums integrate 'second-person interpretation' in their theatrical presentations.[121] Rather than observe, or play inconsequential roles of villagers or citizens, visitors could play central roles and participate more meaningfully in improvisations of history. Even if they 'got history wrong', Magelssen argues, visitors would have a more active and personal experience of how characters made choices that led to significant events, and could be made aware of unhistorical choices and the potential consequences of those choices, in later discussions.[122] In summarizing Freddie Rokem in *Performing History*, Magelssen emphasizes that 'the very presence of the human performer is the element of live performance that separates it from other historiographic discourses and makes it a more forceful mode of creating and disseminating narratives about the past'.[123] Following its mandate of developing an interactive museum, although not going so far as to ascribe roles to actual visitors, the Canadian War Museum has created an online war game called 'Over the Top' where virtual visitors can experience a choose-your-own personalized adventure through some of the experiences of Canadian soldiers who lived and died in the trenches during the First World War and select an array of different outcomes. The idea is that when the player experiences 'living' in the trenches and making decisions in that world, it brings a sense of history alive into the present moment and makes a lasting impression.[124]

Carey's 'Best Pet Shop in the World' has a forceful impact on its visitors, who meet and speak with the performers/inhabitants and, from that

120 Magelssen, 'Making History in the Second Person', 303.
121 Magelssen, 'Making History in the Second Person', 303.
122 Magelssen, 'Making History in the Second Person', 303.
123 Magelssen, 'Making History in the Second Person', 303.
124 'Over the Top', Canadian War Museum <http://www.warmuseum.ca/overthetop/> accessed 24 July 2016.

interaction, may go on to embrace or question conventional representations of Australian nationalism. The reader's presence in the novel is theatricalized and positioned just outside of the 'live' inner audience. The performative energy in the last chapter supports Magelssen's claim that 'theatre and performance are powerful historiographic tools',[125] and the impact of the 'live' performance can be felt even when it is transcribed to the novel. The performance may stir up feelings of spontaneity, recognizable from the theatre, in readers who may be affectively charged by human elements engaged in performative roles. The final chapter, due to this performative energy, has revitalizing capabilities and a certain energy that a document-based fiction based on history and historiography does not generally produce.

Anderson identifies the museum as a contributing factor to the development of an imagined community and explains how museums represented the nation's narratives and desired reflections which led to the development of the nation's values and sense of identity.[126] Carey's live emporium showcases how he suggests the hegemonic Australian majority at a certain point in history wanted to perceive itself through serialized characters that are preserved indefinitely. Frederic Jameson's discussion of pastiche in 'Postmodernism and Consumer Society' resonates uncannily with the living stereotypes in Carey's museum. Jameson writes: 'Pastiche is like parody but without a sense of humour or any norm.'[127] It signals 'a world in which stylistic innovation is no longer possible, all that is left is to imitate dead styles, to speak through the masks and with the voices of the styles in the imaginary museum.'[128] Jameson's concept of the 'imaginary museum' is anticipated in Carey's novel in the 'Best Pet Shop in the World' which dramatizes the 'dead styles', 'masks', and echoed 'voices' of stereotyped Australian identities. The pathetic entrapment of the living stereotypes suggests a thwarted sense of humour that is emptied of humanity and a consumer-driven impulse to reproduce Australian stereotypes

---

125   Magelssen, 'Making History in the Second Person', 303.
126   Anderson, *Imagined Communities: Reflections on the Origin and Spread of Nationalism*, 184.
127   Frederic Jameson, 'Postmodernism and Consumer Society', in E. Ann Kaplan, ed., *Postmodernism and its Discontents: Theories and Practices* (London: Verso, 1988), 18.
128   Jameson, 'Postmodernism and Consumer Society', 18.

that provide nostalgic comfort. Jameson identifies how, in postmodernism, 'we live in a perpetual present' as 'our social system has little by little begun to lose its capacity to retain its past'.[129] Perhaps theatre in fiction is a way of engineering such perpetual presents, a way of refuting the idea that 'stylistic innovation' is impossible; as one cuts and pastes, and splices one form into another, it may create a pastiche that amounts to more than the sum of its parts and, at the very least, points to our inability to express using old forms in old ways.

Illywhacker is an overtly theatrical novel that explores performances of national identity and cultural stereotypes and offers readers insight into a backstage version of a twentieth-century theatricalized historiography of Australia delivered by Badgery. Displaying theatrical qualities of the picaresque genre, Badgery highlights his physicality and constant role-playing and plays with the distance at which he places readers in relation to his story. Carey creates an imagined community of Australians and exposes theatrical qualities of nationalism. Carey's approach to writing Australia's historiography seems to be to introduce one or more central impossibilities – in *Illywhacker*, there are a few in the lying narrator, a dystopic future and elements of magic realism – to destabilize the project, and with it, his readers' assumptions about how one might typically go about constructing historiography in fiction. Thus disarmed and potentially less concerned with separating truths and lies, readers may gain insights into national character where they least suspect it. Some of the most intriguing performances in the novel are performed by members of minority groups who stage their marginality in various ways through parodies or over-acting to survive in postcolonial multicultural Australian society. Carey explores the particular trope of the disappearing acts performed by minorities in order to survive in a predominantly white society. *Illywhacker* encourages readers to evaluate Badgery's and other characters' performances of nationalism by showcasing national identities created for home and away. Carey's dramatic mode in *Illywhacker* lends itself well to exploring issues of performing the body in history, parodying national stereotypes, and dramatizing the artifice and illusions of a postcolonial nation.

129   Jameson, 'Postmodernism and Consumer Society', 28.

CHAPTER 4

Dramatic Modes and the Feminist Poetics of Enactment in Daphne Marlatt's *Ana Historic*

Canadian poet, essayist, and novelist Daphne Marlatt creates a feminist poetics of enactment through a dramatic mode in her novel *Ana Historic* (1988), as she imagines and animates a previously unwritten life story of a woman from late nineteenth-century Canadian history.[1] Awarded the George Woodcock Lifetime Achievement Award (2012) and the Order of Canada for contributions to Canadian literature (2005), Marlatt is an influential writer who has made significant contributions in feminist and lesbian poetics, writing histories through experimental forms and exploring place and memory. Marlatt exhibits evocative and provocative strategies in her writing to circumvent patriarchal language and assumptions as she translates her perspective of the world and Canadian history onto the page. She describes how she began developing as a writer as human rights movements advanced in Canada in the 1960s: 'My emergence as a poet coincided with large-scale political awakenings: the civil rights, anti-war, feminist, and later post-colonial and lesbian/gay-rights movements of two decades, the 1960s through the 1980s.'[2]

Marlatt was one of the founding editors of and contributors to *TISH*, a Canadian poetry journal at the University of British Columbia, from 1961 to 1969. She has since written more than twenty books including several volumes of poetry, critically acclaimed novels *Ana Historic* (1988) and *Taken* (1996), poetic collaborations *Double Negative* and *Touch to My Tongue* with Betsy Warland, poetic and photographic collaborations *Steveston*

---

1   Daphne Marlatt, *Ana Historic* (Toronto: Coach House Press, 1988).
2   Daphne Marlatt, 'Afterword', in Susan Knutson, *Rivering: The Poetry of Daphne Marlatt*, Laurier Poetry Series (Waterloo: Wilfrid Laurier University Press, 2014), 64.

(1974, 1984, 2000) with Robert Minden, which documents a Canadian town where Japanese people were interned during the Second World War, and a prize-winning play, *The Gull* (2008), staged in Japanese Noh style.[3] Marlatt has revised her earlier Vancouver poems in *Liquidities: Vancouver Poems Then and Now* (2013), and has been lauded for her efforts as a writer, university writing instructor and mentor with two honorary doctorates.[4]

Marlatt's performative writing in *Ana Historic* invites connection and resonance through means deeper than, yet incorporated within, words through embodied poetics and dramatic explorations. Marlatt challenges conventional boundaries of genre in the novel by utilizing conventions from drama and the theatre, observable in her early long-poem novels, *The Sea Haven* and *Frames of a Story*.[5] In *Ana Historic*, her most popular novel, unrecorded histories for women are dramatized to animate a living, breathing past. With a prolific career in poetry and an early background in theatre studies, Marlatt draws on diverse techniques from these areas to create experience in language rather than to represent it or frame it, as she describes how she tried to write about childbirth in *Two Women in a Birth*: 'I wanted to re-enact it in language rather than document it.'[6]

Performative moments in *Ana Historic* present opportunities for re-visioning historical possibilities. A range of dramatic strategies is used to re-enact historical moments in the mind's eye of the protagonist in *Ana Historic* and breathe a sense of life and the present moment into the novel. In *Ana Historic*, a contemporary Canadian woman, Annie, who is a research assistant to her historian husband, imagines a life for Mrs Richards, an

3   'Daphne Marlatt', *The Canadian Encyclopedia* <http://www.thecanadianencyclo pedia.ca/en/article/daphne-marlatt/> accessed 10 October 2016. Daphne Marlatt's play *The Gull* was the first Canadian play set in the Japanese Noh style and won the 2008 Uchimura Naoya Prize.

4   'Daphne Marlatt', *The Canadian Encyclopedia* <http://www.thecanadianencyclo pedia.ca/en/article/daphne-marlatt/> accessed 10 October 2016.

5   George   Bowering,   'Given   This   Body: Interview with   Daphne   Marlatt',   *Open   Letter*   4/3   (1979),   38.

6   Bowering, 'Given This Body: Interview with Daphne Marlatt', 64.

English schoolteacher who immigrated to Canada alone in 1873. Annie dramatizes Mrs Richards, whom she names Ana, in order to experience what life might have been like as a woman in the new colony. While a history book might have summed up Mrs Richards in one line – 'In 1874 Mrs. Richards marries Ben Springer and the Pattersons move to Moodyville. that is all that history says'[7] – Annie begins her imaginative work at the margin where the narratives of history typically stop. She looks critically at what is typically recorded in the history of the colony – facts from historical publications, measurements, building descriptions, newspaper notices, and comments about women's nature – and what is omitted. The novel poses the question, what if speculation and imagination allow us to recover or inhabit marginalized women's history? Marlatt writes, 'we live in history and imagination. but once history's onstage, histrionic as usual (all those wars, all those historic judgements), the a-historic hasn't got a speaking part. What's imagination next to the weight of the (f)actual?'[8]

Marlatt's dramatic mode in *Ana Historic* brings to life new versions of history, some drawn from memories or imagined realities, that present unruly, resonant, and subversive possibilities against masculinist and dominant narratives of history. In an interview, Marlatt describes how she is 'always interested in what gets left out of any official history'[9] and comments on the way that 'much of women's work, a lot of it caretaking, never enters the records' and 'is a-historic as such'.[10]

> I like rubbing the edges of document and memory/fiction against one another. I like the friction that is produced between the stark reporting of document, the pseudo-factual language of journalism, and the more emotional, even poetic, language of memory. That's why I used such a hodgepodge of sources in *Ana Historic*: a little nineteenth-century and very local journalism that sounds like a gossip column, a 1906

---

7   Marlatt, *Ana Historic*, 48.
8   Marlatt, *Ana Historic*, 139.
9   Marlatt qtd in Sue Kossew, 'History and place: An interview with Daphne Marlatt', *Canadian Literature* 178 (Autumn 2003), 55.
10 Marlatt qtd in Kossew, 'History and place: An interview with Daphne Marlatt', 53.

school textbook, various historical accounts, some contemporary feminist theory, and a school teacher's diary from 1873 that was completely fictitious.[11]

Ana Historic received a wave of positive critical reviews upon publication in 1988 for its innovation in critiquing that which is typically perceived as history in a genre that combines fiction and poetry. Jane Rule calls *Ana Historic* 'An experiment of the imagination toward new honesties'[12] and George Bowering comments on the aural qualities of the novel and on the ways in which Marlatt deconstructs familiar expectations of what a novel can be:

> For years we have been asking Daphne Marlatt to write a novel, to get that novel finished, please. [...] And as one might have expected, she first had to tear down The Novel. What she has put up in its place is too beautiful to keep to oneself. Please read it. While you are at it, read it out loud. Make oral history.[13]

Since the publication of *Ana Historic*, literary critics have engaged with a range of critical perspectives emerging from it, including queer identity construction in a postcolonial nation,[14] re-writing maternal history,[15] eco-critical approaches[16] and issues of translation.[17] This chapter looks closely at the dramatic mode at work within *Ana Historic* as a strategy for enlivening

---

11   Marlatt qtd in Sue Kossew, 'History and Place: An Interview with Daphne Marlatt', 55.

12   Jane Rule, 'Back Cover', *Ana Historic* (Toronto: Coach House Press, 1988).

13   George Bowering, 'Back Cover', *Ana Historic* (Toronto: Coach House Press, 1988).

14   Heather Zwicker, '*Ana Historic*: Queering the Postcolonial Nation', *ARIEL: A Review of International English Literature* 30/2 (April 1999), 161–75.

15   *Rishma Dunlop*, 'Archives of Desire: Rewriting Maternal History in Daphne Marlatt's *Ana Historic*', *Journal of the Association for Research on Mothering* 4/2 (Autumn/ Winter 2002), 65–72; C. Annette Grisé, '"A Bedtime Story for You, Ina": Resisting Amnesia of the Maternal in Daphne Marlatt's *Ana Historic*', *Tessera* 15 (Winter 1993), 90–8.

16   Renee Jackson Harper, 'Forests, Clearings, and the Spaces in Between: Reading Land Claims and the Actuality of Context in *Ana Historic*', *Canadian Literature/Etudes en Littérature Canadienne* 40/2 (2015), 128–42.

17   Pamela Banting, *Body Inc.: Daphne Marlatt's Translation Poetics* (Winnipeg: Turnstone Press, 1995); Beverley Curran, 'Reading Us into the Page Ahead: Translation as a Narrative Strategy in Daphne Marlatt's *Ana Historic* and Nicole

a re-imagined history for a woman in nineteenth-century Canada for con-temporary readers. While *Ana Historic* cannot escape representation on some level – it still uses words on a page as a means of signification – its transposition of dramatic strategies to fiction draws focus inward and diminishes the conventional critical distance from which readers perceive a novel. Marlatt positions her narrator Annie, and by extension, readers, to imagine a way into the mind and body of Mrs Richards, an historical woman the records tell little about, to explore her backstory, desires, and motivations in a sensuous embodiment of nineteenth-century Canadian life.

In *Ana Historic*, Annie imagines a world outside of what is convention-ally written about historical settler women and focuses on female bodies that are perceived as somehow unwieldy – the immigrant body, the hysteri-cal body, the lesbian body, and the birthing body – to re-enact, rather than to document, in words, a possible version of history. Marlatt experiments with language so that it constitutes experiences for readers that are physi-cal and affective. Her techniques follow a similar paradox of textuality and feeling to what Roland Barthes explores in *The Pleasure of the Text*: 'how can a text, which consists of language, be outside language?'[18] Marlatt's per-formative fiction which brings the female body to life in *Ana Historic* builds on feminist and performative theoretical groundwork by Luce Irigaray, Hélène Cixous, Julia Kristeva and Della Pollock that focus on writing the female body and creating performative texts.[19] I will compare how Marlatt describes Annie imagining herself into inhabiting the historical character Ana to the system Constantin Stanislavski created for actors to develop their characters by delving into the emotional desires and an awareness of the body and its stories.[20] The chapter will also consider writing as an act

---

Brossard's *Le Désert mauve*, in Leiven D'Hulst and John Milton, eds, *Reconstructing Cultural Memory: Translation, Scripts, Literacy* (Amsterdam: Rodopi, 2000).

18   Barthes, *The Pleasure of the Text*, 30.

19   Luce Irigarary, *Ce sexe qui n'en est pas un*, trans. Catherine Porter (Paris: Minuit, 1977); Julia Kristeva, *Revolution in Poetic Language*, trans. Margaret Waller (New York: Columbia University Press, 1984); Hélène Cixous, 'The Laugh of the Medusa', *Signs* (Summer 1976), 245–64; Della Pollock, 'Performing Writing', 73–103.

20   Constantin Stanislavski, *An Actor Prepares*, trans. Elizabeth Reynolds Hapgood [1936] (London: Methuen, 1986).

of translation and examine how Marlatt translates aspects of drama to the page, supported by translation theories of the body by Pamela Banting in *Body Inc.*,[21] to create new endings for women and explore possibilities of performative fictive histories.

Opening the Text: How to Break through Representative Language

In *Ana Historic*, Marlatt wages an attack on more conventional novels that examine history in at least two ways: in the language itself – which translates the body and eschews conventional sentence structure, delineations of time and place, punctuation, and capitalization – and in Marlatt's incorporation of dramatic strategies in fiction, which offer perpetual 'present' moments in the text for its characters and, on some level, for readers. As Annie dramatizes Ana's consciousness, Annie enters history, and readers may feel, on some occasions, a sense of being present in both Ana's and Annie's worlds. Annie re-imagines the past dramatically as part of her strategy of reclaiming history from conventional frames. She says, 'but when you're so framed, caught in the act, the (f) stop of act, fact – what recourse? step inside the picture and open it up'.[22]

Marlatt's dramatic mode in fiction works similarly to how Roland Barthes's *punctum* pierces the *studium* in photographs. Barthes describes the *studium* of a photograph as the general theme that can be interesting to a viewer but lacks a compelling hook.[23] The *studium* contains cultural and historical elements which may intrigue but do not arrest the viewer. Barthes suggests that a photograph which is all *studium* is a passive object; a photograph made up entirely of a *studium* may put forward interesting

21   Banting, *Body Inc.: A Theory of Translation Poetics*.
22   Marlatt, *Ana Historic*, 56.
23   Roland Barthes, *Camera Lucida: Reflections on Photography*, trans. Richard Howard [1981] (New York: Hill, 2000), 26.

ideas but because the ideas do not continue to live outside the picture, the photograph will not connect with the viewer and will remain representative. The *punctum*, according to Barthes, is the element that 'will break (or punctuate) the *studium*'.[24] It 'pricks or wounds' the viewer.[25] Barthes describes how the *punctum* affects him: 'it is this element which rises from the scene, shoots out of it like an arrow, and pierces me'.[26] It allows a vital quality of 'what Barthes calls 'life' to pass through, to permeate the frame'[27] and 'create the adventure'.[28] Barthes describes the sensation of reciprocity that the *punctum* creates between the photograph and its viewer: 'suddenly a specific photograph reaches me; it animates me, and I animate it'.[29] The *punctum* provides an opening in the photograph through which the viewer can enter or an image can leap from the page. In a similar way, Marlatt's dramatic mode, which engages characters and readers in a heightened awareness of role-playing, serves as a kind of *punctum* that breaks through the representative language of the novel.

Barthes describes a photograph without a *punctum* as static: 'When we define the Photograph as a motionless image, this does not mean only that the figures it represents do not move; it means that they do not emerge, do not leave: they are anaesthetized and fastened down, like butterflies.'[30] Dramatized bodies in *Ana Historic* act as a *punctum* in the novel; they do not stay 'fastened down' and are far from 'anaesthetized'. Marlatt's dramatic mode offers a way of exploring characters that have been neglected or restrained within traditional literary and historical representations – particularly, in this case, female immigrants to Canada in the nineteenth century – and works as part of a feminist writing strategy within and against language. A dramatic mode in fiction is particularly appropriate

---

24   Barthes, *Camera Lucida: Reflections on Photography*, 26.
25   Barthes, *Camera Lucida: Reflections on Photography*, 26.
26   Barthes, *Camera Lucida: Reflections on Photography*, 48.
27   Jane Gallop, *Thinking Through the Body* (New York: Columbia University Press, 1988), 153.
28   Barthes, *Camera Lucida: Reflections on Photography*, 20.
29   Barthes, *Camera Lucida: Reflections on Photography*, 26.
30   Barthes, *Camera Lucida: Reflections on Photography*, 57.

for liberating the story of Ina, Annie's mother, who has been trapped twice: in language, and in a medical system that advocates electric shock therapy to treat women's hysteria and depression. Annie imagines that her mother is alive again and interfering in the narration of her novel. She re-creates Ina in the way she was before she lost her imagination, memory, and the 'will to create things differently'.[31] Annie dramatizes Ina to prevent her from remaining 'a character flattened by destiny, caught between the covers of a book'.[32] The deployment of a dramatic mode in the novel is, in part, created through writing that focuses on the body in the present moment.

Marlatt's bodily poetics build on the groundwork of women's writing or *écriture féminine* introduced by French feminist theorists Hélène Cixous, Luce Irigaray, and others in the 1970s.[33] In *Ce sexe qui n'en est pas un*, Luce Irigaray writes, 'If we don't invent a language for our body, there will be too few gestures to portray our history. We will weary of the same few gestures, and our desires will remain latent, and in limbo. Lulled to sleep, unsatisfied. And delivered over to the words of men.'[34] While Sarah Harasym criticizes Marlatt's writing for stereotypical representations of class and race and for resting on biological and essentialist claims of what constitutes a woman,[35] Marlatt's work has been commended for inscribing feminist and lesbian desire in a radical and corporeal way.[36] Marlatt's

31   Marlatt, *Ana Historic*, 150.
32   Marlatt, *Ana Historic*, 150.
33   Marlatt also draws on the work of feminist writers from Quebec, supporting the idea of a 'pre-syntatic' woman's language. See Daphne Marlatt, *Touch to My Tongue and musing with mothertongue* (Edmonton: Longspoon, 1984).
34   Luce Irigarary, *Ce sexe qui n'en est pas un*, trans. Catherine Porter (Paris: Minuit, 1977), 213.
35   Sarah Harasym criticizes Marlatt's equation of women and sexuality and her privileging of l'écriture féminine, which Harasym suggests does not look critically at the ethico-political concerns which re-iterate and separate 'first' and 'third' world constructions of women. See Sarah Harasym, 'EACH MOVE MADE HERE (me) MOVES THERE (you)', *boundary 2* 18/1 (1991), 104–26.
36   See Barbara Godard's '"Body I": Daphne Marlatt's Feminist Poetics', *The American Review of Canadian Studies* 15/4 (1985), 481–96 and Heather Zwicker's 'Daphne Marlatt's *Ana Historic*: Queering the Postcolonial Nation', *ARIEL* 30/2 (1999),

writing style does not follow conventional rules of grammar and sentence structure. As Annie suggests in *Ana Historic*, Marlatt's writing style translates 'the words that flow out from within, running too quick to catch sometimes, at other times just an agonizingly slow trickle. the words of an interior history doesn't include.'[37] Writing from the body recuperates physical experiences, gestures, sensations, and desires that are missing from many conventional historical and heterosexual narratives. Marlatt examines how words carry networks of associations, support teleological and phallogocentric values, and constantly divide, define, and contain. Marlatt deconstructs phallogocentric language to make the body of language she enters fit her like a second skin.

Translations and Transpositions

In *Body Inc.*, Pamela Banting suggests that Marlatt does not represent the body on the page but rather translates the body to the page through intersemiotic translations. Banting borrows the term 'intersemiotic translation' from Roman Jakobson, who distinguishes between three kinds of translations: intralingual (within the same language, yet between different codes or registers), interlingual (between two languages) and intersemiotic (from one sign system to another).[38] Several acts of translation occur in *Ana Historic*. Marlatt describes the intralingual translation between her mother's English from England and the English spoken by herself and her sisters as children in Canada. Marlatt translates masculinist language into a body-centred feminist poetics, for example, when Annie sees a determined logger in a photo and wonders how he is so confident of his role and place in society when she is so unsure of herself and the roles she is meant to play.

161–75. Marlatt explores language and the female body in *Touch to My Tongue and musing with mothertongue*, 48.

37   Marlatt, *Ana Historic*, 90.

38   Qtd in Banting, *Body Inc.: A Theory of Translation Poetics*, 11.

The caption under the photo of the logger says, '*Bull puncher and oxen relax momentarily, sullenly conscious of their ability to get any job done, no matter how tough*.'[39] Annie describes the logger, 'the woodsman look. Self-evident. the pose',[40] and then meditates on her struggle to play the role of a woman with a similarly unified and confident identity:

> there was the look you gave yourself, the look you looked (like) in the mirror. making up someone who was not you but someone you might be. a desperate attempt to make up for the gap – between the way you actually looked in your blue dressing gown round and woolly in the mornings, your scrubbed shining cheeks, anger in two humps between your brows, hair fine as a baby's wisping away in the rush of porridge-making – the gap between that and how you meant to look, how you ought to look ... caught between despair at being nothing ('just' a mother, 'just' a wife) ... and the endless effort to live a lie.[41]

However, the most pertinent translations for the purpose of this chapter are Marlatt's intersemiotic translations from the body to the text and from drama to the novel. Jakobson defines intersemiotic translation as 'an interpretation of verbal signs by means of nonverbal signs'.[42] In *Body Inc.*, Banting extends Jakobson's concept of inter-semiotic translation to include translations between different media; words and images (paintings, photos, drawings); and between text and flesh.[43] Drama is an intersemiotic element Marlatt translates in the novel that Banting does not address specifically in her analysis of Marlatt's writing, although Banting alludes to dance and how it can be translated to the page.[44] In some scenes in *Ana Historic*, intersemiotic translations occur as Marlatt translates the sense of dramatic enactments to text – for example when Annie dives deep inside the character of Ana, when Annie revisits her childhood self, or when Annie invites readers to engage in her intimate connection with Zoe at

39   Marlatt, *Ana Historic*, 56.
40   Marlatt, *Ana Historic*, 56.
41   Marlatt, *Ana Historic*, 56–7.
42   Roman Jakobson, 'On Linguistic Aspects of Translation', *Selected Writings: Word and Language* 2 (The Hague: Mouton, 1971), 261.
43   Banting, *Body Inc.: A Theory of Translation Poetics*, 11.
44   Banting, *Body Inc.: A Theory of Translation Poetics*, 204.

the novel's end; each enactment, translated to the page, generates a sense of evocation, sensory experience and theatrical presence.

Jakobson's definition of intersemiotic translation is similar to what Julia Kristeva calls 'inter-textuality', which describes a transposition between sign systems.[45] A transposition between sign systems involves 'the destruction of the old position and the formation of a new one'.[46] Within each transposition, Kristeva emphasizes that the thetic break is re-articulated anew: the thetic break being the point at which a subject emerges from the mirror stage and the semiotic to enter the symbolic and take up a position of identification.[47] As the thetic break is constructed, reconstructed, and deconstructed in different sign systems in a single text – for example, in Marlatt's novel between the poetic language from the body, written dramatizations and more conventional fictive sections – it carries permutations of its passage from one sign system to another. Kristeva notes that a transposition from one sign system to another may use the same signifying material, such as language moving from an oral narrative to a text, or 'different signifying materials', as seen in 'the transposition from a carnival scene to [a] written text'.[48] Kristeva observes how a novel may contain 'a redistribution of several different sign systems: carnival, courtly poetry, scholastic discourse'.[49]

Marlatt integrates several signifying systems into *Ana Historic*: journal entries, historical descriptions, nineteenth-century poetry, songs, conversations, and dramatizations. There is play and exploration of what Kristeva calls thetic positioning, as Annie inhabits herself, first, as a young girl, then inhabits Ana Richards, and finally, her mother, Ina. At times, Annie's

45 Because 'inter-textuality' is now often used to describe 'a study of sources' in a single work, Kristeva prefers the term 'transposition' which she uses to describe more than one signifying system in a work. See Julia Kristeva, *Revolution in Poetic Language*, trans. Margaret Waller (New York: Columbia University Press, 1984), 60.

46 Kristeva, *Revolution in Poetic Language*, 59.

47 Kelly Oliver, in Michael Grodin and Martin Kreiswirth, eds, *Julia Kristeva: The Johns Hopkins Guide to Literary Theory and Criticism* (Baltimore, MD: Johns Hopkins University Press, 1997), 2.

48 Kristeva, *Revolution in Poetic Language*, 59.

49 Kristeva, *Revolution in Poetic Language*, 59.

enunciative positions are strategically blurred in the narrative; the speaking positions overlap and intersect, and slippages between subject and object lure a reader into occupying the consciousness of a character before a reader knows whose consciousness s/he is in: Annie's, Ana's, or Ina's. As Annie remembers what it was like to be in the body and mind of a little girl, she switches pronouns and, with these, consciousnesses. Changing she/her to me/my, Annie occupies the body of her younger self with a leap of imagination as an actor does while playing a part. This results in fractured or, what Kristeva calls, '"polysemic" enunciative positions in the text'.[50] Additionally, Marlatt omits the conventional representations of dialogue, such as 'Ana said' or 'Ina asked', to put the reader directly in active moments. In 'Given This Body', Marlatt discusses her preference for enactment over conventional frames: 'Once you say, "she says," you get the frame in there. I don't want the frame. I want it just transmitted straight.'[51] In *Ana Historic*, the perspective switches seamlessly from an onlooker outside watching Ana write to Ana writing in her journal inside her cabin without conventional framing devices of 'she said' or 'Ana wrote'.[52]

Early in the novel, there is another abrupt shift in Anna's speaking position. The passage begins with a third-person narration of a young girl who guards her sisters from the monster in the wardrobe and dramatically shifts to the first-person narration of the young girl who calls out at night to her parents:

> who? her parents who went out leaving her alone to defend the house. her mother who ... my mother (who) ... voice that carries through all rooms, imperative, imperious. don't be silly. soft breast under blue wool dressing gown, tea breath, warm touch ... gone.[53]

50   Kristeva, *Revolution in Poetic Language*, 59.
51   Marlatt qtd in Bowering, 'Given This Body: An interview with Daphne Marlatt', 77–8.
52   Marlatt, *Ana Historic*, 54.
53   Marlatt, *Ana Historic*, 10.

Annie becomes young Annie hearing her mother's voice, smelling her breath, and feeling her touch.[54] The shift in perspective effects a dramatization of sorts, short-lived yet evocative. For Annie, it is more than a memory; it is an active portal to her past. In dramatizing her younger self, Annie experiences the memory in the present again. Marlatt's technique of dramatization suggests that there is knowledge stored in Annie's body and sense memory that is evoked by words yet, on some level, elides description by them. Annie writes, 'I-na, I-no- longer, i can't turn you into a story. there is this absence here, where the words stop.'[55] The limitations of the symbolic order are exposed as the dramatization allows Annie to experience her history in a way that privileges physicality and sensation and acknowledges the limitations of representation.

Annie also dramatizes Ana Richards to imagine the kind of writing she might have written or might have wanted to write. She is not convinced that romantic nineteenth-century poetry, with its 'touch of the sublime, that nineteenth-century sense of grandeur',[56] would have suited the private and unsettling experiences Ana would have felt in her new home. Annie conceives of the difficulties Ana would have had in adapting the conventions of nineteenth-century British poetry to Canada where the flora, fauna, climate, and social environment were so unfamiliar.[57] As an extension of the novel's focus on physicality in language, Annie writes women's bodies onto the landscape to conceive of the country newly and as a place where women belong. She describes the soft cedar stump that she used to sit in with her sister as a womb,[58] and has Ana imagine, upon the occasion of the birth of the first settler baby in the colony, the scarlet autumn leaves as 'lips all bleeding into the air',[59] greeting women and welcoming them to a country (and a language) in which they feel at home:

54　Marlatt, *Ana Historic*, 10.
55　Marlatt, *Ana Historic*, 11.
56　Marlatt, *Ana Historic*, 20.
57　Margaret Atwood explores similar themes in *The Journals of Susanna Moodie* (Toronto: Oxford University Press, 1970).
58　Marlatt, *Ana Historic*, 12.
59　Marlatt, *Ana Historic*, 127.

to be born in, enter from birth that place (that shoreline place of scarlet maples, since cut down) with no known name – see it, risen in waves these scarlet leaves, lips all bleeding into the air, given (birth), given in greeting, the given surrounds him now, surrounds her, her country she has come into, the country of her body.[60]

Annie explores the traps, claims, and associations of patriarchal language and encounters what she expects Ana would have left out of her poetry: her living, sensing, and female body.

Living Writing versus Representative Writing

Marlatt's dramatic mode creates experience more than it represents experience. Marlatt began experimenting with immediate and experiential kinds of writing in graduate school. She wrote an essay on etymology for American poet Charles Olson that analysed how conventional devices such as similes force readers to intellectualize experiences without feeling them.[61] In 'Human Universe', Olson explains how writing, which depends on substitution and definition, can isolate readers from more 'active intellectual states' of 'metaphor and performance' that allow them to feel the experience more closely in terms of their own relevance to it.[62] Olson theorizes how writers are 'led to partition reality' by seeking comparisons and reference points.[63] Analysing how one experience is similar to or different from another, Olson suggests, cuts off a reader from feeling it. Aggrieved

---

60   Marlatt, *Ana Historic*, 127. While linking menstruation and gestation with the Canadian woods makes, perhaps, too easy or essentialist a correlation between motherhood, women, and nature, Annie meets such an equation with the subversive possibility that Ana may not mother should she swerve from her expected trajectory and choose a life with Birdie Stuart as a lesbian in the 1870s.

61   Banting, *Body Inc.: A Theory of Translation Poetics*, 156.

62   Charles Olson, 'Human Universe', in Donald Allen and Warren Tallman, eds, *The Poetics of the New American Poetry* (New York: Grove, 1973), 164.

63   Olson, 'Human Universe', 164.

by the comparative nature of descriptions and similes, Olson maintains, 'there must be a way which bears *in* instead of away, which meets head on what goes on each split second, a way which does not – in order to define – prevent, deter, distract, and so cease the act of, discovering'.[64]

Olson's solution lies in a 'proprioceptive' poetics.[65] In physiology, proprioception refers to the perception of sensory information that is mediated by nerve receptors throughout the body. Olson's poetry is concerned with how the body mediates the sensory environment and feels an understanding of the world. Olson wants the body to feel something more than reported pleasures and experiences.[66] Influenced by Olson's poetics, Marlatt offers readers her proprioceptive method that she has developed into a female-centred poetics of enactment. Her writing draws readers inward to the experience inside bodies and consciousnesses. The deployment of dramatic conventions and strategies works in *Ana Historic* through writing that owes more to 'evocation than description', which is what Della Pollock suggests is the essence of performative writing.[67] Both Marlatt's and Olson's work resonate with Della Pollock's theory in 'Performing Writing' that suggests 'writing as "doing" displaces writing as meaning'.[68] Pollock describes the evocative powers of performative writing which collapse the 'distinctions by which creative and critical writing are typically isolated'.[69] The dramatic potential of performative writing, according to Pollock, lies in the shift 'from the scientific paradigm "What if" to its performative counterpart, "As if" and then "what now?"'[70] Marlatt's metaphoric positioning of characters and readers inside a range of dramatizations in *Ana Historic* favours what Pollock might call 'the generative and ludic capacities of language

---

64   Olson, 'Human Universe', 164–5.
65   Banting, *Body Inc.: A Theory of Translation Poetics*, 156.
66   Barthes also champions a proprioceptive poetics in *The Pleasures of the Text*. He writes, 'The pleasure of the text is that moment when my body pursues its own ideas – for my body does not have the same ideas I do' (17).
67   Pollock, 'Performing Writing', 73–103.
68   Pollock, 'Performing Writing', 75.
69   Pollock, 'Performing Writing', 80.
70   Pollock, 'Performing Writing', 81.

and language encounters' rather than the 'illusion of full presence' that a writer using mimetic or realistic perspectives might strive to represent.[71]

Stanislavski's System and Marlatt's Dramatic Mode

In much historical or historically based fiction, characters are limited in their representations by the roles they play in the nation's historical and imperial narrative. Women's roles, in particular, are too often ignored, marginalized, or presented as one-dimensional. In *Ana Historic*, Annie studies Ana Richards in a way that an actor following Constantin Stanislavski's system would flesh out a character: by focusing on emotional truths and knowledge from the body. Marlatt describes Annie's process of dramatization in detail as Annie embodies Ana Richards. After researching historical facts, Annie imagines Ana's body. She holds the pen like Ana would have held it and imagines what the other woman would have seen, thought, felt, heard, and feared. Annie conjures up far more than what would have been provided in historical records:

> she was looking for the company of another who was also reading – out through the words, through the wall that separated her, an arm, a hand – and so she began, 'a woman sitting at her kitchen table writing,' as if her hand holding the pen could embody the very feel of a life. as if she could reach out and touch her, those lashes cast down over blue (brown) eyes, the long line of nose, the lips doubting or pleased, that curve of a shoulder, upper arm, wrist at another table in a different kind of light.[72]

Annie draws on knowledge from the body to guide her into inhabiting Ana's character. She focuses on physical details and connections. She imagines the space on the wall where Ana would have stared, lost in thought, looking for the right word. In a trance-like meditation on Ana's subconscious, Annie begins to write what she imagines it would be like to be inside Ana's

71 Pollock, 'Performing Writing', 80.
72 Marlatt, *Ana Historic*, 45.

mind and body. She encounters what she calls 'the unspoken urge of a body insisting itself in the words'.[73]

There are significant connections between Stanislavski's system in theatre and Marlatt's dramatic mode in writing. Stanislavski codified his influential system of acting in *An Actor Prepares* and in *My Life in Art*. Unlike Bertolt Brecht's epic theatre[74] or Charles Marowitz's style in *The Other Way*,[75] Stanislavski's system is highly naturalistic and requires actors to live truthful moments in imaginary circumstances. Stanislavski believed the actor must create the soul of the character. With the understanding that a script provides 'only a few minutes out of the whole life' of a character,[76] the actor is required to create a fuller life outside of the text that fills in the spaces. The task falls to the actor to 'bring to life what is hidden under the words'.[77] To do this, the actor draws on physical impulses, emotional memories from his or her own life, and imagination. The actor develops what is known as a super-objective for the entire play and finds emotional and physical motivations to accomplish a series of smaller objectives. Attention to minute details is crucial in capturing physical, mental, and emotional realities. Actors translate desire, fear, and joy through gestures, resistance, and embraces. Stanislavski insists that an actor 'lives the part' rather than represents, or indicates, it: 'His [the artist's] job is not to present merely the external life of his character. He must fit his own human qualities to the life of this other person, and pour into it all of his own soul. The fundamental aim of our art is the creation of this inner life of a human spirit, and its expression in an artistic form.'[78] Marlatt explores a similar process in Annie's explorations of Ana. While Annie inhabits Ana – sits like her, speaks like her – she finds new ideas and inspirations about the character,

73   Marlatt, *Ana Historic*, 46.
74   See Brecht, *Brecht on Theatre: The Development of an Aesthetic*.
75   Charles Marowitz, *The Other Way: An Alternative Approach to Acting and Directing* (New York: Applause, 1999).
76   Konstantin Stanislavskiy, *My Life in Art*, trans. G. Ivanov-Mumjiev [1924] (Moscow: Foreign Languages Publishing, 1970), 257.
77   Constantin Stanislavski, *An Actor Prepares*, 52. Variations in the spelling are taken from the particular translations from Russian to English.
78   Stanislavski, *An Actor Prepares*, 14.

as though Ana were 'real' and she had gone 'fishing' in Ana's subconscious. The dramatic mode adds flesh to the story. Annie senses the 'skeletal bones of a suppressed body the story is'[79] and dramatizes the characters in it in order to re-enact what might have been through dramatic modes that extend beyond language.

While in university, Marlatt acted in a number of plays and her onstage experiences of discovering 'what is beyond the self, outside the self'[80] continued to inform her work. Her play, *The Gull: The Steveston Noh Project* (2006), based on the Japanese Noh style of theatre, uses stylized drama, music, dance, and poetry to portray the experiences of two orphaned brothers who return to Steveston, British Columbia after wartime restrictions on interned Japanese Canadians have been lifted in 1950. The brothers encounter the ghost of their mother who perished in the camp. *The Gull* was a theatrical collaboration with international Noh masters Richard Emmert, Akira Matsui and Hakuzan Kubo, who created two Noh masks and wrote original Noh music played by a troupe of musicians from Japan.[81] In an early interview with Bowering, Marlatt described how dramatic techniques helped her as a writer come close to uncovering the 'other': 'Of course you can't experience being it. But you have to somehow let it in. You have to let that dark flood the stage, you have to turn off all the lights.'[82] Marlatt discriminates here between acting that is characterized by stock theatrical gestures and imitative emotions, and acting that comes out of physical and emotional explorations and surrendering to the unknown. In her first book, *Frames of a Story*, she differentiates between the two styles: '& when will I give up *acting* & step into the dark of the other?'[83] Annie creates Ana using recognizable techniques from Stanislavski's system in order to tap into the unknown possibilities of the private life of an early female Canadian settler.

79   Marlatt, *Ana Historic*, 29.
80   Marlatt qtd in Bowering, 'Given This Body: An interview with Daphne Marlatt', 44–5.
81   Susan Knutson and Daphne Marlatt, eds, *Rivering* (Waterloo: Wilfrid Laurier University Press, 2014), xvii.
82   Marlatt qtd in Bowering, 'Given This Body: An interview with Daphne Marlatt', 45.
83   Daphne Marlatt, *Frames of a Story* (Toronto: Ryerson, 1968). Emphasis mine.

Stanislavski requires that the body should be involved in the development
of a character to avoid an over-intellectualized performance:

> Our art demands that an actor's whole nature be actively involved, that he give himself
> up, both mind and body, to his part. He must feel the challenge to action physically
> as well as intellectually because the imagination, which has no substance or body,
> can reflexively affect our physical nature and make it act.[84]

Annie first conceives of the possibility of a sexual attraction between Ana
and Birdie Stewart by imagining herself in Ana's body. Annie speaks to Ana
through second-person narration, placing the reader in Ana's character and
recognizing the possibility of a historical lesbian love affair:

> you turn intrigued, and your body turning in its long skirt, its fitted waist that hugs
> your hips, is caught in the act, you have caught yourself turning in Birdie's eyes. turn-
> ing because of a spark, a gleam, your eyes are green (you had forgotten that) and you
> know them lit with the look of something you almost meet in Birdie's brown. you
> had not imagined – this / as history. unwritten [85]

By imagining intimate physical details – the feel of Ana's clothing, the
'warmth and solidity' of Birdie's body beside her, the second glance at Birdie
that clarifies the desire that runs both ways[86] – Annie enacts a possibility
at odds with the heteronormative ideals of a nation's history. In this case, a
scene is not performed *for* the reader's passive entertainment, but rather the
reader is engaged in dramatic enactment through the second-person narration and the invitation to embody a physical poetics. Annie puts herself,
with her contemporary experiences and her imagination, into role-playing

---

84 Constantin Stanislavski, *An Actor Prepares*, 70. Stanislavski's examples are based on
    a masculine model. See Krasner's *Method Acting Reconsidered* for further analysis
    of Stanislavski's masculine bias and its effects on female actors in David Krasner, ed.
    Method Acting Reconsidered: Theory, Practice, Future (New York: St Martin's, 2000),
    13, 112. See also Elizabeth Stroppel's 'Reconciling the Past and the Present: Feminist
    Perspectives on the Method in the Classroom and on the Stage', in *Method Acting
    Reconsidered* (New York: St Martin's, 2000), 111–23 and Sue-Ellen Case, *Feminism
    and Theatre* (Basingstoke: Macmillan, 1986).
85 Marlatt, *Ana Historic*, 109.
86 Marlatt, *Ana Historic*, 139.

the unwritten possibility of sexual love between Ana and Birdie. Through the process of dramatizing Ana's relationship with Birdie in her writing, Annie begins to recognize the sexual feelings she has for Zoe in her own life. While there are instances of more overtly theatrical public performances at other points in the novel (the ballet, the teenage girls performing for each other), Marlatt creates private and reflective opportunities in which the reader may accompany Annie in her dramatizations of Ina and Ana. These interiorized passages do not convey the sensation of a public watching a performance but rather the quiet, inner sensation of an actor rehearsing the embodiment and inhabitation of another soul. As the reader follows Annie's imaginative work, her dramatic strategies offer engagement and connection that reach beyond the words that convey them.

Issues of fidelity concern Annie as she dramatizes historical characters. Annie feels a sense of obligation to Mrs (Ana) Richards, along with other historical foremothers, 'Mrs. Alexander, and Birdie Stewart, and Susan Patterson'.[87] She says, 'they all existed, they all really lived. i owe them something.'[88] Zoe counters Annie's lament with 'truth, I suppose? fidelity? she sneers. as if you were *impersonating* them.'[89] By definition, to 'impersonate' is 'to invest with an actual personality; to manifest or embody in one's own person; to assume the person or character of; to play the part of'.[90] Zoe suggests that Annie's impersonations of the historical characters can, and will, only be approximate because they are filtered through Annie's imagination before she enacts them. In the end, Annie decides that history and imagination should not be considered as opposite poles when creating a portrayal of a historical person. Annie recognizes the inherent difficulties of portraying herself – let alone someone else – with the plurality of inner contradictions, longings, and fantasies. Despite her mother's discouraging

---

87   Marlatt, *Ana Historic*, 140.
88   Marlatt, *Ana Historic*, 140.
89   Marlatt, *Ana Historic*, 141.
90   'Impersonate', *Oxford English Dictionary* (2nd edn, 1989) <http://www.oed.com. ez.library.latrobe.edu.au/view/Entry/92330?rskey=eXx7wa&result=2&isAdvanc ed=false#eid> accessed 3 July 2012.

words, 'you should've gone into theatre, not history,'[91] Annie acknowledges that her own way into imagining history requires a dramatic mode. She asks, 'what if they balance each other (it's one of those half-cloudy, half-sunny days) and we live in history and imagination'.[92] Where a historian might leave out the imaginary and, as a result, construct a more contained and discrete portrait, Annie impersonates the mind and body of a historical character without allowing herself to dismiss the project, as others might, as indulgent speculation.[93] Both Marlatt and Annie write the risk into their historically based fictions and indulge in speculations, creating possibilities of alternative and subversive histories.

In theatre, an actor influences an audience member's interpretation of a character to a large extent.[94] Essentially, the actor is the medium through which a character, historical or otherwise, is portrayed, and the actor is inseparable from the dramatization. The actor uses his or her voice, body, memories, and imagination to create the rendering. While historians generally aim to erase their fingerprints from their written accounts of history, Marlatt uses a dramatic mode in her novel to illustrate that an objective distance when animating history in fiction is unattainable and undesirable. For Marlatt, imagination is a way of transcending the limitations of one body and one consciousness[95] and embodying another. A combination of intersemiotic modes leads to more corporeal experiences of a historical character. Marlatt values the connection to the past that Ana's dramatization facilitates:

> in inventing a life from Mrs. Richards, i as Annie (and Annie isn't me though she may be one of the selves I could be) invented a historical leak, a hole in the sieve of fact that let the shadow of a possibility leak through into full-blown life. History is

91   Marlatt, *Ana Historic*, 22.
92   Marlatt, *Ana Historic*, 139.
93   Daphne Marlatt asks 'why isn't the imaginary part of one's life story?' in 'Self-Representation and Fictionalysis', in Barbara Godard, ed., *Collaboration in the Feminine: Writings on Women and Culture from Tessera* (Toronto: Second Story, 1994), 204.
94   Naturally, the playwright and director also influence the audience's interpretation.
95   Bowering, 'Given This Body: An interview with Daphne Marlatt', 71.

not the dead and gone, it lives on in us in the way it shapes our thought and especially our thought about what is possible. Mrs. Richards is a historical leak for the
possibility of a lesbian life in Victorian British Columbia.[96]

By dramatizing a possible life for Ana, Annie experiences a personal connection to a historical foremother. History is made personal to Annie
through a dramatic mode and, for the first time, she becomes interested
in Canadian history and women's roles in it. The dramatic mode creates
a continuum by, in Marlatt's words, 'intersect[ing] the present with the
past'.[97] Annie had believed that history was 'the real story the city fathers
tell of the only important events in the world', and finally comes to ask,
'where are the city mothers?'[98] After internalizing the idea that 'ladies keep
to the background' and 'ladies *are* the soothing background their men
come home to',[99] Annie redefines the patriarchal and heterosexist teleologies of history and rehearses an alternate mode through which the lives of
the 'minor players' can be portrayed. *Ana Historic* explores the continuum
between three women in history in their 'backstage' roles.

Positioning the Reader: Fractured Subjectivities in a Colonial Nation

One of the novel's most effective dramatic strategies of connecting history to
the present is the way in which Annie positions the reader in multiple roles
using second-person narration. The reader is invoked alternately through
the pronoun 'you' as Ina and 'you' as Ana, while remaining 'the reader'.
These direct addresses give the reader the sensation of inhabiting Ina and
Ana at different times. A sense of doubleness is common in Stanislavski's

---

96   Marlatt, 'Self-Representation and Fictionalysis', 204.
97   Qtd in Bowering, 'Given This Body: An interview with Daphne Marlatt', 71.
98   Marlatt, *Ana Historic*, 28.
99   Marlatt, *Ana Historic*, 35.

system, in which an actor is both himself or herself and the character he or she plays at the same time. Actors draw on emotions from their lives with a simultaneous awareness of spectators watching them do it.

A sense of a doubled, or fractured, identity is not unusual for immigrants; both Ana and Ina are, at once, British emigrants and Canadian immigrants. Ina's national identity revolves around an England in which she briefly lived. Ina was born in India, where her parents were stationed, before moving to boarding school in England and, later, re-locating to Canada.[100] 'Home' for Ina is illusory; it is not located in a country but in familial customs and memories. Ina's past is similar to Marlatt's own parents' past: Marlatt's mother was born into a colonial medical family in India and met Marlatt's father in Malaysia after completing an English private school education.[101] Marlatt's father was from a military family and lived in India, Malta, Australia and Malaysia before immigrating with his wife and children to Canada. Marlatt was born in Melbourne, Australia and moved at the age of three to Penang where she lived until she immigrated to Canada at the age of nine. As a child in Penang, Marlatt was accustomed to 'a colonial multicultural situation' where five languages – English, Malay, Cantonese, Tamil, and Thai – were spoken by her family and the servants who worked in her home.[102] Marlatt's mother, like Ina, shifted from the role of *memsahib* in a colonial household to the role of a housewife in Vancouver where she emphasized English values to her Canadian daughters.[103] Marlatt, like Annie, was particularly attuned to the language and culture in North Vancouver because it was dramatically different from her colonial childhood in Penang: 'It seems to me that the situation of being such an immigrant is a perfect seedbed for the writing sensibility. If you don't belong, you can *imagine* you belong and you can

100 Marlatt, *Ana Historic*, 98.
101 Daphne Marlatt, 'Entering In: The Immigrant Imagination', *Canadian Literature* 100 (1984), 220.
102 Marlatt, 'Entering In: The Immigrant Imagination', 220.
103 Banting writes about Marlatt's cultural background and linguistic exposure in *Body Inc.*, 179. See also Marlatt, 'Entering In: The Immigrant Imagination', 220.

construct in writing a world where you do belong.'[104] Marlatt referred to
her colonial childhood in Malaysia as a 'phantom limb' that was 'not quite
cut off ... and wanted acknowledging'.[105]

While Marlatt observes that her colonial and immigrant past has
been of benefit to her sensibility as a writer, interestingly, Krasner observes
that a conflict of cultural identity lies at the heart of the method actor's
soul in *Method Acting Reconsidered*.[106] Many of the American method
teachers, including Lee Strasberg, Stella Adler, Sanford Meisner, and Paul
Mann, describe how they reconciled traditions of Judaism with American
assimilation.[107] Some of the most successful contemporary method actors,
including Al Pacino and Sidney Poitier, draw on a doubled sense of cultural
identity, from Italian-American and Bahamian-American contexts respectively. Method acting encourages actors to draw on their life experiences;
a doubled or split cultural identity can be useful on stage in portraying a
character with similarly complex identity formations. Through Marlatt's
dramatic mode in *Ana Historic*, a reader is invited to explore Annie's similar
sense of cultural indeterminacy as Annie explores Ana's and Ina's histories.

Annie looks to history for a semblance of the fractured subjectivity that she experiences in postcolonial Canadian society. She comes up
against hegemonic heterosexual and patriarchal narratives that present
uncomplicated performances of national idealism. The conventional performances of colonial settlers, against which Annie writes, obscure ambivalent
feelings of dissent or anxiety that deviate from the ontology of the early
colonial nation. While Annie's novel is limited to a white female settler's
perspective, it is sensitive to ways in which white female settlers were complicit with power dynamics of class and race in early Canadian history.[108]

104 Marlatt, 'Entering In: The Immigrant Imagination', 222.
105 Marlatt, 'Entering In: The Immigrant Imagination', 221.
106 Krasner, ed., *Method Acting Reconsidered: Theory, Practice, Future*, 30.
107 In addition to the Jewish-American context, Krasner describes how African-American
     and Italian-American method actors draw on their 'double consciousnesses' as sources
     of 'inner, personal conflict' in Krasner, ed. *Method Acting Reconsidered: Theory,
     Practice, Future*, 30–2.
108 Marlatt produced some less critical constructions of race in her early piece, 'In the
     Month of the Hungry Ghosts', *Capilano Review* 16/17 (1979), 45–95, which Harasym

Through the dramatic mode, Annie imagines how Ana might analyse her own performance of a colonial white woman – quaking with fear as she walks by two Siwash men in the woods – for her inherited and stereotypical assumptions about race.[109] The confrontation is further complicated by the notion that Ana's fear is not instant but gradual; she talks herself into feeling the fear after conjuring up the stories that have circulated among the settlers. In essence, Ana rehearses the fear, which, on some level, Ana finds titillating, 'as they crowded past her as if she were a bush, a fern shaking in their way', with 'foolishness quivering through her legs' for the rest of the day.[110] Zwicker suggests that the stereotype of terror in the confrontation of a white colonial woman and Siwash men is, in the manner Bhabha speaks of in 'The Other Question', never far from the stereotype of fetish.[111] Ana's confrontation with the Siwash men depicts how gender, race, and sexuality complicate the white colonial woman's 'desire for and fear of miscegenation that underlies the colonial nation'.[112]

Ana is witness to the occasion of the 'first white birth' at Kum-Kum-lee, later called Burrard Inlet.[113] In terms of imperial history, the moment symbolizes the birth of the white nation, yet the novel does not reproduce the values of this new nation uncritically. Annie goes beyond the historic significance of this occasion for the empire to imagine how Ana herself, not a white male historian imbued with colonial values, would have recorded it; Ana through Annie's eyes saw 'not the "first white child born on Burrard Inlet" but a woman's body in its intimacy, giving birth'.[114] Ana, through Annie's contemporary imagination, views the event as the birth of women's expression and of the possibility of women's control over their sexuality,

---

explores in 'EACH MOVE MADE HERE (me) MOVES THERE (you)', 120. She isolates dichotomies that perpetuate Manichean allegories of race and class.

109   Marlatt, *Ana Historic*, 41–2.
110   Marlatt, *Ana Historic*, 42.
111   Qtd in Heather Zwicker, 'Daphne Marlatt's *Ana Historic*: Queering the Postcolonial Nation', *ARIEL* 30/2 (1999), 168.
112   Zwicker, 'Daphne Marlatt's *Ana Historic*: Queering the Postcolonial Nation', 168.
113   Marlatt, *Ana Historic*, 126–7.
114   Marlatt, *Ana Historic*, 131.

including lesbian relationships, all of which are at odds with the imperial view of a new nation.

The novel is not predominantly concerned with the landmark events of colonial history, but with how a contemporary reader like Annie might scrutinize and represent history.

Annie imagines a range of different performances Ana would have given in her society and how those performances would carry the values of the time in which they were performed. Annie imagines how Ana Richards practises the role of a young widow in her colonial society in order to secure the freedom she needs to immigrate to Canada, live alone, and hold a job. Annie sees Ana Richards coaching herself before confronting the father of an impudent male student. 'Remember it's a role, a part to play', she tells herself. '*Mrs.* Richards, if you please. A woman of some authority, surely.'[115] In dramatizing the performances, Annie bestows cultural significance upon particular unrecorded moments in history and, in the process, learns about limitations in her own contemporary society. While the Siwash men and Ruth, Mrs Patterson's 'Siwash woman',[116] are represented as inscrutable and described in terms of noble savage stereotypes – representations in keeping with the colonial perspective suited to Ana's time – Annie's critical thinking suggests an ontological shift in the area of sexuality. Where Annie imagines how Ana would fear *and* desire miscegenation with the Siwash men, Annie recognizes a similar feeling of fear and desire in her own lesbian relationship with Zoe.

The novel ends with Annie's leap as she presents herself to Zoe and realizes, 'terror has to do with the trembling that takes you out of yourself'.[117] In writing the possibility of a lesbian sexuality for Ana, Annie disrupts the expected heterosexual trajectory of her own life. Where Ana's fate was marriage, and Ina's was death, Annie chooses Zoe, in what Zwicker aptly calls 'a parodic rewriting of the continuist national narrative'.[118]

115   Marlatt, *Ana Historic*, 97.
116   Marlatt, *Ana Historic*, 69.
117   Marlatt, *Ana Historic*, 152.
118   Zwicker, 'Daphne Marlatt's *Ana Historic*: Queering the Postcolonial Nation', 167.

Words Move the Body, Bodies Move the Words

Ana Historic conveys a theatrical sense of orality. Readers discover near the
novel's end that the text in hand has been read aloud by Annie to Zoe at a
writer's workshop in a local café. As the reader hears Annie reading the novel
to Zoe, the text is reconstituted as an oral performance. The sounds of the
poetic prose encourage a reader to feel Marlatt's physical impulses within
it. As Banting observes, the translation from the body to language requires
a composition of the body: 'Learning a new language you are compelled to
curl your tongue, roll your "r"s, pull down deeper into previously hidden
recesses of the throat, thrust your lower jaw forward, experience your lips,
click your tongue, activate your shoulders, eyebrows, hands, even implicate
your hips.'[119] The attention to sound in the novel urges one to think about
the bodies behind and within it making the sounds.

Marlatt explores several aspects of orality: she experiments with how
the cadence of a line creates its own momentum and leads to a deconstruction of the conventional meanings of words. Annie's memory of the word
wardrobes leads to 'wordrobes' and a recurring meditation on how language
conceals meanings.[120] Marlatt includes common sayings about women
from the 1950s and places them in italics for ironic isolation. She contrasts
the different accents and colloquialisms of Canadian English and British
English.[121] Annie catches herself uttering sayings she has learned from her
mother, her husband and her critics. Language is pre-conceived; phrases
echo and recur, leading the speaker to pre-existing and ready-made meanings. In a language full of word traps and pitfalls, where women's experience
is related through male norms, all words are quotations to some degree:
'words, that shifting territory. never one's own. full of deadfalls and hidden
claims to a reality others have made.'[122] In a way similar to the lines that
an actor memorizes and performs, *Ana Historic* suggests that the language

119   Banting, *Body Inc.*, 18.
120   Marlatt, *Ana Historic*, 9, 21.
121   Marlatt, *Ana Historic*, 17.
122   Marlatt, *Ana Historic*, 32.

people use in dialogue has a rehearsed and pre-scripted quality. People may choose *how* to say something but to some extent, not *what* they say; they play roles and follow scripts they may be unconscious of voicing. Annie finds that much of her dialogue is unoriginal and does not resonate with what she means to say. When she catches herself saying 'my very words',[123] she realizes that it is actually her mother's phrase that she repeats. Later, Annie imagines that her husband, Richard, would not understand the way she has approached her project of inventing Mrs Richards. She thinks he would say, 'this doesn't go anywhere, you're just circling around the same idea – and all these bits and pieces thrown in – that's not how to use quotations.'[124] She comes to realize that all the words she can possibly use are not her own: '(and what if our heads are full of other people's words? nothing without quotation marks)'.[125]

The novel examines the performances of language at the etymological level. With a feminist perspective, Marlatt deconstructs meanings and presumptions that are buried in words, thereby exposing how words beguile and control the speaker. By paring words back to their origins, Marlatt acknowledges certain performances of deceit and associations that have been integrated into language. Although Marlatt's penchant for etymology has been criticized as a search for origins that demonstrates a dependence on patriarchal authority,[126] her unpacking of words seems to be in an effort not to find an answer or an origin but to introduce multiple directions that exist within a word so as to create new associations and to allow the word to perform differently.

Marlatt's deconstructions continue the work of feminist etymologist and theologist Mary Daly, who claimed to have made 'ovular' rather than 'seminal' contributions to the etymology field with her publication *Beyond God the Father*. In *Ana Historic*, Annie recalls her astonishment as a girl

---

123   Marlatt, *Ana Historic*, 23.
124   Marlatt, *Ana Historic*, 9.
125   Marlatt, *Ana Historic*, 81.
126   See Harasym's 'EACH MOVE MADE HERE (me) MOVES THERE (you)', and Lola Lemire Tostevin's 'Daphne Marlatt: Writing in the Space That Is Her Mother's Face', *Line* 13 (Spring 1989), 36.

to discover that the French word for vagina is masculine, 'le vagin'; years later, she discovered that it derives from 'sheath, the cover of a sword'[127] and realized the phallic origins of the word for her own female genitals. The novel's etymological searches reveal the masquerading and performative qualities of words themselves.

Many of the words Marlatt uses to describe communication, in the novel and in her poetry, connect with the body's physicality. In 'musing with mothertongue', Marlatt explores the intimate connections between the language of communication and the language of the body.[128] Her list includes:

> matter (the import of what you say) and matter and by extension mother; language and tongue; to utter and outer (give birth again); a part of speech and a part of the body; pregnant with meaning; to mouth (speak) and the mouth with which we also eat and make love; sense (meaning) and that with which we sense the world; to relate (a story) and to relate to somebody, related (carried back) with its connection with bearing (a child); intimate and to intimate; vulva and voluble; even sentence which comes from a verb meaning to feel.[129]

These powerful correlations position the reader to experience communication in a physical way beyond conventional narrative. In 'Touch to my Tongue', Marlatt meditates on an unpublished essay by poet Alexandra Grilikhes called 'Dancing in Animal Skins'.[130] Grilikhes saw the moment of reading poetry as a 'shamanic act' where 'the poet dances in animal skins to evoke in you what longs to be evoked or released'.[131] The poem is not fully realized until it is performed for a reader and involves the reader in a connective moment. Grilikhes believed 'the performance of the poem *is* the poem'.[132] In a similar way, Marlatt's novel only reaches its potential

127   Marlatt, *Ana Historic*, 163.
128   Daphne Marlatt, *Touch to My Tongue and musing with mothertongue* (Edmonton: Longspoon, 1984), 46.
129   Marlatt, *Touch to My Tongue and musing with mothertongue*, 46.
130   Marlatt, *Touch to My Tongue and musing with mothertongue*, 36.
131   Qtd in Marlatt, *Touch to My Tongue and musing with mothertongue*, 36.
132   Qtd in Marlatt, *Touch to My Tongue and musing with mothertongue*, 36.

as an artistic form when it engages the readers in its oral and physical performance of the past.

Endings

Ana Historic concludes with a cluster of endings that resist conclusion. Under the subtitle *Not a Bad End*, Annie hypothesizes an ending to Ana's story in which Ana chooses Birdie Stewart over Ben Springer. In doing so, Annie boldly imposes an alternative version of history on Mrs Richards. Annie's story ends not with her mother, Ina, receiving electric shock therapy for hysteria, but with Annie's torrent of anger. In taking the new last name, Torrent, Annie leaves her husband Richard's claim, separates herself from the Ana Richards of history, and creates a new identity that inscribes both her anger and her passion. Annie resists writing the likely ending that Ina would have endured and creates the possibility a new ending for women in history that doesn't end in marriage, childbirth or death: 'that fiction, that lie that you can't change the ending! it's already pre-ordained, pre-scribed – just what the doctor ordered – in the incontrovertible logic of cause and effect.'[133]

Marlatt writes the reader into the final embrace of Annie and Zoe. The reader becomes, in an intimate and indeterminate way, absorbed into Annie's and Zoe's lovemaking and into their newly found desires. The reader is called upon to join their intimate bond:

> we give place, giving words, giving birth, to each other – she and me. you. hot skin writing skin. fluid edge, wick, wick. she draws me out. you she breathes, is where we meet. Breeze from the window reaching you now ... the luxury of being has woken you, the reach of your desire, reading us into the page ahead.[134]

133 Marlatt, *Ana Historic*, 147.
134 Marlatt, *Ana Historic*, 153.

The reader can move in and out of the scene; into the 'you' that Zoe intends for Annie, and into the 'you' at his or her own desk and window, turning the pages of a sensuous history and future. The reader witnesses the labour of a different kind of birth: of a novel, a new form of dramatized history in fiction and a poetics of enactment and connectivity.

CHAPTER 5

Performing History, Violence, and the Unsayable in Richard Flanagan's *Gould's Book of Fish*

Internationally acclaimed novelist, historian, and environmental activist Richard Flanagan has published an inventive body of fiction concerned with history and its representations in recent times. His third novel, *Gould's Book of Fish: A Novel in Twelve Fish* (2001), won several prestigious awards, including the Commonwealth Writers Overall Best Book Award in 2002[1] and explores the violent colonization of the indigenous people of Tasmania, the brutalities of the British penal colonies, and how one makes sense of history while situated in the present. Flanagan experiments with theatrical and performative modes of representation in this novel using dramatic re-envisioning of the past, self-reflexive satirical and tragic frames, distancing techniques and direct addresses to readers which position readers to be spectators and, ideally, critical thinkers. Flanagan creates performative narrators across a few temporalities who play multiple roles in their attempts to understand a more collective identity in a colonial context. It is not conventionally realistic, romantic or linear historical fiction that Flanagan creates here.[2] Rather, emerging from a genre born in the postmodern era, *Gould's Book of Fish* is

---

1   *Gould's Book of Fish* was also awarded the Miles Franklin Literary Award (2002), the Victorian Premier's Literary Award, the Vance Palmer Prize for Fiction (2002) and the Australian Literary Society Gold Medal (2002). It was shortlisted for the Booksellers Choice Award (2001).

2   Some more conventional Australian historical fictions that focus on nation-building events, famous or infamous historical characters or construct a sense of historical reality, include the twelve-volume *Australians Series* by William Stuart Long, aka Vivian Stuart (New York: Dell, 1979–1990) containing *The Settlers* (1980), *The Traitors* (1981), and *The Colonialists* (1984). See also Eleanor Dark's trilogy of novels about European settlement and the exploration of Australia beginning with *The Timeless*

a hybrid novel that incorporates fiction, history, performativity, and a self-reflexive critique of 'history proper' as Flanagan searches for an expressive form that both animates and interrogates the possibility of writing about colonial history from Van Diemen's Land.[3] The novel explores aspects of history that can be elusive and ephemeral and it is attuned to the presence and materiality of bodies, some of which have experienced trauma, mutilation or death, in colonial and postcolonial Tasmanian history.

Gould's Book of Fish (2001) tells the tale of unreliable narrator and scam artist Sid Hammett who re-constructs the lost journal of William Buelow Gould, an artist and convict, who was sent in 1828 to a penal colony in Van Diemen's Land and ordered to paint a book of fish. Through paintings and annotations, Gould offers an imaginative and nightmarish version of the penal colony on Sarah Island and the indigenous people of Tasmania, convicts, and colonial officials who lived and died there. The character of William Buelow Gould is based on an historical person and each chapter of Flanagan's Gould's Book of Fish is prefaced with a portrait of a fish or sea creature painted by the historical Gould that conveys the essence of the central character described in each chapter.[4] Characters include a despotic Commandant who wants to create the grandeur of European cities in the colony, a prison clerk who falsifies records and a surgeon phrenologist who ships the skulls of indigenous people back to London. When Sid

---

Land (1941), set in 1788 describing the first ships of transported convicts and featuring historian Watkin Tench as a character.

3   Other notable examples of postmodern novels that engage with history while critiquing its limitations and conventions include Salman Rushdie's Midnight's Children [1981] (Toronto: Vintage, 1987) and Julian Barnes' A History of the World in 10 ½ Chapters (Cambridge: Cambridge University Press, 1989).

4   The historical watercolour portraits by William Buelow Gould can be viewed online through the State Library of Tasmania Heritage Collection, Tasmanian Images databases, Gould's sketchbook of fishes <https://www.linc.tas.gov.au/allport/Pages/gould.aspx> or at the Allport Library and Museum of Fine Arts in Tasmania. UNESCO honoured William Buelow Gould's book of illustrations as an item of world significance. See Linda Hunt, 'Convict sketchbook makes UNESCO world register', ABC News, 1 April 2011 <http://www.abc.net.au/news/2011-04-01/convict-sketchbook-makes-unesco-world-register/2631788> accessed 22 January 2017.

Hammet loses the annotated version of the book, he sets out to re-create it from memory. Like all fish stories, Sid Hammett's re-constructed version is impossible to trust. The fantastical parts are hard to fathom, and the horrific aspects beyond belief. In the re-constructed journal, Gould proposes new and experimental forms of literary expression for the new world, as Flanagan is doing with the novel, knowing that existing forms of representation are bound to fail to capture the history of Tasmania:

> this place & its pathetick people will be far happier being eaten up over & over again by the same dreary story [...] – what here I write, & what here I paint are Experiment & Prophecy – do not judge any of it by the shorten'd yardstick of what they call Literature & Art, those sick & broken compasses [5]

Gould, imagined by Sid Hammett, worries how he will ever represent the quick and slippery 'truth of a fish' which is not unlike a slippery and elusive historical moment, and confesses he has 'no idea how to tell a truth, far less paint it'.[6] Called 'a masterpiece',[7] 'savage, phosphorescent'[8] and a 'work of significant genius'[9] by some reviewers, and a 'monstrosity'[10] and 'postcolonial revisionism'[11] by others, *Gould's Book of Fish* launched Flanagan into the spotlight of the international literati in 2001 and the book has since been published in more than twenty-five countries.

5   Richard Flanagan, *Gould's Book of Fish: A Novel in Twelve Fish* [2001] (Sydney: Picador Pan Macmillan Australia, 2002), 60.
6   Flanagan, *Gould's Book of Fish*, 153.
7   John Burnside, 'Authenticity rises to the surface in a masterpiece', Books, *The Times*, London, 5 June 2002, 15.
8   Kate Kellaway, 'Hook, Line and thinker', *The Guardian*, 9 June 2002 <https://www.theguardian.com/books/2002/jun/09/fiction.australia> accessed 2 January 2017.
9   E. William Smethurst, Jr, 'Imaginative reflections on art, nature and corruption', in *Chicago Tribune*, 28 April 2002 <http://articles.chicagotribune.com/2002-04-28/entertainment/0204270054_1_natural-world-richard-flanagan-con-man> accessed 2 January 2017.
10 Peter Craven, 'Something Fishy', in Angela Bennie, ed., *Crème de la Phlegm: Unforgettable Australian Reviews* (Carlton: Miegunyah Press, 2006), 382.
11 Camilla Nelson, 'Faking It, History and Creative Writing', *TEXT* 11/2 (October 2007) <http://www.textjournal.com.au/oct07/nelson.htm> accessed 7 July 2008.

Born in Tasmania and educated as a Rhodes scholar at Oxford, Flanagan is the recipient of numerous national and international awards for his six novels and has worked in and across more than a few media. He won the Man Booker Prize in 2014 for *The Narrow Road to the Deep North* (2013) about the experiences of Australian POWs who built the Thai-Burma railway and were exposed to starvation, beatings, cholera, and death.[12] Flanagan was the director of the film version of his own novel *The Sound of One Hand Clapping* (1998) and a screenwriter with director Baz Luhrmann on *Australia* (2008),[13] the second highest grossing Australian film of all time,[14] which tells the story, to musical refrains from *The Wizard of Oz*, of the forced removal of Indigenous children from their parents and the Japanese bombing of Darwin. Flanagan's novel *Wanting* (2009)[15] follows the longings of Charles Dickens, who produces and stars in a play inspired by the life and disappearance of Sir John Franklin, Governor of Van Diemen's Land. Sir Franklin and his wife adopted an indigenous girl from Tasmania whom they thought to be the last member of her race and threw her to the streets years later when they no longer wanted her.

The artistic diversity in Flanagan's work points to the author's predilection for experimenting with a range of postmodern and performative modes through which engagements with history are designed to create emotional and political resonance and aesthetic interest among contemporary readers. In its integration of theatrical and other artistic modes, including visual art and representations of dance between its covers, *Gould's Book of Fish* offers an implicit critique to more conventional linear and authoritative representations of historical fiction that document certain recorded events

---

12   Richard Flanagan, *The Narrow Road to the Deep North* (North Sydney, NSW: Random House Australia, 2013.) This novel, dedicated to Flanagan's father who was an Australian POW, also won the Western Australian Premier's Book Award and the Independent Booksellers Award in 2014.

13   *Australia*, dir. Baz Luhrmann (Twentieth Century-Fox Film Corporation, 2009) [DVD].

14   'Top 100 Australian Feature Films of All Time', *Screen Australia*, 9 May 2016 <http://www.screenaustralia.gov.au/fact-finders/cinema/australian-films/top-films-at-the-box-office> accessed 21 January 2017.

15   Richard Flanagan, *Wanting* (North Sydney, NSW: Knopf, 2008).

of colonization but can never know or express the full story: the zeitgeist of the time, the vitality of ordinary characters in whom readers may see reflections of themselves, or the extent of the trauma coming from the systemic killing of indigenous people in Tasmania and the psychological legacy of colonial violence. *Gould's Book of Fish* does not provide accuracy in its historical characterizations or totality in its scope; rather, it animates glimpses of the human condition and interrogates the possibility of how literary artifice, or in this case, the 'art of fish', could ever fully succeed in capturing such a slippery, elusive, and brutal entity as the history of Tasmania when records were often inaccurate, partial, or recorded only by colonizers.

In an interview, Flanagan says *Gould's Book of Fish* is an 'anti-historical novel' which Chris Wright suggests is 'closer to the real Tasmania for it'.[16] Flanagan pushes the performative narration of Sid Hammett and Gould in *Gould's Book of Fish* to the point that readers become suspicious of all storytellers, historians, and the tales they tell. He explains:

> Historians create these hermetic systems that don't allow for any chaos or disorder. But life is chaos and disorder. It seems to me to be such a wonderfully European way of thinking: this railway line of thought stopping at all the stations of human progress. But in Tasmania, that's a completely useless way of looking at things. It doesn't explain a place like that.[17]

Flanagan suggests instead that Tasmania needs to be represented in a literary form that resembles the kind of circular stories that Tasmanians tell, the ones 'that don't have a beginning or an end, that digress relentlessly, that somehow envelop the past and also explain the present, that remain with you'.[18]

This chapter will examine Flanagan's dramatic modes and performativity in *Gould's Book of Fish* and draw connections between these and the strategies of three celebrated twentieth-century thinkers, Samuel Beckett, Wolfgang Iser, and Bertolt Brecht, who have engendered possibilities for

---

16   Richard Flanagan qtd in Chris Wright, 'Swimming to Tasmania', *The Phoenix.com*, 2–9 May 2002 <http://www.bostonphoenix.com/boston/news_features/other_stories/multipage/documents/02253069.htm> accessed 12 November 2016.

17   Flanagan qtd in Wright, 'Swimming to Tasmania', n.p.

18   Flanagan qtd in Wright, 'Swimming to Tasmania', n.p.

imagining social and political change through their work in either theatre or in theories of play in texts. Samuel Beckett, Nobel prize-winning modernist playwright and novelist, who wrote between 1930 and 1990, developed techniques of incorporating 'Being' and a sense of presence into his writing that included paying attention to ruptures, repetition, rhythm, gestures, and silences.[19] There are illuminating connections to be made between Beckett's techniques of working with language and Flanagan's methods of punctuating the text of *Gould's Book of Fish* with a sense of presence and breaking through familiar patterns of expression in Gould's search for a compelling form and mode of representation that gestures to and incorporates realms beyond words. One of Beckett's primary concerns was the failure of words to capture living experience and to create new forms in his fiction and plays to express the inexplicable; Flanagan reflects similar concerns to Beckett's in Gould's ongoing search for a means of expression that does not obscure the horrors of colonial violence that lie beneath it, exploring rhymes, silences, fragments, and representations of other artistic forms.

Wolfgang Iser, a German theorist and one of the founders of reader-response criticism and reception aesthetics, beginning in the late 1960s, maintains that imaginative play in a text gives readers the potential to transform their understandings and potentially themselves as they join with an author in creating meanings from a text and in imagining what may have previously lain outside their grasp.[20] To Iser, the 'act of fictionalizing' is a 'crossing of boundaries'.[21] Play holds a central importance for fictionality, according to Iserian theory, because it accommodates the 'coexistence of mutually exclusive' ideas.[22] Games within texts may entice readers to play and interact where their own 'experiential horizon[s]' are juxtaposed with 'the worlds opened up by the text'.[23] A range of dramatic modes, staging,

19   Samuel Beckett, *Disjecta: Miscellaneous Writings and a Dramatic Fragment*, 171–2.
20   Iser, 'The Play of the Text', 325–39.
21   Wolfgang Iser, *The Fictive and the Imaginary: Charting Literary Anthropology* (Baltimore, MD: Johns Hopkins Press, 1993).
22   Iser, *The Fictive and the Imaginary: Charting Literary Anthropology*, 79.
23   Paul B. Armstrong, 'The Politics of Play: The Social Implications of Iser's Aesthetic Theory', *New Literary History* 31/1 (Winter 2000), 219.

and metafictional games guide readers to imagine events and characters from history in Flanagan's *Gould's Book of Fish* which have significance beyond that of mere play; there is an oscillating, 'to-and-from' energy[24] created by the temporal slippages and role-playing in the novel that informs a conception of history where the past and present re-enter one another as seen through Sid Hammet's and Gould's unusual and flawed attempts to situate themselves in almost all the roles in the Tasmanian colonial context. Play and self-reflective games in Flanagan's novel destabilize readers into seeing the content of a scene doubly or with intensifying magnification, for example, when Tracker Mark's body is burnt along with Gould's journal of the horrific account of the cremation that keeps writing itself[25] in a Borges-like conflation of time and space.

In addition to incorporating presence and play in *Gould's Book of Fish*, Flanagan devises an effective literary variation on German playwright and director Bertolt Brecht's theatrical strategy of *Verfremdungseffekt* (translated as a 'defamiliarization effect' or 'estrangement effect').[26] This effect, designed in the mid-1920s for epic theatre, which sought to historicize and call attention to pertinent social, economic, and political issues involves 'stripping the event of its self-evident, familiar, obvious quality and creating a sense of astonishment and curiosity' about it.[27] Brecht used placards, stark stage lighting, truncated scenes, direct addresses and songs to interrupt the action in his plays in order to remind spectators that his theatre was representational and not reality itself.[28] Through these distancing effects, Brecht believed spectators could be prevented from being overwhelmed with empathy. Excesses of empathy derived from the theatre could potentially lead spectators to experience catharsis or a purging of that empathy

24 Armstrong, 'The Politics of Play: The Social Implications of Iser's Aesthetic Theory', 215.
25 Flanagan, *Gould's Book of Fish*, 374.
26 Brecht, *Brecht on Theatre: The Development of an Aesthetic*, 91.
27 Brecht in Peter Brooker, 'Key Words in Brecht's Theory and Practice of Theatre', in Peter Thomson and Glendyr Sacks, eds, *The Cambridge Companion to Brecht* (Cambridge: Cambridge University Press, 1994), 191.
28 Brecht, *Brecht on Theatre: The Development of an Aesthetic*, 138.

and the danger of this, in Brecht's view, was that complacency would follow
catharsis and prevent the spectator from taking social action relating to the
cause that so moved them.[29] In *Gould's Book of Fish*, Flanagan develops a
literary version of *Verfremdungseffekt* as he consistently interrupts his vision
of the past with direct addresses, confounding and disintegrating literary
frames and attention to the artifice of his staging of the past.

While Beckett, Iser and Brecht may not be typical writers to draw upon
in a study of the representation of postcolonial history in postmodern fiction, their work is preoccupied with creating meaning that extends beyond
that which can be represented on a textual level alone. Their theories and
writing which rely on creating a sense of presence in language and on the
active engagement and participation of readers provide useful touchstones
for the work Flanagan develops in *Gould's Book of Fish*.

Although *Gould's Book of Fish* may confound readers at times with its
performative narrative that blurs the identities and times of Sid Hammett
and William Buelow Gould and its aesthetic modes that distance readers
from a range of comic and horrifying scenes, the novel that results is far
more than the exercise in postmodern artistic indulgence that some reviewers have deemed it to be.[30] Critical responses to the novel have focused on a
range of issues central to colonial and postcolonial literary representation,
including fluid temporalities of the past and the present,[31] the question-
able authority and materiality of historical sources,[32] and approaching

29   Brecht, *Brecht on Theatre: The Development of an Aesthetic*, 138.
30   Craven, 'Something Fishy Going On', 382–5 <http://books.guardian.co.uk/reviews/
     generalfiction/0,6121,722129,00.html> accessed March 2014. See also Alex Clark, 'In
     the hands of madmen; Review of Gould's Book of Fish', *The Guardian*, 1 June 2002
     <https://www.theguardian.com/books/2002/jun/01/featuresreviews.guardianre
     view23> accessed 8 April 2008.
31   Jesse Shipway, 'Wishing for modernity: temporality and desire in *Gould's Book of
     Fish*', *Australian Literary Studies* 21/1 (May 2003), 43–53. Shipway focuses on fluid
     temporalities and suggests that the novel 'radically fictionalises' Tasmania's first
     modern age and 'imbue[s] it with the residue of collective longing' in order to envi-
     sion 'an alternative future' for present-day Tasmania (43–4).
32   Ashley Rose Whitmore, 'Reconfigurations of History and Embodying Books in
     Gould's Book of Fish', *Postcolonial Text* 7/2 (2012), 1–16.

representations of history through a sense of the sublime with a focus on the body as a source of knowledge.[33] These responses illustrate the rich scope of the novel's enigmatic possibilities, yet few literary critics have approached the novel from the angle of its dramatic modes and its inherent potential for re-conceiving of postcolonial identity through theatrical play and performative exploration.

In 'Set Adrift: Identity and the Postcolonial Present in *Gould's Book of Fish*', Zach Weir identifies a few performative and participatory elements of Flanagan's novel that intersect with the focus on dramatic modes in this chapter. Weir observes how Gould's song, 'I am William Buelow Gould & my name is a song which will be sung, click-clack – rat-a-tat-a-tat, a penny a painting, silly Billy Gould riding a seahorse to Banbury Cross,'[34] attempts to interrupt the 'flow of symbolic and representational language'[35] in the narrative. I will extend Weir's analysis of the performative elements in Flanagan's novel by connecting them to Samuel Beckett's strategies in breaking through what Beckett called the prison of representational language.[36] Weir emphasizes a 'pact' between the reader and the characters in the novel, suggesting that 'both have a participatory role in the development of [Flanagan's] postcolonial critique' and its 'interpretation and translation.'[37] While Weir does not explicitly situate the participatory roles of the novel's readers within an Iserian context as I will do, he outlines an important interaction between the reader and characters in Flanagan's novel that can be usefully contextualized through an examination of Iser's reader-response critical approach.[38]

---

33 Jo Jones, '"Dancing the Old Enlightenment": *Gould's Book of Fish*, the Historical Novel and the Postmodern Sublime', *Journal of the Association for the Study of Australian Literature*, Supplement (2008), 114–29.

34 Flanagan, *Gould's Book of Fish*, 445.

35 Zach Weir, 'Set Adrift: Identity and the Postcolonial Present in *Gould's Book of Fish*', *Postcolonial Text* 1/2 (2005) <http://postcolonial.org/index.php/pct/article/view/345/803> accessed 12 November 2016.

36 Beckett, *Disjecta: Miscellaneous Writings and a Dramatic Fragment*, 172.

37 Weir, 'Set Adrift: Identity and the Postcolonial Present in *Gould's Book of Fish*'.

38 Iser, *The Fictive and the Imaginary: Charting Literary Anthropology*, 19.

Jo Jones, in '"Dancing the Old Enlightenment": *Gould's Book of Fish*, the Historical Novel and the Postmodern Sublime', argues that Flanagan's foregrounding of physical bodies 'contests the primacy of reason' of the Enlightenment with its emphasis on rationalism, scientific reason and progress 'by insisting on the realities of bodily experience.'[39] Jones describes the physical body in Flanagan's novel as 'an anchor for the "truth" of human existence'[40] and suggests that the reader plays a witnessing role. Jones' emphasis on bodies and the reader as witness intersects in intriguing ways with the exploration of dramatic modes in this chapter and I will extend Jones' focus on the body in dance to Flanagan's portrayal of the body in dramatic modes.

Even as the proverbial seams of the novel show, as Gould's voice blurs with the voices of the present day narrator Sid Hammet and others, Flanagan persists with the experimental form of the novel for the ineffable insights, emotional connections, and sense of presence his range of dramatic and performative modes in his novel offers readers. Just as moments in the theatre have a sense of always being present despite having been written in the past or focusing on a moment from history, Flanagan experiments with creating similar 'now-moments' of theatrical presence in his fiction about the postcolonial history of Tasmania.

Failing Better and Tearing through Language: Echoes of Beckett

In *Gould's Book of Fish*, Sid Hammet continually laments that language fails to express the violence and terror of colonization. The novel uses language because it must, but draws on other artistic forms to develop alternate modes of expression that speak extra-linguistically. Perhaps the writer most famously concerned with expression and language's inherent failings is the

---

39   Jones, '"Dancing the Old Enlightenment": *Gould's Book of Fish*, the Historical Novel and the Postmodern Sublime', 118.

40   Douglass in Jones, '"Dancing the Old Enlightenment": *Gould's Book of Fish*, the Historical Novel and the Postmodern Sublime', 119.

1969 Nobel prize-winning writer and playwright Samuel Beckett, whose influence can be seen in Flanagan's writing, and who strove throughout his career in his plays and novels to create 'a literature of the unword'.[41] In a letter to Axel Kaun in 1937, Beckett wrote:

> It is indeed becoming more and more difficult, even *senseless*, for me to write an official English. And more and more my own language appears to me like a veil that must be torn apart in order to get at the things (or the Nothingness) behind it. A mask.[42]

When Beckett argues that it is 'senseless' for him to write in an official English, both meanings of the word resonate: senseless, as illogical or meaningless, and, more importantly, as devoid of sensations. In Beckett's view, the veil of language obscures intangible physical and sensual qualities behind it. When Beckett's idea of the veil of language is held closely to a similar passage in *Gould's Book of Fish*, there is a striking parallel about language's inability to describe the world:

> Because, you see, it sometimes seems so elusive, this book, a series of veils, each of which must be lifted and parted to reveal only another of its kind, to arrive finally at emptiness, a lack of words, at the sound of the sea, of the great Indian Ocean.[43]

In Beckett's plays, failed communication is the norm and the place where characters always begin. The protagonist in Beckett's play *Worstward Ho* shares his life's philosophy that anticipates negativity yet will not abandon hope: 'Ever tried. Ever failed. No matter. Try again. Fail again. Fail better.'[44] *Gould's Book of Fish*, with its implausible temporality, historical caricatures and impossible narrative, seems to rise with innovation to the challenge of what Samuel Beckett calls, 'failing better.'[45] Beckett identifies certain qualities in the dramatic arts that he cannot replicate through language and uses a variety of dramatic techniques in his writing, including pauses, self-reflexive dialogue,

---

41   Beckett, *Disjecta: Miscellaneous Writings and a Dramatic Fragment*, 173.
42   Beckett, *Disjecta: Miscellaneous Writings and a Dramatic Fragment*, 171. My italics.
43   Flanagan, *Gould's Book of Fish*, 38.
44   Samuel Beckett, *Worstward Ho* (London: Calder, 1983), 7.
45   Beckett, *Worstward Ho*, 7.

and visual cues to light and darkness, in order to 'fail better' and tear through language. His late modernist and minimalist plays, including *Endgame* (1957), *Happy Days* (1960), *Waiting for Godot* (1963) and *Not I* (1972) are characterized by tragic farce, the grotesque and minimalist poetry. Characters are stripped down to the essences of their souls. Beckett experiments with form and language in these plays to access the physical, the metaphysical and the dramatic reverberations of the world behind and beyond words.

Signs that Beckett was striving toward a new and dramatic form long before he moved from novels to plays are clear in his early novel, *Mercier and Camier* (1946), where, as Richard W. Seaver observes, Beckett was 'using more and more frequently methods and techniques that required dramatic presentation'.[46] Seaver suggests that the 'brisk exchanges of dialogue' between Mercier and Camier in Beckett's novel anticipated the existential repartee of Didi and Gogo in *Waiting for Godot* (1952), and the 'music-hall routines' and high and low comedy in *Mercier and Camier* indicated that Beckett 'was heading, almost ineluctably, for the theater'.[47]

Beckett maintained that if writers were able to destroy the familiarized patterns of language which always lead to the same realizations, then other expressions, such as those from other non-verbal arts, might emerge:[48]

> As we cannot eliminate language all at once, we should at least leave nothing undone that might contribute to its falling into disrepute. To bore one hole after another in it, until what lurks behind it – begins to seep through [...]. Or is literature alone to remain behind in the old lazy ways that have been so long ago abandoned by music and painting? [49]

An evocative array of arts is assembled in the form and content of Flanagan's novel to gesture towards all that typically resists articulation in words. *Gould's Book of Fish* explores the ways in which elements of drama, painting, and dance can be integrated into literature to create an extra-linguistic mode through which to examine history in fiction. Flanagan's integration of these

46   Samuel Beckett, *I Can't Go On, I Will Go On*, ed. and intro. Richard W. Seaver (New York: Grove Press, 1976), 160.

47   Seaver in Beckett, *I Can't Go On, I Will Go On*, 160.

48   Beckett, *Disjecta: Miscellaneous Writings and a Dramatic Fragment*, 172.

49   Beckett, *Disjecta: Miscellaneous Writings and a Dramatic Fragment*, 172.

forms can be seen to rally against what Beckett calls the 'old lazy ways' or 'the complacency of words'.[50] Theatrical structures proliferate in the novel, drawing on epic theatre, satire, restoration comedy, and, most noticeably, the performative narration in Sid Hammet's dramatization of Gould and in Gould's dramatizations of the other main characters. Visual art comprises a large part of not just the content but also the form of the novel with Gould's watercolour portraits which seemed so '*human*'.[51] Flanagan said in an interview,

> No paintings exist of any of the convicts who were sent to Sarah Island. So you have this death camp with no images of anyone who went there. All we have left are these fish. It just charmed me the way [Gould] had somehow smuggled out something of the people within. He had pleased his masters, but at the same time had done something completely subversive.[52]

Dance, particularly the one between Twopenny Sal and Gould at Tracker Marks' funeral pyre, conveys profound moments of connection, ritual, and intimacy: 'It was a joy & it was a sadness & it was inexplicable [...] We were dancing something beyond words.'[53] Gould expresses his desire to have the movements tell the story that his words cannot encompass.[54] He comes to realize there is something vital and significant in other art forms that he longs to integrate into his book. He writes:

> I continued making this Book of Fish because I could not laugh it or dance it like Twopenny Sal might have, because I could not swim it & live it like my subjects had, because this most inadequate form of communication – images & words falling stillborn from my brush & quill – was all I was capable of realising.[55]

Like Beckett who declared that 'language is most efficiently used where it is being most efficiently misused',[56] Flanagan's Gould takes an anarchistic

---

50   Beckett, *Disjecta: Miscellaneous Writings and a Dramatic Fragment*, 172.
51   Flanagan qtd in Wright, 'Swimming to Tasmania', n.p.
52   Flanagan qtd in Wright, 'Swimming to Tasmania', n.p.
53   Flanagan, *Gould's Book of Fish*, 377.
54   Flanagan, *Gould's Book of Fish*, 377.
55   Flanagan, *Gould's Book of Fish*, 428.
56   Beckett, *Disjecta: Miscellaneous Writings and a Dramatic Fragment*, 172.

stance and cries: 'I shall confine myself to no man's rule. Next to my paintings I intend to make a bonfire of words, say anything if it illuminates a
paltry moment of truth in my poor pictures.'[57] Gould creates virtual verbal
and artistic explosions in the hopes of igniting something in the language
that reaches beyond its conventional capabilities.

Flanagan illustrates where language, as an expressive mode, fails his characters. Gould makes a confession to God, in his darkest hour, of all his sins,
fears, and loves.[58] The prayer 'A-B-C-D-E-F-G-H-I-J-K-L-M-N-O-P-Q-R-
S-T-U-V-W-X-Y-Z' technically holds everything Gould wants to say, but it
'did no good whatsoever' except to highlight the shortcomings of language.[59]

Another way in which Flanagan endeavours to escape language or, at
the very least, to expose its inadequacies, is by emphasizing the physical
presence of bodies in the story and gesturing to the untold stories they
convey. *Gould's Book of Fish* foregrounds the bodies of convicts and indigenous Tasmanians who are decapitated, burned, tagged, and pored over
by white colonialists; in doing so, the novel insists upon a consideration of
the physical body as a source of knowledge from a historical period where
phrenology and genocide occurred. Jones writes,

> By making visible the remnants of traumatized bodies including tagged and classi-
> fied Aboriginal bones and the preserved, tattooed skin of executed convicts, there
> is a recognition of the reality of certain events – such as genocide – that occurred
> on the Tasmanian frontier. While the 'truth' of numbers dead, the motivations and
> exact manner of death can never be known in a scientific way, a recognition of the
> incontestable reality of violence grounds Flanagan's critique.[60]

One of the trademarks of Beckett's work is the awareness of the present
moment and physical bodies in his writing.[61] In 'Exorcising Beckett', Beckett

57   Flanagan, *Gould's Book of Fish*, 106.
58   Flanagan, *Gould's Book of Fish*, 384.
59   Flanagan, *Gould's Book of Fish*, 385.
60   Jones, '"Dancing the Old Enlightenment": *Gould's Book of Fish*, the Historical Novel
      and the Postmodern Sublime', 119.
61   See Lawrence Shainberg, 'Exorcising Beckett', *Playwrights at Work: The Paris Review*,
      intro. John Lahr [1987] (New York: The Modern Library, 2000), 50–86. Shainberg
      provides a clear discussion on Beckett's attempts to incorporate Being in his writing.

says, 'If anything new and exciting is going on today, it is the attempt to let Being into Art.'[62] Flanagan addresses this struggle explicitly as Sid Hámmet recreates Gould's journal with attention to physicality and the present moment and creates junctures for readers to perceive moments of connection and immediacy with characters at various times. Gould often refers to his own body in the process of writing the book in various fluids and home-made inks: 'Having paint but no ink I have to use whatever is at hand to write – today, for example, I have knocked a few scabs off my elbow & am dipping my quill carved from a shark's rib into the blood that oozes slowly forth to write what you are now reading.'[63] In the Picador hard-cover edition, the words of whole chapters are printed in green, purple, blue, red, and brown ink, produced (ostensibly) from natural ingredients Gould finds, including laudanum, ground lapis lazuli, blood, and fecal matter. The inks gesture toward a physical connection with the reader, linking Gould's past to the reader's present, through an artefact that exists in the reader's world. If readers sense a closer connection to Gould through the artefact in their hands, or are transported on some level to imagine the musicality and physicality of the funeral dance for Tracker Marks, the novel, in a Beckettian sense, 'fails better' in engaging readers in its aim to simulate moments of physical presence through, and despite, language.

Playing with the Reader: Iserian Play and Readerly Engagement

In *Gould's Book of Fish*, dramatic frames become apertures for play, and for positioning and re-positioning readers before its representation of colonial history. Flanagan uses imaginative play and literary games to give readers active roles in deciphering and creating the worlds that are represented therein. In *The Play of the Text*, Iser describes the relationship between

---

62   Beckett qtd in Shainberg, 'Exorcising Beckett', 57.
63   Flanagan, *Gould's Book of Fish*, 54.

author, text, and reader as 'an ongoing process that produces something that had not existed before'.[64] From the school of reception aesthetics, Iser posits that texts are not mimetic translations of the world, but rather arenas for transformative play, as readers take part in creating, enacting, and completing that which has only been adumbrated.[65] The reader's eventual interpretation can take many possible shapes and, as such, Iser suggests that readers play a role in determining the world that is represented in the text.[66] The play of the text is not like 'a pageant' unfolding, but instead 'both an ongoing event and a happening for the reader, causing his or her direct involvement in the proceedings'.[67] Play has a non-threatening quality to it because it is 'just play' but it has transformative power as well; through make-believe, Iser suggests, readers may be capable of imagining what might otherwise escape their grasp.[68] Play in text requires creativity, innovation, and the freedom to picture what is not there. Iser argues that 'play turns out to be a means whereby we may extend ourselves'.[69]

One game in *Gould's Book of Fish* which can be read in an Iserian vein invites readers to make sense of the Afterword, which forecloses any single or straightforward interpretation of the novel as a whole. The Afterword of the novel appears to be an excerpt taken from the Colonial Secretary's correspondence file in the Archives Office of Tasmania, dated 5 April 1831.[70] It provides the official cause of death for William Buelow Gould – 'Drowned attempting to escape'[71] – and a list of aliases for Gould: '*aliases* Sid Hammet, "the Surgeon", Jorgen Jorgensen, Capois Death, Pobjoy, "the Commandant"'.[72] The list of Gould's aliases suggest that Gould could be just about every main character in the story, including Sid Hammet, the narrator of the main dramatic frame of the novel which contradicts the

---

64   Iser, 'The Play of the Text', 325.
65   Iser, 'The Play of the Text', 327.
66   Iser, 'The Play of the Text', 327.
67   Iser, 'The Play of the Text', 336.
68   Iser, 'The Play of the Text', 338.
69   Iser, 'The Play of the Text', 338.
70   Flanagan, *Gould's Book of Fish*, 447.
71   Flanagan, *Gould's Book of Fish*, 447.
72   Flanagan, *Gould's Book of Fish*, 447.

narrative convention adopted in the body of the work. At the novel's end, any certainty about characters, events, temporalities, and history from the inner and outer narratives is confounded. The Afterword is a *mise-en-abîme* that can be interpreted in several ways depending on the presumed identity of its author.[73] If readers interpret the Afterword to have been written by Gould, outside of Sid Hammet's performative narrative, they are likely to be confused by the inclusion of Sid Hammet's name as one of Gould's aliases. Perhaps Sid Hammet is supposed to have written the Afterword as part of his narrative to show his identification with Gould or to suggest that Gould and many others are complicit in playing multiple roles in a colonial history. If the Afterword is outside both Gould's and Sid Hammet's narrative frames, as an official record, it may serve other purposes – to reflect the general inaccuracy of historical documents or to highlight the compulsion of readers to determine and assign a single interpretation to a slippery fiction.

Ultimately, the Afterword is Flanagan's final playful attempt at undoing conceptions of characters, time, and space constructed earlier in the novel. Readers are left with the notion that history and fiction are inextricably twisted: Gould is somehow role-playing several characters; Sid Hammet is Gould and thus, everyone; official documents are fictitious; and all narrative frames fail to some extent. The irresolvable ambiguity of the Afterword, if we apply Iser's terms, 'forces the reader to play the games of the text'.[74] The back and forth movements require continual involvement and investment as a reader tests, re-assesses, and adjusts his or her interpretations. A reader becomes aware not only of the play in the text, but of being, as Iser would

73   The classic definition of *mise-en-abîme* refers to Dallenbach's coat of arms on a shield that features a smaller but identical coat of arms on a shield and repeats beyond the eye's ability to perceive it. In literature, a *mise-en-abîme* may be found in some post-modern works, where a copy of book rests inside a book that is inside a book and ongoing, for example, in the writing of Jorge Luis Borges. It has a theatrical incarnation in metatheatre. See Lucien Dallenbach's *The Mirror in the Text*, trans. Jeremy Whitely with Emma Hughes (Cambridge: Polity in association with Blackwell, 1989) and Linda Hutcheon's *Narcissistic Narrative: The Metafictional Paradox* (London: Methuen, 1980), 55.

74   Iser, 'The Play of the Text', 332.

say, *played by* the text.[75] This falls into a category of textual game that Iser refers to as 'ilinx', where all of the fixed positions in the text are subverted, so that a 'carnivalization of all the positions in the text' takes place.[76] As Paul Armstrong notes, this subversion of positions 'exposes the boundlessness and multiplicity of possible illusions given the ultimately ineradicable difference between the fictive and the real'.[77] Such textual games in *Gould's Book of Fish* entangle a reader in the novel's multiple temporal frames and prevent linear readings of the Afterword; these games can lead to new ways of interpreting meaning that can be carried to other representations of history in fiction where illusions of linearity and impossible perspectives are not as explicitly rendered as they are in this text.

Another way *Gould's Book of Fish* plays with the reader is through humour which appears in self-reflexive, ironic, and crude forms. Humour creates a presence that is provisional and subversive as it is 'only a joke' in the way that drama is 'only play'. Flanagan positions readers as insiders to his characters' ironic and self-reflexive jokes about fiction and history. When Professor de Silva dismisses *Gould's Book of Fish* as a fraud without historical relevance and suggests that Sid Hammet publish it as a novel instead where it might even win literary prizes, which it has done,[78] Sid Hammet takes offence: 'it had never struck [him] as being sufficiently dull-witted and pompous to be mistaken for national literature'.[79] Flanagan anticipates the very discussion of historical authenticity that his novel invites, which, in turn, leads readers to play more games in the text and participate in the creation of meaning in the novel. In doing so, Flanagan elicits the participation of readers to support a genre of self-reflexive national literature that protests aspects of historicity while dramatizing it.

75   Iser, 'The Play of the Text', 335.
76   Iser, *The Fictive and the Imaginary: Charting Literary Anthropology*, 262.
77   Armstrong, 'The Politics of Play: The Social Implications of Iser's Aesthetic Theory', 217.
78   Flanagan, *Gould's Book of Fish*, 24. See a list of prizes in the first footnote of this chapter.
79   Flanagan, *Gould's Book of Fish*, 25.

Gould's Book of Fish features dramatic role-playing in its performative narration which befits the colonial context in Tasmania where convicts, officials, and Aboriginal characters take on and maintain new roles. Through role-playing, Gould imagines what it is to play other characters in the colonial context, the likes of whom he could not previously conceive. In a visionary moment, Gould sees himself as the 'hanged' and the 'hangman', the 'flogged' and the 'flagellator', the voice of history and the speaker of lies.[80] Over time, Gould sees his role in history as extending beyond his own experience to include the wider range of experiences of colonial officials and assumes a measure of culpability in a collective identity:

> I no longer wished to read lies as to who & why I was. I knew who I was: I was the past that had been flogged on the triangle, but I am the flagellator dipping his cat in the sand bucket to give the tails extra bite; I was the past that fell with choked scream through the gallows' green wood trapdoor, but I am the hangman swinging on the dying man's legs; I was the past bought & chained & raped by sealers, but I am the sealer making the black woman eat her own thigh & ears.[81]

Of course, the character of Gould, who makes this revelation, is imagined by Sid Hammet, who is imagined by Flanagan. Dramatic role-playing provides a means through which Sid Hammet, Flanagan, and readers may consider the implications of a more collective identity in the colonial context.

Flanagan provides other examples of role-playing that are significant in a postcolonial context in *Gould's Book of Fish*. Through a survival strategy of mimicry, Tracker Marks imitates the dress and behaviour of a 'white man' which leads to a sense of disconnection between himself and other indigenous Tasmanians and unsettles his own sense of identity. He dresses, in Gould's view, 'like an Eightways dandy' with a white shirt, lapels, collar, and an American whaling hat,[82] 'more white than a white man',[83] and drifts further away from his culture until it is irretrievable to him. There comes

---

80   Flanagan, *Gould's Book of Fish*, 375.
81   Flanagan, *Gould's Book of Fish*, 375.
82   Flanagan, *Gould's Book of Fish*, 247.
83   Flanagan, *Gould's Book of Fish*, 249.

a point where Tracker Marks' performance of the 'whitefella dance' no longer has an audience:

> Once he had excelled at the emu dance & the kangaroo dance; then his talent led him to the whitefella dance, only now no-one was left of his tribe to stand around the fire & laugh & praise his talent for observation & stealthy imitation.[84]

The Commandant, who has seized his position unofficially, hides behind a theatrical gold mask of Apollo as he builds confidence in his new role as leader of the colony.[85] In time, the mask fuses into his flesh, 'fixing forever his image in that of somebody who was not him but had now become so'.[86] While most of the projects of the Commandant in the novel are ahistorical and are too theatrical to be believed, in particular, the enormous painted backdrops of Europe and Africa surrounding a circular railway that goes nowhere,[87] they gesture to other actual 'nation-building' projects in modern-day Tasmania that have exploited and depleted natural resources as political leaders have followed the lead of more established nations.[88] Outside literature, Flanagan has led an impassioned and long-standing campaign against the destruction and logging of old-growth forests in Tasmania and has criticized collusion between Gunns, the largest logging company in Australia and largest exporter of wood chips in the world, and the Tasmanian government led by former Tasmanian Premiers Jim Bacon and Paul Lennon. Flanagan's lengthy essay on the subject, 'Out of Control: The Tragedy of Tasmania's Forests', won the John Curtin award for journalism in 2008.[89]

---

84   Flanagan, *Gould's Book of Fish*, 249.
85   Flanagan, *Gould's Book of Fish*, 409.
86   Flanagan, *Gould's Book of Fish*, 414.
87   Flanagan, *Gould's Book of Fish*, 203–5.
88   See Shipway, 'Wishing for modernity: temporality and desire in Gould's Book of Fish', 10.
89   Richard Flanagan, 'Out of Control: The Tragedy of Tasmania's forests', *The Monthly*, May 2007 <https://www.themonthly.com.au/issue/2007/may/1348543148/richard-flanagan/out-control> accessed 20 January 2017.

Gould's Book of Fish alludes to the de-forestation of Tasmania[90] by dramatizing how the Commandant sells off every natural resource to which he can and cannot lay claim, including 'the Gordon River & the Great Barrier Reef'[91] and 'the entire Transylvanian wilderness'.[92] Flanagan creates a satirical and theatrical portrait of the Commandant in his gold mask for his greed and adoration of England and Europe and suggests that key theatrical processes of imagination and role-playing are vital stages within the development of colonial leaders' identities.

Epic Theatre and Conveying the Unsayable: Brechtian Techniques in Flanagan's Novel

Flanagan uses theatrical direct addresses, Shakespearean-inspired narration, and a number of conventions similar to those introduced by Bertolt Brecht in epic theatre to position readers at varying critical distances from the tale, engage them creatively and critically, and prompt questions about historical representation. Gould's narration, performed by Sid Hammet, is conspicuously theatrical. Gould addresses readers directly, in passionate and colloquial tones, and, like the Chorus figure in Shakespeare's *Henry V*, takes readers on an imaginative odyssey, expanding and collapsing time and distance to create a present moment of action, as moments in theatre

---

90 Richard Flanagan, 'The Stars and the Mountains', *Island* 63 (Winter 1995), 38–4; Flanagan, 'Does Tasmania have a Future?', *Island* 72–3 (Spring/Summer 1997), 134–58; and Flanagan, 'The Selling Out of Tasmania', *The Age*, 22 July 2004 <http://www.theage.com.au/articles/2004/07/21/1090089215626.html> accessed 18 October 2007. See also Shipway, 'Wishing for modernity: temporality and desire in *Gould's Book of Fish*', which explores the political implications of the historical sale of Gordon River. Shipway discusses the current-day fears of foreign ownership of Tasmania's natural resources and the way Flanagan transmogrifies history into his novel.
91 Flanagan, *Gould's Book of Fish*, 190.
92 Flanagan, *Gould's Book of Fish*, 194.

are often represented. He says: 'So permit me to change tack, swoop back
down into Sarah Island, over the Commandant's Moluccan guards, &
tumble down Mr Lempriere's sooty chimney into the smoky living room
where the Commandant in his cups is admitting to the outrage of his
ambition.'[93] Properties of time and space collide in the Commandant's
dramatic monologue about how history 'far from being past, was ever
present'.[94] Gould describes how the Commandant believed he saw all the
traders, pirates, and discoverers who had ever found Van Diemen's Land
'sailing into Two-penny Sal's bedroom'[95] while Gould hides under Twopenny Sal's cot, like a lover in a Restoration comedy.

   Brecht's epic theatre, which uses a variety of estrangement techniques
to prevent the audience from empathetic involvement and to stimulate
critical thinking, foregrounds some of the performative and metafictional
aspects of Flanagan's novel which reveals its seams and flaunts its theatrical
'fictionality' so as to prevent a lulling effect or passive reading. The novel
uses distancing techniques, including a highly performative narrative frame
and the integration of ahistorical and fantastical details about the colony,
which forestall empathy from readers and prompt further contempla-
tion about the ways in which stories from Australia's past that are hard
to imagine and come to terms with are represented in fiction. Without
empathy, Brecht believed his audience could think more clearly about the
ideological and socio-economic context of the play. Brecht clarified his
position: 'Neither the public nor the actor must be stopped from taking
part emotionally [...]. Only one out of many possible sources of emotion
needs to be left unused, or at least treated as a subsidiary source – empathy.'[96]
Flanagan's novel hinders empathy in many instances with its larger-than-
life characters and layered temporal structure, and tells readers again and
again that the violence, chaos, and horror of colonization are not readily
comprehensible despite all outlandish efforts to convey it. Readers are left

93 Flanagan, *Gould's Book of Fish*, 235.
94 Flanagan, *Gould's Book of Fish*, 272.
95 Flanagan, *Gould's Book of Fish*, 272.
96 Brecht, *Brecht on Theatre: The Development of an Aesthetic*, 169–70.

to contemplate the strange truths and misrepresentations of history and where they overlap in the novel.

Flanagan incorporates gaps in the meta-fictional structure of his novel as a means of exploring the unsayable. Gould's journal is a fragment that comes to Sid Hammet with the first forty-five pages missing. Sid Hammet fills in the missing pages with his introduction, and Gould's journal begins, for readers as well, on page 46.[97] This hyper-performative novel brings an awareness of artifice to the fore and flaunts the novel's very failure to express history. In *Roland Barthes*, Barthes quotes Brecht on the limitations of representing the world in literature in a realistic mode:

> On the one hand, literature cannot transcend the knowledge of its period; and on the other, it cannot say everything: as language, as finite generality, it cannot account for objects, spectacles, events which would surprise it to the point of stupefying it: this is what Brecht sees when he says: 'The events of Auschwitz, of the Warsaw ghetto, of Buchenwald certainly would not tolerate a description of literary character. Literature was not prepared for such events, and has not given itself the means to account for them.'[98]

In a world too horrible to copy or represent, Barthes argues that 'knowledge deserts literature which can no longer be Mimesis or Mathesis, [a means to understand the world] but merely Semiosis, the adventure of what is impossible to language'.[99] Similarly, in theatre, Brecht made no attempt at creating realistic depictions of the world. By interrupting enduring conventions and revealing the illusions of storytelling, he created the estrangement that he felt was 'necessary to all understanding'.[100] Brecht differentiated between two kinds of plays: the 'essentially static' Aristotelian play, that tries to show the world as it is, or was, and the epic style play, 'which is

---

97 Flanagan, *Gould's Book of Fish*, 46.
98 Roland Barthes, *Roland Barthes*, trans. Richard Howard (Berkeley: University of California Press, 1977), 119.
99 Barthes, *Roland Barthes*, 119.
100 Brecht, *Brecht on Theatre: The Development of an Aesthetic*, 71.

essentially dynamic' and tries to show the world 'as it changes (and how it might be changed)'.[101]

Gould's Book of Fish protests against a static representation of history and suggests that while a wholly realistic representation is unattainable and ultimately undesirable in the way it may limit the comprehensive reach of the reader and make the assumption that a violent colonial history is something that could be absorbed in a literary sitting. The novel suggests that colonial Tasmanian history is more complex, violent, and unwieldy than can be portrayed through realism and demands a dramatic and meta-fictional mode. The novel gestures toward this Tasmanian world, and particularly to its violence and horror, by disintegrating the frames of literary familiarity.[102]

Horror beyond Words

In 'Art and the Holocaust: Trivializing Memory', Elie Wiesel addresses the paradox of speaking the unspeakable, or what Beckett called the 'unnameable'[103] in reference to Auschwitz. Wiesel believes that Auschwitz always defeats the attempts of artists who try to represent it: 'Auschwitz is something else, always something else.'[104] Elusively incomprehensible and inexpressible, the Holocaust looms outside the periphery of the imagination. Wiesel advocates representations which incorporate the silences of

---

101   Brecht, *Brecht on Theatre: The Development of an Aesthetic*, 79.
102   See the ending in D. M. Thomas, *The White Hotel* (New York: Viking Press, 1981) and the way in which the realistic framework disintegrates into postmodern fragments when it describes the Holocaust.
103   Elie Wiesel, 'Art and the Holocaust: Trivializing Memory', *The New York Times*, 11 June 1989.
104   Wiesel, 'Art and the Holocaust: Trivializing Memory', n.p.

impossible expression and the stories of the survivors, so that one hears, intermingling, the voices of the living and the echoes of the dead.[105]

Horrific violence is explored incrementally through the senses at varying levels of closeness in *Gould's Book of Fish* as Flanagan experiments with how to represent tragic and incomprehensible historical acts upon indigenous people and convicts. On arriving in the colony, Gould smells death and rotting flesh although he does not see bodies or any violence.[106] The first account of horrific violence Gould hears is provided by Conciliator Robinson, imagined by Gould, and re-written by Sid Hammet, is one in which Clucas, a sealer, steals a baby boy from Twopenny Sal and bashes the baby's head in against some rocks before abducting Twopenny Sal and forcing her to live as his slave (246).[107] While the details of the story are gruesome and tragic, the immediacy and impact of this first encounter with violence is diminished to some degree as it is related to readers third-hand.

The ill fate of the Surgeon Lempriere is described in Gould's journal through a description of stage imagery which distances the reader from the action. Gould writes, 'And when finally I reopened my eyes & saw that the acrid mist had parted like a theatre curtain, there was no way of mistaking what now rose up in the muddy horror of that stage before me.'[108] The novel toys with the expectations of the reader who imagines the theatrical frame to set up something deeply horrific about history, yet instead, it prefaces an ironic, comic, and clearly fictional end for Lempriere. Behind the mist that Gould describes as 'a theatre curtain'[109] is a giant turd containing what is left of Lempriere who has been eaten and excreted by his own pet pig.

As the horrors continue, however, the narrative disintegrates and becomes more fractured. Sid Hammet's presence shows through the cracks of Gould's narration and the narrative strains before it bursts into a self-reflexive, nightmarish explosion. Gould sees mutilated bodies and severed body parts in his escape from Sarah Island with his friend, Capois Death,

---

105 Wiesel, 'Art and the Holocaust: Trivializing Memory', n.p.
106 Flanagan, *Gould's Book of Fish*, 118.
107 Flanagan, *Gould's Book of Fish*, 246.
108 Flanagan, *Gould's Book of Fish*, 245.
109 Flanagan, *Gould's Book of Fish*, 245.

and meditates on how words cannot convey the bodily horrors of the world.[110] Sid Hammet performs the inadequacies of language when he, as Gould, describes Capois Death as he is speared to death:

> & he felt language starting to drift
>
> away,
>
> words tendingto fall intooneanother an dlittlemade sen se & thenthes centof aguavareturned&tommytalkingwalking withme& farfarfaraway&tommy! tommy! cold&cold &
>
> &-------[111]

Sid Hammet's sustained performance of Gould falters as bodies are dismembered. Gould self-reflexively criticizes his own abilities to historicize: 'I was hauling a sled of lies called history through a wilderness [...]. I was writing a book in another time trying to understand why there were no words for what had taken place.'[112] When Gould knows more than he should or could about the narrative, he asks the reader not to pry: 'Please don't ask how I know such things, please: where fish are concerned I know everything – or as good as – & besides, it's rude to interrupt when I am in the middle of telling you.'[113]

The performance of Gould becomes unimaginable for Sid Hammet in such a violent history. The bodies, mutilated and dismembered, are reflected in the fractured text and in the breakdown of Sid Hammet's performance of Gould. The bodies are the haunting doubles that guide the narrative to, and beyond, the limit of expression. Gould moves through a landscape of 'mounds of bones & a host of human skulls, long since picked clean by animals & birds & insects'.[114] He sees skulls with holes from musket balls and 'Tracker Marks' mutilated face and scattered remains on the funeral pyre.[115] The emphasis on the presence of the bodies in the text inverts

---

110   Flanagan, *Gould's Book of Fish*, 343.
111   Flanagan, *Gould's Book of Fish*, 357.
112   Flanagan, *Gould's Book of Fish*, 359.
113   Flanagan, *Gould's Book of Fish*, 423.
114   Flanagan, *Gould's Book of Fish*, 380.
115   Flanagan, *Gould's Book of Fish*, 381.

the hierarchical dichotomy of mind and body. Words in the novel are de-emphasized as bodies convey extralinguistic stories.

The narrative doubles back on itself reflexively. During Tracker Marks' cremation, Gould discovers a scrap of paper that has the same sentence on it that he has just written in an historical account which seems to be writing itself.[116] Soon the bodies are the only clear images amongst a chaos of words, literary form, and content. Gould throws his journal on the funeral fire to rid himself of 'those descriptions of so many individual pasts, their implicit idea of a single future'.[117]

> Onto that pyre I threw so many, many words – that entire untrue literature of the past which had shackled & subjugated [him] as surely as the spiked iron collars & leg locks & jagged basils & balls & chains & headshaving – that had so long denied me my free voice & the stories I needed to tell.[118]

A Fishy End

The novel's array of overly dramatic forms and conventions emphasizes the performative aspects of representing history in fiction and the necessary involvement of an active audience, or readership, as it were. Readers play the games of the text and become witnesses to Sid Hammet's role-playing, boundary crossings, and epic conventions from the theatre. The novel suggests the possibility that there are narratives from history that have escaped records yet are vitally significant in history and, through the inclusion of over-blown scenarios and caricatured characters, readers are conditioned to become dubious to some extent of all versions they receive and participate in the play of the text and invest in creating its meanings. The text offers the experience of imagining the horror and violence of the colonization

116 Flanagan, *Gould's Book of Fish*, 374.
117 Flanagan, *Gould's Book of Fish*, 375.
118 Flanagan, *Gould's Book of Fish*, 375.

of Tasmania through play beyond the limitations imposed by narratives of history and language for a dramatic envisioning of history.

Gould cautions readers that people will 'forget what happened [...] for a hundred years or more'[119] before they start to re-imagine the history, because forgetting is easier than admitting to various complicit roles in history. People will keep telling the same story, Gould says, because

> any story will be better than the sorry truth that it wasn't the English who did this to us but ourselves, that convicts flogged convicts & pissed on blackfellas & spied on each other, that blackfellas sold black women for dogs and escaping convicts, that white sealers killed & raped black women & black women killed the children that resulted.[120]

The novel ends with Gould's transformation into a fish where he is 'unburdened by speech & its complications',[121] yet Gould misses the power of speech in order to be able to explain how his account fell so far short of the explosion of colour, life, and sensation he had hoped to produce. The novel warns readers against the trappings of literary representation through Gould's image of the fish net which awaits, 'ever ready to trap & then rise with us tangled within'.[122] Flanagan's text lures the reader to swim through the net, fill in the gaps, and take part in creating a dynamic, dramatic world. In *Narcissistic Narrative*, Linda Hutcheon argues that if metafiction can entice a reader to participate in creating the universe of the novel, it could lead the reader to action – 'even direct political action'.[123] Similarly, metafiction of this kind, that employs dramatic modes and theatricality to examine history and highlight the implausibility of capturing it in fiction, may lead readers to new approaches of reading, creating, and remembering history as a living part of a collective present. Through its engaging and participatory

119   Flanagan, *Gould's Book of Fish*, 443.
120   Flanagan, *Gould's Book of Fish*, 443.
121   Flanagan, *Gould's Book of Fish*, 439.
122   Flanagan, *Gould's Book of Fish*, 445.
123   Hutcheon, *Narcissistic Narrative: The Metafictional Paradox*, 155.

form, shifting subjectivities, confounding temporalities, range of dramatic forms and frames around horrific violence, *Gould's Book of Fish* may entice a reader who is willing to swim in transformative waters to embrace or, at least, become critically invigorated by aesthetic forms that resonate, provoke, and endure in the bones.

CHAPTER 6

Filmic and Dramatic Modes in Guy Vanderhaeghe's
The Englishman's Boy

The Englishman's Boy (1996) by Canadian writer Guy Vanderhaeghe, alternates between the wild frontier of Montana and Saskatchewan in the 1870s and the world of cinema in Hollywood in the 1920s, and integrates filmic and dramatic conventions in its exploration of how the history of the Wild West is perceived and produced by characters with diverging agendas over time.[1] In *The Englishman's Boy*, Vanderhaeghe questions the values of various history-makers as they represent their versions of history through multi-discursive modes. A 1920s' Hollywood film producer is motivated by profit and creating a white nationalist American mythology; a young 1920s' Canadian writer plays a role in exploiting a source and later writes a memoir to restore the 'truth'; and an Assiniboine elder in the 1870s records his history for future generations in drawings. Through techniques transposed to the text from film and theatre, Vanderhaeghe develops literary deployments of multi-discursive modes in his novel using filmic structures of narrative, dramatic gestures from theatre and immersive moments of 'being there' in each time period to de-emphasize the hegemony of text in writing history even as he reproduces it.

Coming to fiction after a career as a historian, Vanderhaeghe addresses in *The Englishman's Boy* some of the challenges of writing history that are inherent in reflexive historical fiction, or Hutcheon's 'historiographic metafiction',[2] through close attention to discursive modes of representation. Juxtaposing filmic and dramatic modes in the novel, Vanderhaeghe creates

---

1   Guy Vanderhaeghe, *The Englishman's Boy* [1996] (London: Anchor/ Transworld Publishers, 1998).
2   Hutcheon, *Narcissistic Narrative: The Metafictional Paradox*, 22–46.

an oscillating effect for readers between affective immersion in scenes and an awareness of the distance created by various technological processes of preserving and constructing the past. The hallmark characteristics associated with postmodern 'historiographic metafiction' as outlined by Hutcheon in *The Canadian Postmodern* contain a central defining paradox in that they are 'intensely self-reflexively, art, but [...] also grounded in historical, social, and political realities'.[3] Common literary criticisms of postmodern historiographic metafiction maintain that such novels often focus less on the social realities of the world and the located and distinct aspects of the historical past than on their own textual processes and homogenizing impulses of the present time.[4] Félix Guattari in 'The Postmodern Impasse' contends that the postmodern condition is reiterative of modernism, tends to submit to compromises to appease the status quo, lacks innovation and focuses on 'linguistic performance' at the cost of 'ethological and ecological dimensions'.[5] The path out of the impasse, in Guattari's view, requires a movement toward writing that considers ethics, ecology, and sociology as well as the 'semiotic components, aesthetic, corporeal and fantasmatic ones that are irreducible to the semiology of language.'[6]

Another criticism of literature characterized by postmodernism centres on its erasure of local specificity arising from particular cultural contexts and histories. While these contentions have some bearing in works of postmodern literature that, as Larry McDonald suggests, comply 'with the homogenizing tendencies of multinational postmodernism [that] has worked to preclude the study of what is historically specific to our postcolonial experience and our present cultural condition,'[7] not all postmodern

---

3   Hutcheon, *The Canadian Postmodern*, 13.
4   See Larry McDonald, 'I Looked for It and There It Was – Gone: History in Postmodern Criticism', *Essays on Canadian Writing* 56 (Autumn 1995), 37–50; Sylvia Söderlind, 'The Contest of Marginalities', *Essays on Canadian Writing* 56 (Autumn 1995), 96–109.
5   Pierre-Félix Guattari, 'The Postmodern Impasse', in Gary Genosko, ed., *The Guattari Reader* (Oxford: Blackwell Publishers Ltd, 1996), 110.
6   Guattari, 'The Postmodern Impasse', 111.
7   McDonald, 'I Looked for It and There It Was – Gone: History in Postmodern Criticism', 43.

novels move away from local origins and specific contexts. Vanderhaeghe's *The Englishman's Boy* indicates a locatedness and an awareness of postcolonial specificity with its examination of the destruction of Assiniboine people at Cypress Hills, American imperialism in the North American West,[8] and, more to the purposes of this chapter, a shift in focus in more affective and corporeal means and modes of representations that engage with historical stories from the past. Jennifer Blair observes this continuing shift in more recent Canadian postmodern literature that addresses history with a 'significant emphasis on embodiment, perception, and the physical environment'.[9] Blair suggests 'that whether or not this may be considered an effort to navigate beyond the postmodern impasse', these novels 'focus on the physical world (including the physicality of the human body)' and 'the affective impact of literature on both the mind and body' as a key part of their exploration of 'exploring the function and parameters of history'.[10] Blair includes Vanderhaeghe's *The Englishman's Boy* in this group of novels, along with Michael Ondaatje's *The Collected Works of Billy the Kid*, Madeleine Thien's *Certainty* and others,[11] to which I would add Daphne Marlatt's *Ana Historic*, Tomson Highway's *Kiss of the Fur Queen*, and Dionne Brand's *In Another Place, Not Here*. Similar assertions about an affective shift toward addressing the body in literature that addresses history and colonization through self-reflexive and performative modes have been made by Della Pollock who argues such writing can be both welcome and radical within social and cultural discourses that are saturated

8   See Mei-Chuen Wang, 'Wilderness, the West and the national imaginary in Guy Vanderhaeghe's *The Englishman's Boy*', *British Journal of Canadian Studies* 26/1 (2016), 21–38. Wang investigates how *The Englishman's Boy* rewrites the past of the North American West in spatial terms to re-map the landscape as a space inscribed by diverse social discourses.

9   Jennifer Blair, '"The Postmodern Impasse" and Guy Vanderhaeghe's *The Englishman's Boy*', in Robert David Stacey, ed., *RE: Reading the Postmodern: Canadian Literature and Criticism after Modernism* (Ottawa: University of Ottawa Press, 2010), 205.

10 Blair, '"The Postmodern Impasse" and Guy Vanderhaeghe's *The Englishman's Boy*', 205.

11 Blair, '"The Postmodern Impasse" and Guy Vanderhaeghe's *The Englishman's Boy*', 205.

with textuality,[12] and Ross Gibson with his call for modes of representing history that make readers or spectators feel that they encounter it palpably through affective modes.[13]

The Englishman's Boy was critically acclaimed upon its publication, winning the Governor General's Award of Canada (1996)[14] and several other prestigious awards,[15] yet the novel itself is not easily categorized. It has been called a 'revisionist western',[16] the 'Great Canadian Western',[17] 'postmodern historical fiction'[18] and, in Herb Wyile's assessment in 1999, 'characteristic of the more muted self-consciousness of [...] English-Canadian historical fiction'[19] rather than the overtly self-reflexive and aesthetically focused post-modern historiographic metafictions typical of the late 1980s. Two of the reviews on the novel's back cover draw attention to its performativity and dramatic narrative mode, which speak to Vanderhaeghe's inclination toward an affective sensibility in his narration of history and finding evocative and resonant means of representing it in fiction: Mordecai Richler declares the

---

12   Della Pollock, 'Performing Writing', 73–103.

13   Ross Gibson, 'Palpable History', 179–86.

14   Vanderhaeghe is a three-time winner of the Governor General's Award of Canada; in addition to *The Englishman's Boy* (1996), he won for *Man Descending* (1982) and *Daddy Lenin and Other Stories* (2015).

15   *The Englishman's Boy* won the Saskatchewan Book Award for Fiction and Best Book of the Year (1996) and was nominated for the 1996 Scotiabank Giller Prize. Vanderhaeghe's *The Last Crossing* won the 2003 Libris Award and the Saskatoon Book Award for Fiction and Book of the Year (2002). Vanderhaeghe's *A Good Man* was nominated for the 2012 Langum Prize for Historical Literature-Historical Fiction. Vanderhaeghe has won an Order of Canada (2003) and the Lieutenant Governor's Arts Award for Lifetime Achievement in the Arts (2013).

16   David H. Evans, 'True West and Lying Marks: *The Englishman's Boy*, *Blood Meridian*, and the Paradox of the Revisionist Western', *Texas Studies in Literature and Language* 55/4 (Winter 2003), 406–33.

17   Canadian Forum review, qtd in hardcover edition of Vanderhaeghe's *The Englishman's Boy* (Toronto: McClelland & Stewart, 2012).

18   Blair, '"The Postmodern Impasse" and Guy Vanderhaeghe's *The Englishman's Boy*', 207.

19   Herb Wyile, 'Dances With Wolfers: Choreographing History in *The Englishman's Boy*', *Essays on Canadian Writing* 76 (Spring 1999), 23–52.

novel 'A stunning performance', and Julia Flynn writes, 'Bristles with rare vitality. [...] it is hard not to admire the skill with which Vanderhaeghe dramatizes two quite different worlds.'[20]

The two main storylines of Vanderhaeghe's *The Englishman's Boy* follow the life of a young, unnamed English immigrant who takes part in the relatively obscure Cypress Hills Massacre of 1873 where American wolf hunters freely cross the Canadian border in search of their stolen horses and violate and murder a group of Assiniboine people,[21] and, alternately, the life of Canadian screenwriter Harry Vincent who is hired by a Hollywood film producer, Damon Ira Chance, to write the quintessential American Western in the 1920s. Harry Vincent's intentions to adapt a 'true' story from cowboy Shorty McAdoo's past, honour the memory, and create a sense of 'being there' stand in contrast to those of Hollywood film producer Damon Ira Chance who exploits his subjects for commercial gain as well to construct a mythology for America that celebrates white nationalism and obscures the violent realities of the exploitation of indigenous people and the land. Form mimics content as the narrative approximates filmic sutures and splices; sharp cross-cuts link apparently unrelated events creating historical connections and reverberations between seemingly disparate characters. This chapter examines Vanderhaeghe's efforts to create sensory

20   Mordecai Richler and Julia Flynn qtd in Vanderhaeghe, *The Englishman's Boy*, back cover.
21   See Philip Goldring, 'Cypress Hills Massacre', *Canadian Encyclopedia*, Historica Dominica Institute <http://www.thecanadianencyclopedia.ca/en/article/cypress-hills-massacre-feature> accessed 19 August 2013. In summary, on 1 June 1873 a group of American wolf hunters entered the valley of Cypress Hills between Montana and what later became known as Saskatchewan, seeking to recover their missing horses. A battle ensued between the Assiniboine people, the whiskey traders, the Métis, and the American wolf hunters, which resulted in open fire upon the Assiniboine camp and deaths of approximately twenty Assiniboine people, along with one wolf hunter. Canadians, under British rule at the time, felt threatened by the free movement of the Americans across the border and the government experienced difficulties in extraditing and prosecuting several of the American wolf hunters involved. The Cypress Hills Massacre is regarded as instrumental in the creation of the North West Mounted Police in Canada.

traces and a sense of presence in *The Englishman's Boy* through the use of dramatic and filmic modes, and evaluates how these modes of expression are incorporated into diverse perceptions and constructions of history in the novel. This focus on dramatic and filmic modes branches outward from an already established body of criticism built on epistemological questions pertaining to the complex relationships between history, politics, truth, and their representations in postmodern historical fiction.[22]

Before looking at the dramatic and filmic modes in the novel, it is useful to consider Laura U. Marks' approach in *The Skin of the Film: Intercultural Cinema, Embodiment, and the Senses* (2000), which examines how film-makers from diverse cultures who create affective films about historical and cultural events – Marks calls this genre 'intercultural cinema' – explore sensory traces behind print, speech, and images, and 'read significance in what official history overlooks'.[23] Marks analyses some intercultural films that 'confront the limits of thought' by 'showing what stories cannot be told through [...] official histories', and other films that 'begin to work at the limits of what can be thought, by referring to the memories of objects, the body, and the senses'.[24] She proposes that 'a mimetic and synesthetic relationship to the world underlies language and other sign systems' and is conveyed in cinema through translation into the image on the screen.[25] Marks writes:

22   See Daniela Janes, 'Truth and History: Representing the Aura in *The Englishman's Boy*', *Studies in Canadian Literature* 27/1 (2002), 88–104; Wyile, 'Dances With Wolfers: Choreographing History in *The Englishman's Boy*', 23–52; Blair, '"The Postmodern Impasse" and Guy Vanderhaeghe's *The Englishman's Boy*', 203–28; Evans, 'True West and Lying Marks: *The Englishman's Boy, Blood Meridian*, and the Paradox of the Revisionist Western', 406–33; Wang, 'Wilderness, the West and the national imagi-nary in Guy Vanderhaeghe's *The Englishman's Boy*', 21–38.

23   Marks, *The Skin of the Film: Intercultural Cinema, Embodiment, and the Senses*, 28. Marks includes *Surname Viet, Surname Nam* (1998) by Trinh T. Minh-ha, *Kanehsatake: 270 Years of Resistance* (1993) by Anishnabek filmmaker Alanis Obomsawin, and *Calendar* (1993) by Atom Egoyan in the genre of films she calls 'intercultural cinema'.

24   Marks, *The Skin of the Film: Intercultural Cinema, Embodiment, and the Senses*, 29.

25   Marks, *The Skin of the Film: Intercultural Cinema, Embodiment, and the Senses*, 214.

> While the mimetic traces of the world are harder to recognize in the demanding systems of signs that constitute the technological world [...] they are still at work in our understanding of it. We are constantly recreating the world in our bodies, even as our representational systems become more abstract. Even when language is mediated through printed words, an invocatory trace of speech and its mimetic relationship to the world remains.[26]

She proposes that new expressions are created by speaking between historical discourses, layering them, or breaking from conventions in significant ways.[27] In Marks' view, societal and political change is made through 'a sort of a dance between sedimented, historical discourses and lines of flight, between containment and breaking free'.[28] *The Englishman's Boy* follows a line of thought similar to Marks' by delving into the internal histories of events, studying the reverberations between historical events as part of the stories themselves and taking into account memories, senses, and objects that are typically outside of historical exploration. This can first be seen with an examination of the novel's use of dramatic techniques which connect the Englishman's boy from the 1870s to Shorty McAdoo in Hollywood in the 1920s and position readers to experience something somatic and meta-textual from both time periods, through ceremony, ritual, and memories layered with historical traces.

Dramatic Discourse and Traces of Presence in the Novel

Vanderhaeghe develops a sense of presence in *The Englishman's Boy* by contrasting narrative modes that 'show' and 'describe' (*mimesis*) with dramatizations that endeavour, with varying levels of success, to enact moments (*methexis*). The novel dramatizes rituals of friendship and death, highlights the physical bodies of the characters and their theatrical presences and

26 Marks, *The Skin of the Film: Intercultural Cinema, Embodiment, and the Senses*, 214.
27 Marks, *The Skin of the Film: Intercultural Cinema, Embodiment, and the Senses*, 28.
28 Marks, *The Skin of the Film: Intercultural Cinema, Embodiment, and the Senses*, 28.

gestures, and invokes the ritualistic power associated with ceremonies. In the 1870s' narrative, on the night before the Cypress Hills Massacre, the Englishman's boy and Ed Grace sense impending danger. The boy asks Grace if he will agree to a protective pact: 'You stand by me – I'll stand by you.'[29] The novel highlights a sense of ceremony as the men seal the pact with a firm handshake:

> Nothing more was said. [....] The boy felt a sense of occasion, his father had been a ceremonious man, gravely polite in a backwoods fashion. The kid laid aside his stick, and with his blanket hanging off his shoulders like a cape, shyly held out his hand. Grace shook it three times, emphatically.[30]

A similar sense of ritual and ceremony resonates in Harry Vincent's narrative as the physicality of the characters tells its own story at Miles's funeral. When Vincent, Shorty McAdoo, and Wylie bury Wylie's brother Miles, the men communicate to one another through body language and silence that marks the solemnity of the occasion and acknowledges the futility of words in the wake of Wylie's grief. Vincent writes: 'We lower the coffin to the ground, take a quick blow, and then McAdoo curtly bobs his head, the signal to stoop, lift, and scurry on.'[31] The description of Miles' funeral provides physical details that bring a sensory immediacy to the scene: the taste of earth 'souring the back of [Vincent's] throat';[32] and the body language of the men, 'McAdoo stiff-backed in his black coat, Wylie with the burial ropes knotted in his hands, and me'.[33] In contrast to the dramatized mode in which the story of Miles' burial is told, another death is mentioned during this scene with very few details of presence or physicality. As the men dig Miles' grave, Shorty McAdoo tells Vincent about Old Harp Lewis' Indian wife who cut off two of her own fingers when her husband died.[34] While the second story is powerful in its emotion, the mode of narration

29   Vanderhaeghe, *The Englishman's Boy*, 169.
30   Vanderhaeghe, *The Englishman's Boy*, 169.
31   Vanderhaeghe, *The Englishman's Boy*, 143.
32   Vanderhaeghe, *The Englishman's Boy*, 148.
33   Vanderhaeghe, *The Englishman's Boy*, 148.
34   Vanderhaeghe, *The Englishman's Boy*, 146.

is that of straight dialogue frames without any description of *being there*. The two storytelling modes are markedly different from one another and highlight how effective physical and sensory details can be in the first story when dramatizing a moment that brings a reader into its present time.

While the narration of the two stories differs, they are connected; the story of Old Harp Lewis and his wife is a part of the internal history of Wylie's brother's funeral. McAdoo's memory is a part of his present and part of the historical archaeology of the moment. Vanderhaeghe writes: 'So begins the interment of Miles Easton [...] [w]ith this and a memory of the grief of that other stranger, of the funerary rites of a Crow woman, who cut a part of herself away to join whatever she had lost.'[35] In a geological metaphor for history, Deleuze portrays all the 'circles of the past' as:

> constituting so many stretched or shrunk *regions*, *strata* and *sheets*: each region with its own characteristics, its 'tones', its 'aspects', its 'singularities', its 'shining points' and its 'dominant' themes. Depending on the nature of the recollection that we are looking for, we have to jump into a particular circle.[36]

This scene in the novel shows circles of the past overlapping one another and extending into the present. Ceremonies and rituals awaken past stories and memories to create multi-dimensional presents with physical, emotional, and historical depths.

The sense of the past in the present in the novel is developed not only through the dramatizations of ritual but also through a close focus on the aura of objects which carry traces and connections to the objects' original contexts. Walter Benjamin, in 'The Work of Art in the Age of Mechanical Reproduction', describes the aura of an object as 'its presence in time and space' and its 'unique existence at the place where it happens to be.'[37] The essence or authenticity of Benjamin's aura decays as the object is reproduced through technological means. The compelling quality of an historical object and its aura is partly due to its ineffable distance from

---

35   Vanderhaeghe, *The Englishman's Boy*, 148.

36   Gilles Deleuze, *Cinema 2: The Time-Image*, trans. Hugh Tomlinson and Robert Galeta [1985] (London: Athlone Press, 1989), 99.

37   Benjamin, 'The Work of Art in the Age of Mechanical Reproduction', 214.

its modern-day beholder; no matter how much one longs to embrace it, it always remains, on some level, out of the present time and beyond our grasp; and yet it brings stories from the past that cling to its material form. In Vanderhaeghe's novel, the narrative lingers on certain bodies and objects as if searching for or mourning lost auras in the wake of technological discourses (print, film) that preclude tangible or physical connections to historical figures. The novel foregrounds particular bodies and objects as if traces of their historic materiality could be felt or sensed through the discourse of writing and gestures.

When considering certain objects in the novel in light of Benjamin's notion of the aura – Shorty McAdoo's saddle, Harry Vincent's second-hand revolver and Damon Ira Chance's Indian artifacts – a reader may notice a range of provocative effects to unlock memories the objects have on the characters that possess them and release sensuous connections to the past. In *The Skin of the Film*, Marks explores how auratic objects, for example, those which Benjamin calls fetishes,[38] and those which Deleuze calls fossils,[39] 'condense time within themselves' and how 'in excavating them we expand outward in time'.[40] Deleuze's fossils 'acquire their meaning by virtue of an originary contact'[41] while Benjamin's fetish object 'accomplishes its effect by how it is libidinally located upon the body'.[42] Both do not 'represent' that which is powerful but have made actual physical contact with it. Marks groups objects that Benjamin considers fetishes, and Deleuze fossils, as 'recollection objects' with 'the power to witness history'.[43] When such objects are emphasized in literature or film, as they

38 Benjamin believes 'the fetish object encodes truths of collective life, and these truths can be discovered only through a shock that reaches the unconscious', qtd in Marks, *The Skin of the Film*, 86.

39 Deleuze defines fossils as objects from the past that bring a kind of a 'radioactive' presence to the present. Fossils are 'strangely active ... radioactive, inexplicable in the present where they surface, and all the more harmful and autonomous. Not recollections but hallucinations', qtd in Marks, *The Skin of the Film*, 113.

40 Marks, *The Skin of the Film: Intercultural Cinema, Embodiment, and the Senses*, 77.

41 Marks, *The Skin of the Film: Intercultural Cinema, Embodiment, and the Senses*, 84.

42 Marks, *The Skin of the Film: Intercultural Cinema, Embodiment, and the Senses*, 112.

43 Marks, *The Skin of the Film: Intercultural Cinema, Embodiment, and the Senses*, 85.

are in Harry Vincent's narrative and in Chance's obsessive collecting of film props in *The Englishman's Boy*, they have the potential to engage the kind of sense memory that is often overlooked in a technologically focused culture and enthrall spectators who perceive it second-hand. An example of one such object is Shorty McAdoo's saddle which is a powerful talisman to Wylie; it is Wylie's tangible connection to Shorty and Shorty's past, and a fetish object Wylie rides to create his own luck.[44] It is also the means by which Vincent finally locates Shorty by tricking Wylie to return it to Shorty, making possible the physical connection between Vincent and the legendary cowboy.

Not long after Shorty agrees to sell his stories, Vincent is put under pressure by Chance to make Shorty recall the violent memories of 'Indian wars'.[45] To this end, Vincent buys a historic revolver from a pawn shop and leaves it with Shorty as a means of eliciting the stories.[46] The next time the two of them meet, Shorty decides to share the central story of cowboys and Indian warfare that Vincent needs to hear most. While Shorty knows that his version won't see the light of day in Chance's film and says to Vincent, 'He don't want my truth. It ain't to his taste',[47] he tells the story anyway. The materiality of the revolver pulls Shorty back into the past and plays a part in his process of unlocking an authentic memory.

Vanderhaeghe shows how an assemblage of authentic objects aids Chance in perverting history in Chance's white and anti-Semitic cinematic representation of it. Chance is obsessed with acquiring authentic items to be used as props in his film so as to 'generate sensations in the body';[48] however, Chance is more concerned with the authenticity of the items than with preserving the truth of Shorty McAdoo's tale. Before he even has a script, Chance commissions his staff to 'fan out across the country, chequebooks in hand, to dun private collectors, to seduce destitute reservation Indians

44   Vanderhaeghe, *The Englishman's Boy*, 68–73.
45   Vanderhaeghe, *The Englishman's Boy*, 155.
46   Vanderhaeghe, *The Englishman's Boy*, 157.
47   Vanderhaeghe, *The Englishman's Boy*, 194.
48   Henri Bergson, *Matter and Memory*, trans. Nancy Margaret Paul and W. Scott Palmer [1911] (London: Allen & Unwin, 1962), 179.

who might be persuaded to part with Grandpa's medicine bundle, coup stick, or eagle war bonnet for a pittance'.[49] His men ship crates of costumes and props to his home where he 'fingers the booty' himself.[50] Emboldened by the tactile connection to the objects and the effect they will have on viewers of the film, Chance orders the re-writing of the ending of McAdoo's story so the strong defeat the weak, the Assiniboine are aggressors not victims, and his values of American idealism prevail where all immigrants must convert to a white anti-Semitic nation or be damned.[51] Chance's version of history has the Assiniboine girl set fire to her captors[52] instead of Hardwick, the wolfer, setting fire to the house with the girl in it after she has been brutally gang-raped.[53] Chance believes he can 'retain [...] some traces of the fetishist [...], who, by owning the work of art, shares in its ritual power'.[54] Chance has a 'mania for authenticity'[55] in the physical objects only; he draws a sense of power from the historical traces of the items, and, as he commandeers the artefacts, he appropriates the stories to his purposes and creates a view of American history that glorifies the white heroes who conquered the West.

Film Discourse in the Novel

Film is another discourse that influences the narrative structure of *The Englishman's Boy*. A variety of film techniques are transposed into the narrative, including panoramic shots, cross-cuts, close-ups, and flashbacks, some

---

49 Vanderhaeghe, *The Englishman's Boy*, 215.
50 Vanderhaeghe, *The Englishman's Boy*, 215.
51 Vanderhaeghe, *The Englishman's Boy*, 241.
52 Vanderhaeghe, *The Englishman's Boy*, 238–9.
53 Vanderhaeghe, *The Englishman's Boy*, 291.
54 Benjamin qtd in Janes, 'Truth and History: Representing the Aura in *The Englishman's Boy*', 96.
55 Vanderhaeghe, *The Englishman's Boy*, 213.

of which were pioneered by filmmaker D. W. Griffith who is characterized in the novel as Chance's hero and mentor.

In *Cinema 2*, Deleuze introduces a theory that focuses on the spaces between images in film and the generative possibilities of juxtaposition. 'Film', he writes,

> is the method of BETWEEN, 'between two images,' which does away with all cinema of the One. It is the method of AND, 'this and then that,' which does away with all the cinema of Being = is. Between two actions, between two affections, between two perceptions, between two visual images, between the sound and the visual: make the indiscernible, that is the frontier, visible.[56]

What becomes important, in Deleuze's view, is not the association of images, 'but the interstices between [them]'.[57] Sometimes in film, cuts seem merely functional, and at other times they create interactions between two images which 'engender or trace a frontier which belongs to neither one nor the other'.[58] The notion of frontier-crossing is central in *The Englishman's Boy*, not only thematically, in terms of its exploration of a Canadian identity that is between American and British, and physicality, in terms of the historical events that led to more formal policing and defining of the boundaries of the North American frontier, but also structurally through a narrative mode that uses cross-cuts, juxtapositions, and faintly perceptible links to create a whole that is all the more resonant or compelling due to its interstices. Benjamin comments how film spectators are interrupted by the constant and sudden change of images: 'This constitutes the shock effect of the film, which, like all shocks, should be cushioned by heightened presence of mind'.[59] He writes: 'Reception in a state of distraction, which is increasingly noticeable in all fields of art and is symptomatic of profound changes in apperception, finds in the film its true means of exercise.'[60] The contrapuntal structure of the novel resembles the quick and confronting

56 Deleuze, *Cinema 2: The Time-Image*, 180.
57 Deleuze, *Cinema 2: The Time-Image*, 200.
58 Deleuze, *Cinema 2: The Time-Image*, 181.
59 Benjamin, 'The Work of Art in the Age of Mechanical Reproduction', 240.
60 Benjamin, 'The Work of Art in the Age of Mechanical Reproduction', 233.

editing techniques of some films and may contribute to keeping readers in a state of heightened awareness.

The novel imitates a filmic structure in a series of 'narrative cross-cuts' between chapters that connect present and immediate worlds from different eras. Some of the cross-cuts between stories of the 1870s and the 1920s seem rather utilitarian, perhaps the literary equivalent of a fade in/fade out in film, while other cross-cuts suggest that there are pivotal and confronting thematic connections and relationships between characters from the different times. The first cross-cut between narratives connects Fine Man and Broken Horse leading 'a stream of horses' like 'shining strengthening water'[61] to Canada in Chapter 1, and Chapter 2 begins with Vincent's meditation on the recently thawed South Saskatchewan River. While the chapters seem relatively unrelated, the 'stream of horses' flows directly into the description of the 'cold, black water'[62] outside Vincent's window and initiates a connection between the indigenous characters of the 1870s and in Vincent's role in deciphering suppressed narratives from history through his writing.

Other cross-cuts provide more obvious clues about how the narrative strands are related to one another. Chapter 11 concludes with the party of American wolfers feasting on the blood and organs of a freshly slaughtered bull with the narrative drawn closely to the bull's physicality and material presence:

> Hardwick presses the jibbing horse to where the bull waits with black, distended tongue and blood-red eyes, shaking his huge head, flinging threads of slobber into his dirty, matted wool, massive shoulders bridling, the curved, polished horns hooking the air.[63]

Vanderhaeghe emphasizes the smell of gunpowder, the 'greasy shine' on the grass beneath the coiled intestines, and the 'thick and hot' blood which is drunk from tin cups.[64] These sensory details create a scene that is not only

---

61   Vanderhaeghe, *The Englishman's Boy*, 14.
62   Vanderhaeghe, *The Englishman's Boy*, 14–15.
63   Vanderhaeghe, *The Englishman's Boy*, 118.
64   Vanderhaeghe, *The Englishman's Boy*, 118.

easy to visualize but one that provokes an affective response in readers who can very nearly smell, hear, feel, and taste what is described. Directly after this feast at the end of Chapter 11, Chapter 12 opens with another meal, described in sensory-rich detail to engage readers on an affective level. Harry Vincent delivers groceries to Shorty McAdoo as partial payment for his life stories and McAdoo savours every morsel:

> He starts with the cheese, paring cheddar from the wedge, shingling his soda crackers with paper-thin slices. Unhurried, steady chewing, a ruminative savouring of flavour, old turtle eyes squinching up with delight. After that, a can of sardines, forked up with the blade of a jackknife, the empty can mopped clean of the last of the oil, polished shiny with a dry heel of bread.[65]

Lastly, he relishes the canned peaches, 'piece by piece, rolled slippery and sweet in the mouth, mulled over', and washes them down with whisky sloshed around in the syrupy tin.[66] While it is premature at this point in the novel to connect the character of the Englishman's boy with Shorty McAdoo definitively, the juxtaposed feasts suggest an association too deliberate to be inconsequential. Another narrative cross-cut linking the end of Chapter 12 and the beginning of Chapter 13 implies Shorty McAdoo and the Englishman's boy are, most likely, the same person. In Chapter 12, Shorty McAdoo shares details about his past with Harry Vincent, revealing few specifics but that his 'daddy [was] dead' and he had a brother he hated that 'might be dead or alive'.[67] Chapter 13 opens with the Englishman's boy recalling how he was 'trudging his daddy's fields' and 'the stench of a hated brother's shit greeting him when he jerked open the privy door of a morning back home'.[68] Vanderhaeghe does not confirm the connection between the two characters at any point in the novel but leaves the discovery to the reader. Narrative cross-cuts encourage immersions in two present worlds that introduce, as one might see in a film, connections on a sub-conscious level, so that the possibility circulates in a reader's mind, remaining viable

65   Vanderhaeghe, *The Englishman's Boy*, 120.
66   Vanderhaeghe, *The Englishman's Boy*, 120.
67   Vanderhaeghe, *The Englishman's Boy*, 120.
68   Vanderhaeghe, *The Englishman's Boy*, 124.

but unsubstantiated. Ghosts of images occur and recur, leaving trails of possible connections before the mind's eye.

Deleuze describes the cinema's capacity to produce 'the genesis of an "unknown body" which we have in the back of our heads, like the unthought in thought, the birth of the visible which is still hidden from view'.[69] He explores distinctions between the capacities of film and theatre to portray presence; theatre puts spectators in the proximity of the 'real' presence of the body in a way cinema cannot; cinema represents the absences and suspended traces of bodies that are not 'there' in ways that theatre cannot. Cinema, Deleuze suggests,

> spreads an 'experimental night' or a white space over us; it works with 'dancing seeds' and a 'luminous dust'; it affects the visible with a fundamental disturbance, and the world with a suspension, which contradicts all natural perception.[70]

One way in which Vanderhaeghe's novel engages with the element of the 'seen' and the 'unseen' is through meticulous attention to lighting and the illumination of significant moments as though being filmed. After the death of the Englishman, there is a literary equivalent of an establishing shot of the Englishman's boy in the doorway of the Overland Hotel after he stands up to the night clerk and begins his independent life.[71] The boy is described in shades of light and darkness that reflect his haunted past and steely resolve, and it is this ominous vision of the boy, 'lit by the light spilling from the doorway, dwarfed by another man's clothes, dwarfed by the long shadow rooted to his heels and stretched in tortured protraction across the pale dust of the street'[72] that discourages the night clerk from pursuing him. As the boy contemplates his future, a cinematic sunrise floods the sky above the Missouri river: 'There the strong glow of the rising sun lit a mass of shelving cloud so that it appeared a bank of molten lava squeezed from the guts of the earth, each striation distinct and gleaming with a different fire.'[73] From the

69   Deleuze, *Cinema 2: The Time-Image*, 201.
70   Deleuze, *Cinema 2: The Time-Image*, 201.
71   Vanderhaeghe, *The Englishman's Boy*, 50.
72   Vanderhaeghe, *The Englishman's Boy*, 50.
73   Vanderhaeghe, *The Englishman's Boy*, 51.

heart of the sunrise, three tiny black dots gradually become distinguishable in a literary 'long shot' revealing Hardwick, Vogle, and Evans, who become the central players in the Cypress Hills Massacre.

Cinematic Effects in Perceiving and Expressing the World

The Englishman's Boy uses references and strategies from film to explore the impact of technological discourses upon the way writers, historians, and spectators perceive the world. Benjamin begins 'The Work of Art' by analysing the effects technology has on perception expression in art.[74] He suggests that present-day notions of art are intimately entwined with modernist notions of knowledge, power, and technology and argues how the mechanical reproduction displaces art from its traditional, ritualistic, and/or religious origins, and this displacement serves to eradicate the aura surrounding works of art. In arts such as photography and film, the concept of an authentic original object is made redundant. There is no direct tangible or sensory connection to a negative or, in this day, a file that can be digitally reproduced in countless quantities; the connection resides only in the representation of any authentic objects to be found inside the copy. As Benjamin puts it, to ask for the 'authentic print' of a photographic negative, from which any number of prints can be made, 'makes no sense'.[75] Mechanical reproduction does not just affect the dissemination and availability of a work of art, Benjamin argues, but how it is conceived, created, and subsequently perceived.[76] Vanderhaeghe's novel takes up a related point on how film influences the ontological processes of people and articulates it through Chance, who lectures Vincent on film's ability to teach the masses history in the 1920s. Chance tells Vincent that President Woodrow Wilson, after seeing D. W. Griffith's *The Birth of the Nation*, proclaimed it to be

74   Benjamin, 'The Work of Art in the Age of Mechanical Reproduction', 211.
75   Benjamin, 'The Work of Art in the Age of Mechanical Reproduction', 218.
76   Benjamin, 'The Work of Art in the Age of Mechanical Reproduction', 218.

'History written by lightning'[77] and pronounces his era 'to be a century governed by images, one following upon the other with the speed of the steam locomotive that was the darling of the last century and symbolized all its aspirations'.[78] Chance is convinced that film is 'the language of the new century' and that hordes of spectators in the nickelodeons are 'learning to think and feel in the language of pictures'.[79] While Harry Vincent comes to view Chance's politics as didactic, self-serving and anti-Semitic, he too cannot escape the impact that film has on his mode of perception and expression as is made clear in the way he narrates his story in filmic terms.

The narration of the novel, as seen by Vincent, is shaped by filmic references on structural and aesthetic levels and it also integrates some dramatic modes from theatre. Vincent interprets scenes from life as though they appear in films, views people and events as if looking through a lens, and maps the geography of Hollywood in terms of which films were made where in the town. Early in the novel, Vincent watches Fitz, Chance's right-hand man, fire director Bysshe Folkestone in front of the entire cast and crew, using very few words and some deliberate and effective symbolic actions as though they were in a silent film.[80] Vincent describes the scene:

> We all stood watching from a distance. It was like a silent movie without subtitles and musical accompaniment. After a few words from Fitz, Bysshe started to wave his arms; his face, in turn, registering outrage, innocence, perplexity, while all around the two of them work continued.[81]

---

77 President Woodrow Wilson's comment – 'It is like writing history with Lightning. And my only regret is that it is all so terribly true' – appears at the beginning of most prints of D. W. Griffith's *Birth of a Nation* (1915). The comment was later denied when the NAACP protested against the heroic representation of the Ku Klux Klan and the derogatory and villainous depiction of African-Americans. See Mark Benbow, 'Birth of a Quotation: Woodrow Wilson and "Like Writing History with Lightning"', *The Journal of the Gilded Age and Progressive Era* 9/4 (October 2010), 509–33 <https://doi.org/10.1017/S1537781400004242> accessed 2 June 2015.

78 Vanderhaeghe, *The Englishman's Boy*, 108.

79 Vanderhaeghe, *The Englishman's Boy*, 108.

80 Vanderhaeghe, *The Englishman's Boy*, 20.

81 Vanderhaeghe, *The Englishman's Boy*, 20.

Vincent describes how Bysshe's 'once emphatic and confident gestures became uncertain and tentative. In the end [Bysshe] shrugs half-heartedly; his arms fell to his sides; he fell silent.'[82] Vincent's cinematic perception of the scene situates readers doubly as spectators where art depicts how life mirrors art. Harry Vincent goes on to describe the dramatic actions in how Fitz ignores the director and proceeds to slowly wipe sand off his hands again and again to indicate that he is wiping his hands clean of Bysshe and the entire situation. Vincent writes, 'Even from a distance from where we stood, you could feel the cold cruelty of this pantomime. Nobody could have stood it for long. The meaning was perfectly clear.'[83] The pantomime functions as a literary 'close-up' of a recognizable symbolic social action which is also known as a *gest* from Brecht's epic theatre. The gest, which Brecht developed as a technique of estrangement in epic theatre, is a gesture or action that carries within it a social value or meaning which, due to its familiarity and relevance in real life, interrupts the audience and provides an awakening shock in the theatre by conveying social and, at times, political messages without language.[84] In Vanderhaeghe's novel, the gest prompts readers to interpret the social significance of the physical action and, by doing so, it interrupts the narrative flow of the text by demanding a different mode of perception. Gests engender a mode of reading which emphasizes the performative.

Another example in the text where a symbolic action speaks volumes is when Hardwick, the leader of the wolfers, refuses to shake the hand of the Métis leader who has told him where the Assiniboine people are camped:

> When the Métis offered his hand to shake, Hardwick ignored it. The Englishman's boy saw the briefest of smiles twitch the Métis' lips and then he ironically and gravely saluted Hardwick, wheeled his horse around, galloped back to the ridge and disappeared behind it.[85]

82 Vanderhaeghe, *The Englishman's Boy*, 20.
83 Vanderhaeghe, *The Englishman's Boy*, 21.
84 John Willett, ed., intro. and trans., *Brecht on Theatre: The Development of an Aesthetic by Bertolt Brecht* (London: Methuen, 1964), 42.
85 Vanderhaeghe, *The Englishman's Boy*, 181.

Some physical details in the novel, such as the glimmer of a smile described above, are presented to the reader through a filmic narrative style of close-ups and isolated shots. A tight focus on the minute detail is provided via the placement of the reader looking with what seems to be a camera's eye. Vanderhaeghe uses elements from both epic theatre and film to emphasize and frame the significance of body language, actions both large and minute, between characters.

At the novel's end, Harry Vincent describes Chance's reaction at the *Besieged* premiere; he makes the sign of victory, hands clasped high above his head. His exuberant gest indicates not only his delight in his accomplishment but also his power and privilege.[86] After Chance is shot by Wylie and lies dying, his gests become harder to interpret: 'He is beyond speech. He makes a gesture to the wall of rain, to whomever, whatever, he imagines lurks behind it.'[87] Positioned to view the scene as spectators, readers are prompted to interpret what nuances of expression the physical gestures can convey through Vanderhaeghe's incorporation of filmic and dramatic modes.

Vincent borrows numerous references from film to describe his world. Rachel Gold's face is softened in the light rain 'like gauze on a lens';[88] Vincent sees Fitz as 'the crazy, loyal servant in Murnau's *Nosferatu* [...] [d] evoted to the master';[89] the dawn is described as tea-coloured 'like tint in a Griffith picture';[90] and McAdoo's shack is captured in words as though it is a tightly framed and stylized cinematic image:

> McAdoo pushes the door open and I follow him in. Because of the tar-papered windows, a kerosene lamp sits on an apple box at the far end of a room long and narrow as a shooting gallery, the light making luminous the sheets of an unmade bed. German expressionism, I think to myself. A lot of cameramen would give their eyeteeth for that shot.[91]

---

86   Vanderhaeghe, *The Englishman's Boy*, 301.
87   Vanderhaeghe, *The Englishman's Boy*, 306.
88   Vanderhaeghe, *The Englishman's Boy*, 256.
89   Vanderhaeghe, *The Englishman's Boy*, 255.
90   Vanderhaeghe, *The Englishman's Boy*, 197.
91   Vanderhaeghe, *The Englishman's Boy*, 186.

Even the pace at which McAdoo delivers his memories is conveyed in filmmaking terms. His reluctance to speak is described as 'rusted locks, suspended action, the camera crank stuck. Suspended action, the failure to find the right key for his rusted lock, is what the rest of the morning turns into.'[92]

Film bleeds into life as Harry Vincent views the geography of Hollywood in terms of how movies map the town. Mother Reardon's boarding house, where Shorty McAdoo once lived, is described in terms of how close it is to where 'Griffith constructed the gargantuan Babylon set for his film *Intolerance*';[93] Rachel and Vincent sit on the beach of the Pacific Ocean, 'which once doubled for the Red Sea in Cecil B. DeMille's *The Ten Commandments*'.[94] The novel highlights other parallels between film and life: Vincent describes a scandal involving the actor Fatty Arbuckle, who went from superstar to public enemy when he was accused of raping a young starlet with a glass bottle: 'there were reports of women attacking the screen when Arbuckle comedies were shown and Wyoming cowboys riddling them with bullet holes'.[95] Chance describes how Erich von Stroheim was attacked in the streets after 'playing so many evil Prussians during the war'[96] and refers to the legendary premiere of the Lumière Brothers' film in which a train appears to hurtle off the screen towards the audience.[97] Such techniques emphasize to readers how Hollywood cinema influenced people to various degrees in how they perceived their worlds; it asks readers not only to consider the modes of expression as inseparable from the messages conveyed but also to regard the modes as influential in the construction of

92   Vanderhaeghe, *The Englishman's Boy*, 120.
93   Vanderhaeghe, *The Englishman's Boy*, 61.
94   Vanderhaeghe, *The Englishman's Boy*, 253.
95   Vanderhaeghe, *The Englishman's Boy*, 24.
96   Vanderhaeghe, *The Englishman's Boy*, 104.
97   Martin Loiperdinger exposes the supposed chaos and terror resulting from Louis Lumière's short film *Arrival of the Train* as 'cinema's founding myth'. Despite the absence of police or eyewitness reports, journalists have promoted the idea that spectators mistook the image of the train on the screen for reality. See Martin Loiperdinger, 'Lumière's *Arrival of the Train*: Cinema's Founding Myth', *The Moving Image* 4/1 (Spring 2004), 89.

the messages themselves. Vanderhaeghe's novel explores how technological advances influence ontological processes and change the way in which
characters view and interpret the past and also their present lives. By the
time Vincent ends up agreeing to take part in Chance's skewed filmic representation of Shorty McAdoo's life, his perception of the world is already
affected by film in ways of which he is unaware.

Key Absences and 'Inadequate' Language to Indicate
Limitations of a Living Presence

While the novel's incorporation of dramatic rituals and auras creates sensations of a 'present' history, Vanderhaeghe indicates in a few places his novel's
inability to create a living historical presence in writing. To foreground this
incongruity and explore the limitations of the discourse, the novel withholds the inclusion of the most significant scene in Shorty McAdoo's life
in Vincent's narrative and calls attention to sections of the novel where
language is somewhat inadequate as an expressive form. Consider the significant absence of Shorty McAdoo's memory of the Cypress Hill Massacre,
the novel's crucial ur-text, from Vincent's memoir. It is the Holy Grail of
stories that Vincent desires and it would also help the reader to link Shorty
McAdoo to the Englishman's boy from the 1870s' narrative conclusively.
Once Shorty McAdoo decides to speak to Vincent, the narrative that ensues
is not the story itself but rather Vincent's description of the storytelling
experience: 'his voice went on, growing slightly frayed and raspy, hoarse
from hours of talk'.[98] The absence of the story itself is worth noting; readers
only glean a sense of the historical event in a later re-telling through the
Englishman's boy's description of it that is included for the reader but not

---

98   Vanderhaeghe, *The Englishman's Boy*, 196.

'mediated' by Shorty or Vincent.[99] When it comes at last, it is delivered with dramatic intensity and visceral force. Dramatic strategies of enactment, physicality, and spatial awareness bring the reader into the present as the Englishman's boy makes a few meta-theatrical observations before returning abruptly to feel base physical sensations:

> He had the strange feeling of fading out of the scene, standing apart from what was happening to him. Where had this second set of eyes come from? He felt himself floating, peering down from above. He saw old Grace lying dead behind him. The horse dead. The Indians dead [...] He wondered if maybe he weren't dead too, maybe a ghost seeing as he could picture it all. He bit his tongue, fiercely, and the salty tang of blood in his mouth told him he wasn't no spectre yet.[100]

In omitting Shorty McAdoo's version of the climactic story from his memoir, Vincent attempts to make up for his part in exploiting the story for Chance's film. The novel examines the consequences that come from the appropriation of personal histories for mass consumption especially in a technological age of film where the construction of an individual's history as-it-happened is secondary to considerations of profit and aesthetics. In an interview, Vanderhaeghe discusses how he also changed certain details from the Cypress Hills Massacre and made artistic decisions that were not strictly historical. He conflated the probable multiple rapes of Assiniboine women into a single rape of a young girl in an attempt to 'create a stronger, more horrific moment.'[101]

There are a few instances in the novel where the language indicates the difficulty of making history present and vivid in literature. Rather than glossing over awkward expressions or anachronisms, Vanderhaeghe highlights them through repetition or, in one case, through a parallel with Vincent's and Rachel Gold's struggle to write language in their scripts that sounds authentic for the time and is comprehensible to their contemporary

---

99 The climatic story from the Englishman's point of view is described in Chapters 27 and 29. See Vanderhaeghe, *The Englishman's Boy*, 265–73, 284–92.
100 Vanderhaeghe, *The Englishman's Boy*, 269.
101 Guy Vanderhaeghe, 'Writing History vs Writing the Historical Novel', *Drumlummon Views* (Spring/Summer 2006), 143.

audience. The first and last chapters of *The Englishman's Boy*, written from a third-person omniscient perspective focused through Assiniboine characters have, at times, a stilted or translated quality to them. They occupy a prominent, albeit 'borderline' position in the novel, which Alison Calder suggests is a 'deliberate creative strategy designed to point to the absences of indigenous voices in Shorty's story',[102] yet feature within them some unconvincing dialogue and characterizations. One Assiniboine character describes one of the white wolfers: 'The one with the ugly hair, red like a fox's, he stood making his water and talking over his shoulder.'[103] The writing represents an attempt to mimic the syntax of an indigenous language transposed to English but comes across as imitative of the classic 'noble savage' created by non-indigenous writers.

Each section of the novel utilizes different modes of speech – Assiniboine 'translations', cowboy idioms, Hollywood shop-talk – and exposes the complex task of connecting the experiences of the characters from the past to contemporary readers without further estrangement through unfamiliar language. While choosing suitable dialogue is not commonly the task of the historian, as Vanderhaeghe points out in an interview, it is necessary, when writing fiction about history, for the author to 'masquerade as an actor present at the events he describes and discusses'.[104] In researching for this novel, Vanderhaeghe read classic Old Westerns and was not convinced by much of the dialogue he encountered.[105] He asked himself whether the writers of such accounts 'may have been influenced by dime novel Westerns they undoubtedly read' or if 'average Montanans of the 1870s actually talked this gibberish'.[106] He writes:

> The problem is that this speech, even if it is authentic and correct, can only strike modern readers as parody, leaving them feeling like they've been dropped in the Mel Brooks' movie *Blazing Saddles* to be harangued by actors cranked on hallucinogens

102 Alison Calder, 'Unsettling the West: Nation and Genre in Guy Vanderhaeghe's *The Englishman's Boy*', *Studies in Canadian Literature* 25/2 (2000), 104.
103 Vanderhaeghe, *The Englishman's Boy*, 11.
104 Vanderhaeghe, 'Writing History vs Writing the Historical Novel', 144.
105 Vanderhaeghe, 'Writing History vs Writing the Historical Novel', 145.
106 Vanderhaeghe, 'Writing History vs Writing the Historical Novel', 145.

and mimicking Gabby Hayes, Walter Brennan, and Slim Pickens. As a literary language it is worse than inadequate, it is laughable. What I settled for was an illusion of authenticity. So my characters all talk an artificial, invented language that I hoped the reader would swallow as historical.[107]

Vanderhaeghe devised the Englishman's boy's dialect in part from the 1878 diaries of L. A. Huffman and pieces of *Huckleberry Finn*; Rachel Gold's character resembles Dorothy Parker and Anita Loos; while Chance is a mixture of Henry Adams and H. L. Mencken.[108] As the illusion of authenticity was Vanderhaeghe's aim, the dialogue was crafted to be authentic-sounding and comprehensible with an awareness of the complex task of reproducing historically accurate language that sounds contemporary out of its time.

Vanderhaeghe dramatizes the dilemma of creating convincing dialogue through Rachel Gold's and Vincent's struggles to write convincing scripts. Rachel Gold tells Vincent:

> For anything prior to 1600, be it Babylon or Tudor England, crib the King James version of the Bible. This satisfies the nose-pickers in Chattanooga who can read, although sometimes they get confused and believe they're conning the word of God, which can later lead to confusion in tent meetings. For American historical costume dramas, the Declaration of Independence is an unfailing model for the speech of the quality. When it comes to frontier gibberish I merely reproduce the kitchen-table conversation of the relatives of my former husband. The Gentile one.[109]

With self-reflexive awareness, the novel incorporates Biblical language and apocalyptic imagery when characters in the Englishman's boy's narrative become fearful and withdrawn. After shooting Hardwick's bull, the Scotchman resorts to mystical and incoherent religious babble, frightening the other American wolfers who believe he has lost his senses. The omniscient narrator of the 1870s' section sets the scene: 'When folks went scare, or off their heads, they'd been known to pile on the Bible talk. The Scotchman seemed to be a bit of both.'[110] The Scotchman rails on about

107 Vanderhaeghe, 'Writing History vs Writing the Historical Novel', 145.
108 Vanderhaeghe, 'Writing History vs Writing the Historical Novel', 144.
109 Vanderhaeghe, *The Englishman's Boy*, 44.
110 Vanderhaeghe, *The Englishman's Boy*, 125.

'the way of the Bible Jews', 'the wild God of dreams and visions' and 'the Devil's Sabbath', which consists of a 'foul cup of blood' and 'uncooked flesh'.[111] Later that night, the Englishman's boy sees an apocalyptic vision of the dead white horse that adds to his sense of foreboding. Despite Rachel's warning about how and why Biblical language is used strategically in her scripts, the Englishman's boy's narrative seems designed to bridge, through mystical and sacred references, a gap between the historical past and the readers' present. While Rachel disparages the technique of symbolic Bible talks, Vanderhaghe employs it in this scene.[112] Readers are situated inside a construction of history that acknowledges the limitations of language but exploits them anyway.

In silent films, language is withheld, yet not absent. The lips of the characters move, and subtitles provide narrative descriptions and/or dialogue to clarify the images, yet the gap between words spoken and words heard remains. Silent films contain trace stories that spectators do not hear or see, yet due to the conventions of silent films, they can fill in the gaps. Technically, in film, half of the time the screen is black or blank and the viewer's eye fills in the interstices. In a similar way, Vanderhaeghe's novel shows that language can be, at times, incomplete and full of gaps; it stands in for what cannot be expressed. While the novel borrows strategies from dramatic and filmic discourses to recreate experiences for the reader, it settles, at times, for representing experience by exposing the failures or limitations of language and the literary discourse within which the novel operates. Roland Barthes begins *Empire of Signs*, a series of observations about Japan, by stating that his aim is to reproduce Japan's inscrutability and decipher its cultural signifiers as a critique of the West rather than to create a more straightforward observation of the Japanese nation.[113] Perhaps this aim is close to what the stilted and obvious 'talk' in Vanderhaeghe's novel accomplishes. It flags an inscrutability that it is more valuable to include and acknowledge than to omit and avoid. The novel suggests that something inaccessible or inexpressible lurks behind language, and what

111   Vanderhaeghe, *The Englishman's Boy*, 125.
112   Vanderhaeghe, *The Englishman's Boy*, 125.
113   Roland Barthes, *Empire of Signs* (New York: Noonday Press, 1989).

it cannot successfully 'access' or 'dramatize' it represents through overt inscrutability.

Transitional Discourses

One of the main thematic concerns in the novel is how discourses transform in rapidly changing worlds. How a story is told, and to what end, is of great concern to several characters in the novel, including Strong Bull, Shorty McAdoo, Harry Vincent, and Damon Ira Chance. The novel's form reflects this concern in its engagement with and acknowledgment of its interdisciplinary discourses such as oral storytelling, scripts, films, theatre, and its attention to the transitions between forms and the need for more than one mode of relating a story, particularly, an historical one. *The Englishman's Boy* itself has been reconstructed through several different forms: oral, written, and cinematic. Before the novel was published, excerpts from the novel were broadcast on CBC Radio's *Ambience*.[114] In 1996, producer Kevin DeWalt began his lengthy project of adapting the novel into a four-hour miniseries for CBC Television, directed by John N. Smith and starring R. H. Thomson and Bob Hoskins. The series eventually premiered in 2008. Vanderhaeghe plays a small role as the barkeeper, and the film focuses on the 1870s' storyline.[115] When asked how he adapted his novel to a screenplay, Vanderhaeghe replied: 'John Irving said it best: First you have to make the decision, which two-thirds of it do I leave out? When you go to tell the story, you have to choose. Which character do you focus on? We decided to place the emphasis on the 1873 part of the story.'[116]

---

114 Vanderhaeghe notes this in his 'Acknowledgements' in *The Englishman's Boy*, 318.

115 Patricia Robertson, 'Deadwood North: CBC TV shoots Western mini-series', *The Globe and Mail*, 21 August 2006 <http://www.theglobeandmail.com/arts/dead wood-north/article1102337/> accessed 23 August 2007.

116 Robertson, 'Deadwood North', n.p.

In *Language, Counter-Memory, Practice*, Michel Foucault writes: 'Discursive practices are not purely and simply ways of producing discourse. They are embodied in technical processes, in institutions, in patterns for general behaviour, in forms for transmission and diffusion, and in pedagogical forms which, at once, impose and maintain them.'[117] *The Englishman's Boy* explores ways in which discourses impact on the telling of stories and capture the moments of transition that accompany them. In the last chapter, Strong Bull tells Fine Man why he 'spent his days drawing pictures in the lying books'.[118] He explains that he draws the pictures 'so the grandchildren will recognize [them]' in a world that is constantly changing.[119] In this, Vanderhaeghe looks for ways to value non-textual testimony that typically escapes recording. I agree with Daniela Janes' contention that 'Vanderhaeghe's endorsement of the text-as-record is a guarded one'.[120] Rather than reifying the 'white' Western way of recording information, Strong Bull's book of drawings, albeit represented within a text, represents a search for an enduring method of storytelling in a time of cultural and technological transition.

Vincent also dreams of a discursive form that will convey the essence of a present historical moment. No single discursive mode, oral, written or filmic, satisfies his desire to 'be there'. When Chance dislikes the written version of Shorty McAdoo's first anecdote, Vincent realizes he needs to tell the story in a different way, yet remains unsure of how to do it:

> I berate myself for my stupid assumption that words on the page can convey what I have learned about McAdoo. [...] Words on the page are not capable of communicating this. It had been the burial, the drawing in of night, the incessant wind, the way McAdoo held himself in the chair, the flick of the boot slamming closed the stove door, the sudden darkness, the voice playing scales in the darkness, beginning flat as

---

117   Michel Foucault, *Language, Counter-Memory, Practice: Selected Essays and Interviews 1963–1972*, ed. Donald F. Bouchard, trans. Donald F. Bouchard and Sherry Simon (Oxford: Blackwell, 1977), 200.
118   Vanderhaeghe, *The Englishman's Boy*, 312.
119   Vanderhaeghe, *The Englishman's Boy*, 314.
120   Janes, 'Truth and History: Representing the Aura in *The Englishman's Boy*', 101.

dictation, then growing troubled, self-questioning. All this I suddenly see as more important than what he said; the *feel* of the night was its meaning.[121]

To resolve his dilemma, Vincent draws on the discourses of drama and film, focusing on bodies, gestures, lighting, and connecting moments in history with the present when writing his memoir. Vanderhaeghe similarly addresses a reader's desire of 'being there' by integrating dramatic and cinematic discourses into a layered, multi-discursive literary form which results in an impression of a palpable past that engages readers to question and interrogate it.

The novel is as suspicious of singular fictive modes used to describe history as it is of clear-cut historical accounts. Vanderhaeghe clarifies this in *Drumlummon Views*: 'In writing *The Englishman's Boy* I had hoped to issue a warning: beware of anyone who hands you history too neatly packaged whether it comes wrapped up in histories, films, or historical novels.'[122] His self-professed take on historical fiction is 'to present the past as a textured, lived experience, experience from the "inside".'[123] By incorporating elements from dramatic and filmic discourses, Vanderhaeghe develops a novel in which readers can immerse themselves in historical representations in sensuous and experiential ways as they recognize the impact the narrative perspective and discursive forms from diverse historical eras have on the story. *The Englishman's Boy* does not gloss over or fill in the unknowns of historical gaps; rather, it draws attention to its own epistemological blind spots as it elicits embodied and critical responses to animate the limitations and possibilities of historiographic metafiction through cinematic and dramatic modes.

121   Vanderhaeghe, *The Englishman's Boy*, 156.
122   Vanderhaeghe, 'Writing History vs Writing the Historical Novel', 146.
123   Vanderhaeghe, 'Writing History vs Writing the Historical Novel', 145.

Taking It Further: Novels that Perform History Inside and Beyond Australian and Canadian Contexts

This book has explored a range of dramatic modes employed in Australian and Canadian historical fiction written between 1985 and 2010. As critical debates about history, fiction, and the interrelations between them have intensified in recent decades, and affective and performative approaches to literature have gained traction, a genre of novels has emerged that utilizes evocative, provocative, and 'palpable' modes for constructing the past as it challenges and critiques certain limitations of literature. Some dramatic modes explored in this book immerse readers in a reconstruction of an historical moment that appeals to affective sensibilities; other modes rely more on theatrical conventions that emphasize distance, and position readers as witnesses at a remove so that they may engage in critical interpretation and perceive strategies of resistance and power in the performances they observe. The dramatic modes establish active connections between the reader and the text. These novels invite a re-consideration of the notion that an unbridgeable divide exists between history and fiction, and that artistic forays between the separate domains are necessarily against fact, entirely fanciful, or threatening to truthful examinations of human existence in history. Dramatic modes in fiction create opportunities for readers to experience an enlivened version of the past in the present – both affectively and intellectually – and provide access to understandings of history that resonate with a contemporary reader or promote active critical thinking about the limitations of historical representation in fiction. This particular genre of fiction that engages with history through dramatic modes is most usefully considered not with regards to how closely the significant moments or events match the historical evidence in history books to the letter but

rather in terms of the potential of the genre to offer readers access to elusive moments in history that may not be accessible through conventional
forms of historical research, examination, or exposition.

   Without audiences of some kind, there can be no history. It exists
for and in relation to those who receive it. And yet, paradoxically, history
excludes audiences from it, to some degree, by the nature of its existence in
the past. As Roland Barthes says: 'History [...] is constituted only if we consider it, only if we look at it – and in order to look at it, we must be excluded
from it.'[1] This is exemplified well in *Ana Historic* and *The Englishman's Boy*
when readers are given the sense of entering and embodying the mind and
body of a character, in the way Stanislavski guides his actors to do, and then
just as suddenly removed from that consciousness to examine the scene from
afar and from alternate perspectives. It is accomplished through a different
approach, for example, in *Gould's Book of Fish* when all the aesthetic and
dramatic frames used to represent the past fall apart as they are examined
too closely. The oscillation of dramatic frames disrupts familiar narrative
strategies and results in some innovative perspectives about history in fiction. Dramatic modes in fiction enable readers to 'look' with more than
just the mind's eye, with pulse and presence, immediacy and remove, and
experience a sense of being in a realm from which a reader is inevitably
excluded. Greg Dening observes that 'both "theatre" and "theory" derive
from the Greek origin "thea" (sight) and, when combined, provide a way
of seeing and knowing that is both sight and insight'.[2] Dening writes,
'Theory [is] a mind-set for viewing; theatre – a space-set for spectatoring;
theatrical – a convention-set for mimesis.'[3] When novels perform history,
theatre and theory inform one another with the energies from disparate
yet connected epistemological fields. Through imaginative speculation,
elusive history comes 'closer' as energies of the past are re-played with the
energies of the present.

1   Barthes, *Camera Lucida: Reflections on Photography*, 65.
2   Dening, *Performances*, 104.
3   Dening, *Performances*, 104.

Theatrical energy, or as Aristotle conceived of it in *Poetics*, *energeia* (force) and *enargeia* (that which shines forth to appear before the listener),[4] thrives when applied to the gaps of history in fiction; while it can, at times, challenge a historian's concept of truth, it stretches the boundaries of what history has been conceived of to be previously and what it can be. Aristotle argues in *Poetics* that the difference between history and poetry (which, for this argument, I extend to literature) is that 'one relates what has happened, the other what may happen'.[5] The theatre, in particular, further challenges the inherent paradox in how one might capture the past definitively; theatre is a medium that uses living bodies as signs with an infinite range of potential expressions in each live performance. When novels integrate dramatic modes to engage with history, they often touch upon the spontaneity and potentiality of the medium of theatre that approximates a sense of what it is to 'capture' history which is another medium of living signs.

The performative modes that writers use to engage with history in this genre of fiction may influence contemporary readers to experience the past in ways beyond the cerebral so that the act of reading provides an occasion or an experience in their present. In *Performances*, Dening suggests that the mode and delivery of performative history become inseparable, so far as to say, 'We only know a past through the histories made of it, by the past becoming in some way a text which we must read not just for the story it tells but also for the occasion of its telling and the mode of its expression.'[6] In novels that perform history, dramatic modes create new 'occasions of telling' each time they play in the minds of readers. Dramatic modes in novels can provide a sense of communing with characters from the past, as in Marlatt's *Ana Historic*, where readers may project their energy and consciousness into roles through guided dramatizations. Other dramatic modes use fractured and disintegrating frames, as in Flanagan's *Gould's Book of Fish*, to estrange readers from historical events and characters through Brechtian techniques of alienation. Metatheatre and melodrama bring

4   Aristotle qtd in Freddie Rokem, *Performing History: Theatrical Representations of the Past in Contemporary Theatre* (Iowa City: University of Iowa Press, 2000), 189.
5   Aristotle, *Poetics*, trans. Samuel H. Butcher (New York: Dover Publications, 1951), 35.
6   Dening, *Performances*, 17.

recognizable theatrical frames to Keneally's *The Playmaker*, and Musgrave's *Glissando*, where scenes of colonial and postcolonial significance are staged doubly and readers recognize symbolic microcosms of the nation through satiric, comic, and tragic conventions. Vanderhaeghe's *The Englishman's Boy* employs a counterpoint strategy of immersion and estrangement that teases readers with the possibility of entering an historic moment and reminds them of the impossibility of doing so. This counterpoint strategy reveals the tension between living moments and textual representations, and creates, by exposing the limitations of various forms, what Laura U. Marks calls 'a dance' between 'established, sedimented discourses' and 'lines of flight'.[7]

Interaction with an audience is a central element within indigenous and other forms of oral storytelling. In *Kiss of the Fur Queen*, Highway conveys that Cree stories are remade with each telling of every story and adapted to suit the social context of each audience. Readers discover in the final chapter of both Marlatt's *Ana Historic* and Carey's *Illywhacker* that each of these novels has been related orally to a listener or a crowd of listeners. This knowledge requires readers to re-conceptualize the novel they have read in the context of an oral performance. The oral form, even while in a text, gives the impression of organicity since it has been shaped to suit its particular telling as it is delivered. A reader may be the only 'audience member' present, but he or she may sense a connection to others 'hearing' or reading the tale, as explored in Benedict Anderson's notion of individual readers in imagined communities who read a narrative that suggests a unifying collective among its many readers.[8] This strategy of placing the reader in an imagined audience is particularly useful in the performances of more marginalized historical narratives that challenge the hegemonic beliefs of nations as they convey a sense that there is a collective readership bearing witness to stories that have not been widely told.

While dramatic modes in fiction range in form and effect, they use words to create, rather than refer to, experiences. Dramatic modes in fiction gesture to life beyond the word, to the impulses and thought processes that

7   Marks, *The Skin of the Film: Intercultural Cinema, Embodiment, and the Senses*, 28.
8   Anderson, *Imagined Communities: Reflections on the Origin and Spread of Nationalism* [1983] (London: Verso, 1991).

lead to the text, and to bodies and extra-linguistic communications that elude written descriptions. One of the most important functions of poetic and theatrical devices, as Sigurd Burckhardt puts it, 'is to release words in some measure from their bondage to meaning, their purely referential role, and to give or restore to them the corporeality which a true medium needs.'[9] Marlatt's deconstructive strategy in *Ana Historic* confronts phallogocentric language and uses the body, specifically women's bodies, to inspire language that awakens sensory awareness and create rhythmic associations between words. Flanagan calls attention to language's inadequacies in capturing living experience, as Beckett did before him,[10] and using art forms that awaken the senses of the body, such as the visual arts, music, dance, and drama, into his novel. Similarly, Highway uses elements from dance, music, drama, and indigenous storytelling in *Kiss of the Fur Queen* to bring corporeal impulses and a sense of the living Cree language into his novel. Carey emphasizes the grotesque and transgressive qualities of Badgery's body in *Illywhacker* to dramatize the material presence of the narrator, while Musgrave, in *Glissando*, illuminates through musically inspired and melodramatic dramatic frames his desire for affective and excessive modes of aesthetic representation that point to inscrutable aspects of postcolonial history. Vanderhaeghe, in *The Englishman's Boy*, focuses on auratic objects as a means of entering the past with an awareness of the lure of physicality and presence. He incorporates theatrical gests as non-linguistic communication and film-inspired narrative strategies of close-ups, cuts, and juxtapositions as a means of viewing the world, and leaves some incomprehensible gaps in between these strategies that resist articulation.

In this book, the novels that perform history are each set in worlds that are in transition. They dramatize conflict and transformation in early colonial settlements and postcolonial societies in Australia and Canada and highlight the changing modes of expression that accompany the transitions. Drama, as well as history, has conflict and transformation at its heart, and when incorporated in fiction, it becomes a fitting and versatile

---

9   Burckhardt qtd in Bert O. States, *Great Reckonings in Little Rooms: On the Phenomenology of Theater* (Berkeley: University of California Press, 1985), 7.
10   Beckett, *Disjecta*, 1983.

mode through which to explore the development of postcolonial nations as they pass through major transitions. Dramatic modes in these novels highlight performative and tumultuous aspects of history. They show how illusions and imagination are central to the conception of a nation and, in particular, a postcolonial nation; how national identity requires ongoing rehearsals; how minoritized groups 'stage their marginality' in various ways in dominant society; and how a nation's founding myth is adapted to suit its audiences.

This study of performative modes in Australian and Canadian historical fiction does not assume the countries do not contain their own complex histories, languages, literary heritages, and culturally diverse populations. This is a growing field and the focus here on only seven examples of the dramatic mode in Australian and Canadian novels is not to suggest that these are the only representations of the genre or that this kind of writing can only arise from these two national contexts in English. Rather, these novels represent a range of the different aims and effects of dramatic modes in this genre of literature. I have compared novels of this kind from Australia and Canada to recognize the interconnections between these two national contexts and the particular suitability and fertility of dramatic modes used to animate history in fiction from two settler/invader postcolonial contexts that share some distinctive elements of their nationhood without disregarding the distinctions of either.

Dramatic modes that investigate history in novels can be found in the literature of other countries in the world, in particular, in nineteenth-century novels from England, and in postcolonial novels from India and the Caribbean. In addition to Litvak's and Allen's books on the theatricality and theatrical modes of the nineteenth-century English novel,[11] critical books and articles about performativity in Indian writing, often linked to magic realism, have been published, for example, on Salman Rushdie's *The Satanic Verses* and *Midnight's Children*, and on performativity and film in

11   Litvak, *Caught in the act: theatricality in the nineteenth-century English novel* [1992]; Allen, *Theater Figures: The Production of the Nineteenth-Century British Novel* [2003]; special issue of *Victorian Network* 13/2 (Winter 2011).

Arundhati Roy's *The God of Small Things*.[12] Michael Dash has written on performativity in Caribbean Literature along with other scholars on Wilson Harris' use of dramatic modes in fiction.[13] While limited critical attention has been paid to this emerging body of work thus far, it has caught the imagination and critical attention of some scholars and readers interested in affect, performativity, and the complexities of writing history in fiction. To introduce the potential for exploring dramatic modes in novels that enact history in literature from other postcolonial contexts, I will study the dramatic modes and kathakali theatre used in *The God of Small Things*[14] by Arundhati Roy, set in Kerala, India in the 1960s, to frame and preserve key moments from the characters' most painful memories against a backdrop of the post-Independence politics of Indian caste and class. I will examine performative identity and the use of dramatic modes in *The Infinite Rehearsal*,[15] by Guyanese writer Wilson Harris, which explores an imaginative process where the protagonist continually re-enacts the Conquest of the Caribbean in order to understand the trauma of colonization and to learn how to transcend the mindset of the colonized. These novels serve as only two examples of how the theoretical model explored here can be extended beyond the frame of Australia and Canada for the purposes of a study that explores dramatic modes in fiction in a wider range of postcolonial and other historical contexts.

12 See Alexandru, *Performance and Performativity in Contemporary Indian Fiction in English*, in which performative language, political and cultural contexts and film styles are explored in Rushdie's and Roy's novels. For observations on Rushdie's self-conscious performativity and its relationship to the postcolonial condition, see Gikandi, *Maps of Englishness: Writing Identity in the Culture of Colonialism*. For a focus on Roy's motif of performance, see Sarkar, 'Performing Narrative: The Motif of Performance in Arundhati Roy's *The God of Small Things*', 217–36.

13 Michael Dash, 'In Search of the Lost Body: Redefining the Subject in Caribbean Literature', *Kunapipi* 9/2 (1987), 8–23; *Theatre of the Arts: Wilson Harris and the Caribbean*, ed. Hena Maes-Jelinek and Benedicte Ledent (Amsterdam: Rodopi, 2002).

14 Roy, *The God of Small Things* (Toronto: Vintage, 1997).

15 Harris, *The Infinite Rehearsal* (London: Faber, 1987.)

In *The God of Small Things* (1997), a novel about memory, trauma, post-Independence violence in India and forbidden love, Arundhati Roy integrates elements from kathakali theatre, an ancient dance-drama form originating in Kerala, India from the late sixteenth and early seventeenth centuries, into the novel to frame through analogy the violence inflicted upon a man who breaks the caste laws. Velutha is an 'undesirable' Hindu and has a love affair with Ammu, a high-caste Christian and mother of the novel's protagonists, twins Rahel and Estha, who revisit tragic events from their childhood through dramatic frames. The integration of dramatic frames, and particularly the historically and regionally rooted kathakali intertext, provides an embodied and culturally specific mode through which to explore Kerala in the late 1960s. It also shows how the tragic episodes portrayed in the novel are at the threshold of textual representation through any one mode.

In Roy's novel, the memories of the traumatic moments are heightened and dramatized as if they have, over time, become re-inscribed in Rahel's and Estha's memories as scenes from a play that are happening on stage. Because the 'Loss of Sophie Mol' has such profound impact on Rahel and Estha, who feel responsible for the death of their cousin Sophie Mol by drowning, the twins experience and re-construct the memory of her arrival, short stay, and death, as a play. In their memories, the scene of Sophie Mol's homecoming plays over again until it becomes the most familiar script they know. Roy describes how Rahel and Estha, as children, exclude themselves from the central action 'while the *Welcome home, our Sophie Mol* Play was being performed in the front verandah.'[16] Roy writes, 'Rahel looked around her and saw that she was in a Play. But she had only a small part. She was just the landscape. A flower perhaps. Or a tree. A face in the crowd. A Townspeople.'[17] Roy writes that Sophie Mol tries to walk 'out of the Play to see what Rahel was doing behind the well. But the Play went with her [...]. Walked when she walked, stopped when she stopped.'[18] Roy's narration demonstrates not only how Sophie Mol is the centre of the

16   Roy, *The God of Small Things*, 184.
17   Roy, *The|God of Small Things*, 164.
18   Roy, *The God of Small Things*, 173.

play because it is her tragedy, but also how she is perceived with discernible awe because she is fair, half-British, and from London. Even in Rahel's and Estha's own memories, the spotlight travels with Sophie Mol.

Throughout the novel at other points of grief and trauma, the characters are described as though they are playing roles. The language of theatre and performance suggests a longing for a structure in which to absorb moments which are too dramatic for regular comprehension. When Rahel re-visits Estha as an adult and is unable to break through to him, Roy describes them as 'a pair of actors trapped in a recondite play with no hint of plot or narrative. Stumbling through their parts [...] Unable, somehow, to change plays.'[19] After Margaret Kochamma's second husband Joe is killed, Roy describes the policeman who delivers the news as though he was acting: 'He had looked strangely comical, like a bad actor auditioning for a solemn part in a play.'[20] These recurring references to theatre and acting direct readers to consider how people structure their memories and particularly difficult memories of grief into recognizable structures that are removed from ordinary life and provide a shape and form for despair. Here, Roy demonstrates how a grieving mind re-shapes memories into available forms for re-enactment as the mind requires.

One way that Roy frames the cyclical brutality of inter-caste violence in *The God of Small Things* is by integrating kathakali into the novel as an analogous mode for representing Velutha's fate and thereby introducing a critical distance through which characters process tragedy by positioning violence as a performance. Kathakali, which translates literally into 'story play', brings to life the themes and characters from the Ramayana and Mahabharata traditional epics.[21] The stories are conveyed through stylized hand gestures, choreography, dance steps and costumes to the rhythm of

19   Roy, *The God of Small Things*, 182.
20   Roy, *The God of Small Things*, 237.
21   Phillip B. Zarrilli, 'kathakali', in Dennis Kelly, ed., *The Oxford Companion to Theatre and Performance* (Oxford: Oxford University Press, 2010) <http://www.oxfordrefe rence.com.ez.library.latrobe.edu.au/view/10.1093/acref/9780199574193.001.0001/ acref-9780199574193-e-2044?rskey=CDA9qx&result=2> accessed 11 February 2016.

drums and onstage vocalists.[22] Kathakali performances traditionally ran from dusk to dawn, although, in post-Independence times, and in Roy's novel, they are truncated to suit the expectations of tourists and constitute a bastardization of the traditional form that has been altered to accommodate foreign and colonial tastes. As Florence Labaune-Demeule observes, 'kathakali becomes the expression of cultural defilement, as is illustrated by the performances for tourists in "God's Own Country", [...] a perversion of art which the dancers try to expiate in full performances at the temples.'[23] Kathakali grounds the novel in the specific regional background of Kerala, distinguished by its religious, political, and linguistic multiplicity within India, and also serves to blend Indian and Western modes of storytelling in a hybrid performative form. Labaune-Demeune observes in novels that incorporate kathakali, 'the more modern theories of reading as an active process meet the more spiritual emotions generated by kathakali, producing a new hybrid aesthetics of writing.'[24]

In the theatrical telling and re-telling of a familiar story, different truths, perspectives, and nuances are revealed with each performance. Roy describes how the Great Stories of kathakali are familiar, yet intensely compelling, in their re-enactments:

> The Great Stories are the ones you have heard and want to hear again. [...] They don't deceive you with thrills and trick endings. They don't surprise you with the unforeseen. They are as familiar as the house you live in. Or the smell of your lover's skin. You know how they end, yet you listen as though you don't [...]. In the Great Stories you know who lives, who dies, who finds love, who doesn't. And yet you want to know again.[25]

---

22   Zarrilli, 'kathakali', n.p.
23   Florence Labaune-Demeule, 'Anita Nair's Aesthetics of Hybridity; *Mistress* as Narrative Kathakali', in Vanessa Guignery, Catherine Pesso-Miquel and Francois Specq, eds, *Hybridity: Forms and Figures in Literature and the Visual Arts* (Newcastle: Cambridge Scholars Publishing, 2011), 228.
24   Labaune-Demeule, 'Anita Nair's Aesthetics of Hybridity; *Mistress* as Narrative Kathakali', 235.
25   Roy, *The God of Small Things*, 218.

In Rahel's memory, the brutal beating of Velutha made such a deep impression that Rahel can only express it fully in the narrative after watching a kathakali performance as an adult. Many aspects of Velutha's beating mirror the theatrical violence of the kathakali performance and to Rahel, after many years, the traumatic memory becomes akin to a legend or a classic tragedy.[26] Roy suggests that it is difficult to process trauma without recognizable frames of understanding. In the novel, the first scene of explicit violence occurs in 'Death of Duryodhana and Dushasana', which Rahel and Estha watch as adults. By inserting the novel's first violent scene as one that has been circulating for centuries, Roy prepares readers to interpret the next scene of violence, Velutha's murder, in terms of a systemic, cyclical death that is not particularly personal; rather, it is born from centuries of division and rigid boundaries between castes.

Shortly after this kathakali scene, the narrative shifts to the consciousnesses of young Rahel and Estha who remember witnessing the brutal battering and murder of Velutha by the policemen. There is an absence of anger and passion in the policemen who seem not to register that their victim is human; in this, a sense of the performance of violence remains. When the policemen arrive, they are described as if they are fulfilling roles in the theatre. They assume the roles they have been given and proceed to brutalize a man because it appears in their script. Roy describes Rahel and Estha as 'an under-age audience' watching 'History in live performance'.[27] Here, the kathakali intertext serves as an allegorical story come-to-life in the scene of Velutha's murder and links this culturally specific dramatic mode as an essential, symbolic, and evocative element of the novel.

The Infinite Rehearsal (1987), by Wilson Harris, is a surrealist, intertextual allegory in the form of a fictive autobiography about Robin Redbreast Glass, who meets archetypal characters through time. Glass meets a ghost who will not leave the world and goes backwards and forwards indefinitely to

---

26   Brian Doerries, *The Theatre of War* (London: Scribe, 2015). Doerries explores the cathartic effects that come from watching live Greek tragedies for American war veterans in this reflective study that stems from Doerries' work as the founder and director of the theatre company Theater of War.

27   Roy, *The God of Small Things*, 293.

rehearse major events in Caribbean history during the European Conquest. The ghost revisits other allegorical historical conquests and conflicts – Hiroshima, Chernobyl, Babylonian slavery – in the forms of several characters to stage history imaginatively through metaphors of theatre. This process of 'an infinite rehearsal of the birth of history' can 'exhume' what Harris calls the 'fossils' of his culture, both personal historical memories and those belonging to a shared unconscious, that have been buried deep in the minds of the colonized survivors long after colonization.[28] According to Harris' philosophy, which builds upon Jung's archetypes and notion of the collective unconscious,[29] the fossils can be used as 'gateways'[30] into the past and back to the future to create an imaginative dialogue that offers a paradigm shift in the ways one conceives the postcolonial past.

The process or dramatic mode of the 'infinite rehearsal', which operates in several of Harris' novels,[31] has characters retrace their steps not to endlessly repeat history but to re-visit it and remove illusions, misconceptions, and prejudices that have become embedded in the characters' unconscious. In rehearsing the past, characters and readers may unlock binary thinking about colonizers and the colonized that prohibits healing and transformation. Robin Redbreast Glass, the first-person narrator, uses the metaphor of the theatre as he enacts his history on an imaginary stage in order to progress beyond the polarized divides created by the Conquest of his family and people:

28   Wilson Harris, *Fossil and Psyche* (Austin: University of Texas, 1974).
29   Carl Gustav Jung, *The Archetypes and the Collective Unconscious* (Princeton, NJ: Princeton University Press, 1980).
30   See also Dominique Dubois, 'Wilson Harris's "Infinite Rehearsal" or the Imaginative Reconstruction of History', *Commonwealth* 21/1 (Autumn 1998), 37.
31   Dubois in 'Wilson Harris's "Infinite Rehearsal" or the Imaginative Reconstruction of History' notes how 'the infinite rehearsal' is prominent in *The Palace of the Peacock* with Donne's men resembling Conquistadors and re-enacting the European Conquest in reverse; Dubois explores how the motif of 'the infinite rehearsal' is used in several of Harris' novels, including, *The Four Banks of the River of Space, The Tree of the Sun, Ascent to Omai,* and *The Eye of the Scarecrow.*

> I know that in unravelling the illusory capture of creation I may still apprehend the obsessional ground of conquest, rehearse its proportions, excavate its consequences, within a play of shadow and light threaded into value; a play that is infinite rehearsal, a play that approaches again and again a sensation of ultimate meaning residing within a deposit of ghosts relating to the conquistadorial body – as well as the victimized body – of new worlds and old worlds, new forests and old forests, new stars and old constellations within the workshop of the gods.[32]

The infinite rehearsal allows for a reinterpretation of history that helps the protagonist, through Robin's guidance and theatrical imagination, reclaim history from the perspective of 'the ruled or apparently eclipsed side of humanity'.[33]

The form of the novel writes back to the realist form of the classic English novel which Harris, in an essay, argues 'coincide[d] with the rise of imperialism'.[34] Harris believed that such a 'consolidated' view of society found in realist novels demonstrated an understanding of reality on a single plane of existence rather than the layered psychic view of identity and extended idea of history as inter-connected through times that Harris suggests exists in Caribbean identity constructions.[35] In taking apart notions of selfhood and proposing a vaster view of life that extends beyond the duration of a lifetime, Harris creates in *The Infinite Rehearsal* a chorus of intersecting characters that spans time and addresses misconceptions of discrete identities that do not take into account the multiracial and multi-cultural population of Guyana from a history of several tribes of indigenous people, indentured labourers from India, stolen people from Africa, and European and South American colonizers. Krishna Ray Lewis observes that the 'dramatization of selfhood, particularly in the postcolonial era as a continual negotiation among identities and pasts, is the fictional and

---

32　Harris, *The Infinite Rehearsal*, 1.
33　Harris, *The Infinite Rehearsal*, vii.
34　Harris, *The Infinite Rehearsal*, vii.
35　Hena Maes-Jelinek, 'Wilson Harris', in Hans Bertens, Theo D'haen, Joris Duytschaever and Richard Todd, eds, *Post-war Literatures in English: A Lexicon of Contemporary Authors* (Alphen aan den Rijn: Samsom and Graningen; Wolters-Noordhoff, 1988 et seq.), 3 <https://orbi.ulg.ac.be/bitstream/2268/201008/1/Maes_Wilson-Harris_Post-War-Literatures-in-English_1997.pdf> accessed 19 February 2017.

theoretical preoccupation of much of Wilson Harris's writing.'[36] *The Infinite Rehearsal* not only writes back through theatrical imaginings to the dominant view of history of Caribbean conquests but also writes back to texts from canonical literature, including Goethe's *Faust*, Marlow's *Dr Faustus*, and elements from T. S. Eliot, James Joyce, Joseph Conrad, and Shakespeare, establishing connections between traditions as it inscribes and re-stages the protagonist's vision as central rather than marginalized.

Harris's prose in *The Infinite Rehearsal* works through intuitive and poetic means to enliven a reader and bring voices from the past into the present in search of connections between oppositional and Manichean binaries of thinking. In 'The Radical Imagination', Harris describes the kind of writing that can make 'bridges' between cultures that are 'tormented and torn and divided':[37]

> They do exist. They can be found. They can be discovered and rediscovered, provided that there is a different kind of rhythm which requires us to read backwards, and forwards, to read an image not simply in a linear way, pressing forward all the time, but sensing what lies behind that image, the way that image appears in a different context, the way it can open itself somewhere else. [...] This is to say that the dead can be brought back into some kind of dialogue with us because of the music of space.[38]

A character in *The Infinite Rehearsal* who shares the same initials as the novel's author, W. H., speaks about the qualities in fiction that can awaken a creative and dynamic stirring in a reader, especially through modes that draw on the 'sensible' body and sense of dramatic imagination of the past:

> Fiction gives buoyancy to us. Fiction explores the partiality of the conditioned mind and the chained body, chained to lust, chained to waste. Fiction's truths are sprung from mind in its illumination of the sensible body again and again and again, in its

---

36   Krishna Ray Lewis, 'The Infinite Rehearsal and Pastoral Revision', *Callaloo* 18/1 (1995), 83.
37   Wilson Harris, *The Radical Imagination: Lectures and Talks*, ed. Alan Riach and Mark Williams (Liege: Universite de liege: L³, 1992), 114.
38   Harris, *The Radical Imagination: Lectures and Talks*, 114.

illumination of our grasp of intuitive theatre and of deprivation in the materials with which one constructs every quantum leap from the sick bed of humanity.[39]

The concept of the infinite rehearsal, as employed by Harris, emphasizes the writing and conceptualizing of postcolonial history in fiction as an ongoing creative process rather than an absolute or completed product.[40] In a similar vein in a discussion about postcolonial literature, Helen Tiffin suggests that decolonization is 'process, not arrival; it invokes an ongoing dialectic between hegemonic centrist systems and peripheral subversions of them; between European or British discourses and their post-colonial dis/mantling'.[41] *The Infinite Rehearsal* forges a fluent, multivocal, and dramatic form through which to explore hybridized cultures of the Caribbean from the side of the subjugated and to address the trauma of colonialism. It presents a conceptual strategy where past and present are inseparable, and dramatizations of allegorical histories are used to revisit conquests, eliminate polarizations and move toward a vast and a vast plural humanity.

Dramatic modes in fiction about history create active and risk-taking readers. With an Iserian sense of 'play', readers may relax boundaries and permit their minds to explore what they might ordinarily reject. Gaps and omissions within and between layered discourses provide fertile ground for readers to make meaning and their own creative connections. Dramatic modes create charged moments of being in novels, for example, in

39 Wilson Harris, *The Infinite Rehearsal* in *The Carnival Trilogy* (London: Faber and Faber, 1993), 221.

40 See Joanne Tompkins, "'The story of rehearsal never ends": Rehearsal, performance, identity in settler culture drama', *Canadian Literature* 144 (Spring 1995), 142–61. In this article, Tompkins points to a number of Canadian and Australian plays which engage the metaphor of rehearsal to create performances of identity which may be subversive, radical, and/or deviate from stereotypical identities: Maria Campbell and Linda Griffiths, *The Book of Jessica: A Theatrical Transformation* (Toronto: Coach House Press, 1989); Mojika, *Princess Pocahontas and the Blue Spots: Two plays*; Djanet Sears, *Afrika Solo* (Toronto: Sister Vision, 1990); and Louis Nowra, *Cosi* (Sydney: Currency Press, 1992).

41 Helen Tiffin, 'Post-Colonial Literature as Counter-Discourse', in Bill Ashcroft, Gareth Griffiths and Helen Tiffin, eds, *The Post-Colonial Studies Reader* (London: Routledge, 1995), 95–8.

embodying sensual possibilities in *Ana Historic*, in the intense gaze created by internal audiences through metatheatre in *Kiss of the Fur Queen* and *The Playmaker*, as characters develop and role-play identities that are advantageous for survival in postcolonial contexts. Dramatic modes usher readers into the event of the text, either through picaresque models of narration in *Illywhacker*, melodramatic frames, in *The Playmaker* and in *Glissando*, or Cree storytelling traditions in *Kiss of the Fur Queen*. This genre explores the intimate and subjective potential rendered through Stanislavski-inspired immersion into a character and where words create affective experiences for the reader, as in *Ana Historic* and *The Englishman's Boy*, or through more estranging theatrical techniques that use, disrupt, and critique the theatrical frames of representation, as in *Gould's Book of Fish*, and prompt readers to confront the ways in which they receive and question history. This book has begun an investigation into how the living spirit we find in the theatre is translated into novels. It explores the inventive and political possibilities and practical limitations of transposing dramatic modes into the representation of history in contemporary Australian and Canadian fiction and illustrates how the genre is at work in literature in other specific postcolonial contexts, offering energizing and affective forms of representation of culture and history.

Dramatic modes in fiction about history condition readers to connect to and expand textual fields with their own experiences of the world. Through this strategy, readers are intimately involved in the storytelling process; the particular version of the story they read cannot exist without them. Readers enter a space of possible transformation and potentiality. This embodied way of looking at the past injects readers into historical scenes they are partially responsible for creating and, as a result, likely to remember. In a manner similar to how we emerge from a theatre after a play, stumbling, eyes adjusting to the light, returning, as the various worlds we have visited swirl in our heads, we emerge from novels that perform history, with sight and insight, turning and returning the past, in physical and sensuous illumination, to the present.

Bibliography

Abrams, M. H., *A Glossary of Literary Terms*, 7th edn (Boston: Heinle & Heinle, 1999).

Acoose, Janice, *Iskwewak Ka' Ki Yaw Ni Wahkomakanak: Neither Indian Princesses nor Easy Squaws* (Toronto: Women's Press, 1995).

——, 'Post Halfbreed: Indigenous Writers as Authors of Their Own Realities', *Looking at the Words of Our People: First Nations Analysis of Literature* (Penticton: Theytus Books, 1993), 27–44.

Adams, Harold, *Prison of Grass: Canada from a Native Point of View* (Saskatoon: Fifth House, 1989).

Alexandru, Maria-Sabina Draga, *Performance and Performativity in Contemporary Indian Fiction in English* (Boston: Brill Rodopi, 2015).

Alfred, Taiaiake, *Peace, Power, Righteousness: An Indigenous Manifesto* (Don Mills, Ontario: Oxford University Press, 1999).

Allen, Emily, *Theater Figures: The Production of the Nineteenth-Century British Novel* (Columbus: Ohio State Press, 2003).

Althusser, Louis, 'Ideology and Ideological State Apparatuses: Notes Toward an Investigation', *Lenin and Philosophy, and Other Essays*, trans. Ben Brewster (New York: Monthly Review Press, 1971), 123–73.

Anderson, Benedict, *Imagined Communities: Reflections on the Origin and Spread of Nationalism* [1983] (London: Verso, 1991).

Aristotle, *De Arte Poetica*, ed. Ingram Bywater (Oxford: Oxford University Press, 1958), 5–7.

——, *Poetics*, trans. Samuel H. Butcher (New York: Dover Publications, 1951).

Armstrong, Jeanette, 'The Disempowerment of First North American Native Peoples and Empowerment Through Their Writing', in Daniel David Moses and Terry Goldie, eds, *An Anthology of Canadian Native Literature in English* (Toronto: Oxford University Press, 1991), 239–42.

——, ed., *Looking at the Words of Our People: First Nations Analysis of Literature* (Penticton: Theytus Books, 1993).

Armstrong, Paul B., 'The Politics of Play: The Social Implications of Iser's Aesthetic Theory', *New Literary History* 31/1, *On the Writings of Wolfgang Iser* (Winter 2000), 211–23.

Arrival of a Train at La Ciotat, dir. Auguste and Louis Lumière, Lumière Brothers, 1896.

Ashcroft, Bill, 'Reading Carey Reading Malley', in *Australian Literary Studies* 21/4 (2004), 28–39.

Ashcroft, Bill, Gareth Griffiths and Helen Tiffin, *The Empire Writes Back: Theory and Practice in Post-Colonial Literatures* [1998] (London: Routledge, 1999).

Atwood, Margaret, *The Journals of Susanna Moodie* (Toronto: Oxford University Press, 1970).

Austin, John, *How To Do Things With Words* [1955] (Boston: Clarendon Press, 1962).

Australia, dir. Baz Luhrmann, USA, Twentieth Century Fox Film Corporation, 2009 [DVD].

Australian Story: A Letter From Richard Flanagan, transcript, 3 November 2008 <http://www.abc.net.au/austory/content/2007/s2410155.htm> accessed 4 April 2009.

Baker, Candida, 'Thomas Keneally', *Yacker 2, Australian Writers Talk About Their Work* (Sydney: Pan, 1987), 116–42.

Bakhtin, Mikhail, *The Dialogic Imagination*, ed. and trans. Michael Holquist and Caryl Emerson (Austin: University of Texas Press, 1981).

——, *Rabelais and his World*, trans. Helene Iswolsky (Cambridge, MA: M. I. T. Press, 1968).

Balzac, Honoré de, *The Comèdie Humaine*, ed. and trans. George Saintsbury (Philadelphia, PA: Gebbie Publishing Company, 1897–1899).

Banting, Pamela, *Body Inc.: A Theory of Translation Poetics* (Winnipeg: Turnstone Press, 1995).

Barnes, Julian, *A History of the World in 10 ½ Chapters* (Cambridge: Cambridge University Press, 1989).

Barthes, Roland, *Camera Lucida: Reflections on Photography*, trans. Richard Howard [1981] (New York: Hill and Wang, 2000).

——, *Empire of Signs* (New York: Noonday Press, 1989).

Beckett, Samuel, *Disjecta: Miscellaneous Writings and a Dramatic Fragment*, ed. Ruby Cohn (London: John Calder, 1983).

——, *Happy Days: A play in two acts* (London: Faber, 1966).

——, *I Can't Go On, I Will Go On*, ed. and intro. Richard Seaver (New York: Grove Press, 1976).

——, *The Pleasure of the Text*, trans. Richard Miller (London: Lowe and Brydone, 1975).

——, *Roland Barthes*, trans. Richard Howard (Berkeley: University of California Press, 1977).

——, *Worstward Ho* (London: Calder, 1983).

Belghiti, Rachid, 'Choreography, Sexuality, and the Indigenous Body in Tomson Highway's *Kiss of the Fur Queen*', Postcolonial Text 5/2 (2009), 1–16.

Benbow, Mark E., 'Birth of a Quotation: Woodrow Wilson and "Like Writing History with Lightning"', *The Journal of the Gilded Age and Progressive Era* 9/4 (October 2010), 509–33 <https://doi.org/10.1017/S1537781400004242 > accessed 2 June 2015.

Benjamin, Walter, *Illuminations* [1955], ed. Hannah Arendt, trans. Harry Zorn (London: Pimlico, 1999).

——, 'On Some Motifs in Baudelaire', in Hannah Arendt, ed., Harry Zorn, trans., *Illuminations* [1955] (London: Pimlico, 1999), 152–90.

——, *Reflections: Essays, Aphorisms, Autobiographical Writing*, ed. Peter Demetz, trans. Edmund Jephcott (New York: Schocken Books, 1978).

——, 'The Work of Art in the Age of Mechanical Reproduction', in Hannah Arendt, ed., Harry Zorn, trans., *Illuminations* [1955] (London: Pimlico, 1999), 211–44.

Bentley, Eric, *The Life of the Drama* (London: Methuen, 1965).

Bergson, Henri, *Matter and Memory*, trans. Nancy Margaret Paul and W. Scott Palmer [1911] (London: Allen & Unwin, 1962).

Bhabha, Homi K., 'Of Mimicry and Man: The Ambivalence of Colonial Discourse', in *The Location of Culture* (London: Routledge, 1994), 85–92.

——, *Nation and Narration* (London: Routledge, 1990).

——, 'Signs Taken for Wonders: Questions of ambivalence and authority a tree outside Delhi, May 1817', in Ed F. Barker, ed., *Europe and Its Others: Proceedings of the Essex Conference on the Sociology of Literature, 1* (Colchester: University of Essex, July 1984).

——, 'Signs Taken for Wonders: Questions of ambivalence and authority under a tree outside Delhi, May 1817', *Critical Inquiry* 12/1 (Autumn 1985), 144–65.

Bilkey, Richard, 'Interview: David Musgrave on Glissando', *Bookseller +Publisher* <http://www.fancygoods.com.au/booksellerpublishermagazine/2010/04/09/interview-david-musgrave-on-%E2%80%98glissando%E2%80%99-sleepers-publishing/> accessed 9 April 2010.

Birth of a Nation, The, dir. D. W. Griffith, perf. Lillian Gish, Mae Marsh, Bessie Love, 1915, Chatsworth, CA. Image, 1992.

Blaber, Ronald, and Marvin Gilman, *Roguery: The Picaresque Tradition in Australian, Canadian and Indian Fiction* (Springwood, New South Wales: Butterfly, 1990).

Blair, Jennifer, 'The Postmodern Impasse and Guy Vanderhaeghe's *The Englishman's Boy*', in Robert David Stacey, ed., *RE: Reading the Postmodern: Canadian Literature and Criticism after Modernism* (Ottawa: University of Ottawa Press, 2010).

Blazing Saddles, dir. Mel Brooks, perf. Cleavon Little, Harvey Korman, Gene Wilder, Warner Bros/Crossbow Productions, 1974.

Bliss, Carolyn, 'Peter Carey', *A Companion to Australian Literature Since 1900*, ed. Nicolas Birns and Rebecca McNeer (New York: Camden House, 2007), 281–92.

Boal, Augusto, 'Theatre as Discourse', in Michael Huxley and Noel Witts, eds, *The Twentieth-Century Performance Reader* (London: Routledge, 1996), 85–98.

Boddy, Michael, and Robert Ellis, *The Legend of King O'Malley*, 1970 (Sydney: Angus & Robertson, 1974).

Boire, Gary, 'Inside Out: Prison Theatre from Australia, Canada, and New Zealand', *Australian-Canadian Studies* 8/1 (1990), 21–34.

Bowering, George, 'Given This Body: An interview with Daphne Marlatt', *Open Letter* 4/3 (1979), 32–88.

Brand, Dionne, *In Another Place, Not Here* (Toronto: Alfred A. Knopf, 1996).

Brecht, Bertolt, *Brecht on Theatre: The Development of an Aesthetic*, ed. and trans. John Willett (New York: Hill and Wang, 1964).

Brisbane, Katharine, 'Not Wrong – Just Different' [1971], *Contemporary Australian Drama*, ed. Peter Holloway, 1981 (Sydney: Currency Press, 1987), 91–6.

Brook, Peter, *The Empty Space* [1968] (London: Penguin, 1990).

Brooker, Peter, 'Key Words in Brecht's Theory and Practice of Theatre', in Peter Thomson and Glendyr Sacks, eds, *The Cambridge Companion to Brecht*, Cambridge Companions to Literature Series (Cambridge: Cambridge University Press, 1994).

Brooks, Peter, *The Melodramatic Imagination: Balzac, Henry James, Melodrama, and the Mode of Excess* (New Haven, CT: Yale University Press, 1976).

Brown, Ruth, 'From Keneally to Wertenbaker: Sanitizing the System', in Ian Duffield and James Bradley, eds, *Representing convicts: new perspectives on convict forced labour migration* (London and Washington: Leicester University Press, 1997).

Bruner, Jerome, *Making Stories: Law, Literature, Life* (Boston: Harvard University Press, 2002).

Budick, Sanford, and Wolfgang Iser, eds, 'Introduction', in *Languages of the Unsayable: The Play of Negativity in Literature and Literary Theory* (New York: Columbia University Press, 1989), xi–xxi.

Burke, Peter, 'Performing History: The Importance of Occasions', *Rethinking History: The Journal of Theory and Practice* 9/1 (2003), 35–52.

Burnside, John, 'Authenticity rises to the surface in a masterpiece', Books, *The Times*, London, 5 June 2002, 15.

Butler, Judith, *Excitable Speech: A Politics of the Performative* (New York: Routledge, 1997).

——, *Gender Trouble; feminism and the subversion of identity* (New York: Routledge, 1990).

Calder, Alison, 'Unsettling the West: Nation and Genre in Guy Vanderhaeghe's *The Englishman's Boy*', *Studies in Canadian Literature* 25/2 (2000), 96–107.

Calendar, dir. Atom Egoyan, perf. Arsinée Khanjian and Ashot Adamyan, New York: Alliance Atlantis, 2000.

Campbell, Maria, *Halfbreed* (Toronto: McClelland & Stewart, 1973).

——, 'Interview', in Harmut Lutz, ed. and comp., *Contemporary Challenges: Conversations with Canadian Native Writers* (Saskatoon: Fifth House Publishing, 1991), 48–56.

Campbell, Maria, and Linda Griffiths, *The Book of Jessica: A Theatrical Transformation* (Toronto: The Coach House Press, 1989).

Cannon, Michael, *Australia, Spirit of a Nation: A Bicentenary Album* (South Yarra, Victoria: Currey O'Neil, 1985).

Carey, Peter, 'American Dreams', in *Collected Stories* (London: Faber, 1995), 171–82.

——, *Amnesia* (Camberwell, Victoria: Hamish Hamilton, 2012).

——, *Bliss* (St Lucia, Queensland: University of Queensland Press, 1981).

——, *The Fat Man in History* (St Lucia: University of Queensland Press, 1974).

——, *His Illegal Self* (Milson's Point, NSW: Random, 2008).

——, *Illywhacker* (St Lucia: Queensland University Press, 1985).

——, *My Life as a Fake* (Milson's Point, NSW: Random House, 2003).

——, *Oscar and Lucinda* (St Lucia: Queensland University Press, 1988).

——, *Parrot and Olivier in America* (Camberwell, Victoria: Hamish Hamilton, 2009).

——, *The Tax Inspector* (St Lucia: University of Queensland Press, 1991).

——, *Theft* (Milson's Point, NSW: Random, 2005).

——, *True History of the Kelly Gang* (St Lucia: Queensland University Press, 2001).

——, *The Unusual Life of Tristan Smith* (St Lucia: University of Queensland Press, 1994).

——, *Wrong About Japan: A Father's Journey with his Son* (London: Vintage, 2004).

Carroll, Dennis, 'Introduction', *Australian Contemporary Drama*, ed. Dennis Carroll [1985] (Sydney: Currency Press, 1995).

Carter, Paul, *The Road to Botany Bay: An Essay in Spatial History* 1987 (New York: Knopf, 1988).

Case, Sue-Ellen, *Feminism and Theatre* (Basingstoke: Macmillan, 1986).

Chatterjee, Partha, 'Whose Imagined Community?', in *The Nation and Its Fragments: Colonial and Postcolonial Histories* (New Jersey: Princeton University Press, 1993), 3–13.

Cixous, Hélène, 'The Laugh of the Medusa', *Signs* 1/4 (1976), 245–64.

Clark, Alex, 'In the hands of madmen', Review of *Gould's Book of Fish*, *The Guardian*, 1 June 2002 <https://www.theguardian.com/books/2002/jun/01/featuresreviews.guardianreview23> accessed 8 April 2008.

Clark, Manning, *A History of Australia* (Carlton, Victoria: Melbourne University Press, 1963).

Clemens, Samuel L. (a.k.a. Mark Twain), *Following the Equator: A Journey around the World* [1897] (New York: AMS Press, 1971).

Conlogue, Ray, 'Another Triumph for Highway', *Globe and Mail*, 10 February 1989, A-18.

Craven, Peter, 'Something Fishy Going On', in Angela Bennie, ed., *Crème de la Phlegm: Unforgettable Australian Reviews* (Carlton: Miegunyah Press, 2006), 382–5.

Culleton, Beatrice, *In Search of April Raintree* (Winnipeg: Pemmican, 1984).

Curran, Beverly, 'In Her Element: Daphne Marlatt, the Lesbian Body, and the Environment', *Ecopoetry: A Critical Introduction*, ed. J. Scott Bryson and John Elder (Salt Lake City: University of Utah Press, 2002), 195–206.

——, 'Reading Us into the Page Ahead: Translation as a Narrative Strategy in Daphne Marlatt's *Ana Historic* and Nicole Brossard's *Le Désert mauve*', in *Reconstructing Cultural Memory: Translation, Scripts, Literacy*, ed. Lieven D'Hulst and John Milton (Amsterdam: Rodopi, 2000), 165–78.

Dallenbach, Lucien, *Recit specularie: essai sur la mise en abyme (The Mirror in the Text)*, trans. Jeremy Whiteley with Emma Hughes (Cambridge: Polity in association with Blackwell, 1989).

Daly, Mary, *Beyond God the Father: Toward a Philosophy of Woman's Liberation* (Boston: Beacon, 1979).

Damm, Kateri, 'Says Who: Colonialism, Identity and Defining Indigenous Literature', in *Looking at the Words of Our People: First Nations Analysis of Literature* (Penticton: Theytus Books, 1993), 9–25.

Dance Me Outside, dir. Bruce McDonald, perf. Ryan Black, Adam Beach, Lisa LaCroix, Michael Greyeyes, Kevin Hicks, Jennifer Podemski, Sandrine Holt, Herbie Barnes, Odeon Films, 1995 [DVD], Ardustry Home Entertainment, 1996.

Dances with Wolves, dir. Kevin Costner, perf. Kevin Costner, Mary McDonnell, Tig Productions/Orion Film, 1990.

'Daphne Marlatt', *The Canadian Encyclopedia* <http://www.thecanadianencyclopedia.com/en/article/daphne-marlatt/> accessed 10 October 2016.

Dash, Michael, 'In Search of the Lost Body: Redefining the Subject in Caribbean Literature', *Kunapipi* 11/1 (1989), 17–26.

Deleuze, Gilles, *Cinema 2: The Time-Image*, trans. Hugh Tomlinson and Robert Galeta [1985] (London: Athlone Press, 1989).

Deleuze, Gilles, and Félix Guattari, *A Thousand Plateaus: Capitalism and Schizophrenia*, trans. Brian Massumi [1980] (Minneapolis: Minnesota University Press, 1987).

Dening, Greg, *History's Anthropology* (Lanham, MD: University Press of America, 1988).

——, *Performances* (Melbourne: Melbourne University Press, 1996).

Dubois, Dominique, 'Wilson Harris's "Infinite Rehearsal" or the Imaginative Reconstruction of History', *Commonwealth* (Dijon) 21/1 (Autumn 1998), 37–45.

Dumont, Marilyn, 'Popular Images of Nativeness', in *Looking at the Words of Our People: First Nations Analysis of Literature* (Penticton: Theytus Books, 1993), 45–50.

Dunlop, Rishma, 'Archives of Desire: Rewriting Maternal History in Daphne Marlatt's *Ana Historic*', *Journal of the Association for Research on Mothering* 4/2 (Autumn/ Winter 2002), 65–72.

Englishman's Boy, The, dir. John N. Smith, perf. Nicholas Campbell, Bob Hoskins, R. H. Thomson, Mind's Eye Entertainment/CBC, 2008.

Evans, David H., 'True West and Lying Marks: *The Englishman's Boy*, Blood Meridian, and the Paradox of the Revisionist Western', *Texas Studies in Literature and Language* 55/4 (Winter 2003), 406–33.

Fanon, Frantz, *Black Skin, White Masks*, trans. Charles Lam Markmann (London: Paladin Press, 1970).

——, *The Wretched of the Earth*, pref. Jean-Paul Sartre, trans. Constance Farrington (Harmondsworth, England: Penguin Books, 1967).

Farquhar, George, *The Recruiting Officer*, ed. Peter Dixon (Manchester, UK: Manchester University Press, 1986).

Feros, Kate, 'The Picaresque as Australian Political Satire: Peter Carey's *The Unusual Life of Tristan Smith*', in unpublished conference paper from 42nd APSA conference at Australian National University, 3–6 October 2000 <http://www. apsa2000.anu.edu.au/confpapers/feros.rtf> accessed 20 January 2006.

Finney, Brian, 'Samuel Beckett's Postmodern Fictions', in *The Columbia History of the British Novel*, ed. John Richetti (New York: Columbia University Press, 1994), 842–66.

Flanagan, Richard, 'Does Tasmania have a Future?', *Island* 72–3 (Spring/Summer 1997), 134–58.

——, *Gould's Book of Fish: A Novel in Twelve Fish* [2001] (Sydney: Picador Pan Macmillan Australia, 2002).

——, 'Out of Control: The Tragedy of Tasmania's forests', *The Monthly*, May 2007 <https://www.themonthly.com.au/issue/2007/may/1348543148/richard-flan agan/out-control> accessed 20 January 2017.

——, *The Narrow Road to the Deep North* (North Sydney, NSW: Random House Australia, 2013).

——, 'The Selling Out of Tasmania', in Opinions in *The Age*, 22 July 2004 <http:// www.theage.com.au/articles/2004/07/21/1090089215626.html> accessed 18 October 2007.

——, *The Sound of One Hand Clapping* (Sydney: Macmillan, 1997).

——, 'The Stars and the Mountains', *Island* 63 (Winter 1995), 38–41.

——, *Wanting* (North Sydney, NSW: Knopf, 2008).

Fletcher, M. D., 'Australian Political Identity: Aboriginal and Otherwise. Carey/ Malouf/Watson', in unpublished conference paper from 42nd APSA conference at Australian National University, 3–6 October 2000 <http://www.apsa2000. anu.edu.au/confpapers/fletcher.rtf> accessed 20 January 2006.

Foucault, Michel, *Language, Counter-Memory, Practice: Selected Essays and Interviews. 1963–1972*, ed. Donald F. Bouchard, trans. Donald F. Bouchard and Sherry Simon (Oxford: Blackwell Publishers, 1977).

——, 'Nietzsche, Genealogy, History', in Donald F. Bouchard, ed., *Language, Counter-Memory, Practice* (Ithaca, NY: Cornell University Press, 1977), 154.

——, *Surveiller et punir* (Paris: Gallimard, 1975).

Frank, Marcie, 'At the Intersections of Mode, Genre, and Media: A Dossier of Essays on Melodrama', *Criticism* 55/4 (Autumn 2013), 535–45.

Gaile, Andreas, *Fabulating Beauty: Perspectives on the Fiction of Peter Carey*, Cross/ Culture 78 (Amsterdam: Rodopi, 2005).

Gallop, Jane, *Thinking Through the Body* (New York: Columbia University Press, 1988).

Gatherings: The En'owkin Journal of First North American Peoples 1/1, ed. En'owkin Centre (Penticton: Theytus Books, 1990).

Gelder, Ken, and Paul Salzman, *After the Celebration: Australian Fiction 1989–2007* (Carlton: Melbourne University Press, 2007).

Gellner, Ernest, *Thought and Change* (London: Weidenfeld and Nicolson, 1964).

George, D. E. R., 'Quantum theatre – potential theatre: a new paradigm?', *New Theatre Quarterly* 18/5 (1989), 171–9.

Gibson, Ross, 'New Media and Digital Culture', unpublished lecture, *What Lies Beneath Conference*, University of Melbourne, 6 November 2003.

——, 'Palpable History', unpublished lecture, *Re-Writing the Past: Experimental Histories in the Arts* Conference, University of Technology Sydney, 28 July 2006.

——, 'Palpable History', *Cultural Studies Review* 14/1 (March 2008), 179–86.

Gikandi, Simon, *Maps of Englishness: Writing Identity in the Culture of Colonialism* (New York: Columbia University Press, 1996).

Gilbert, Helen, 'De-Scribing Orality: Performance and the Recuperation of Voice', in Alan Lawson and Chris Tiffin, eds, *De-Scribing Empire: Post-Colonialism and Textuality* (London: Routledge, 1994), 98–111.

Gilbert, Helen, and Joanne Tompkins, *Post-Colonial Drama: Theory, Practice, Politics* (London: Routledge, 1996).

Gittings, Christopher, *Canadian National Cinema: Ideology, Difference and Representation* (London: Routledge, 2002).

Godard, Barbara, '"Body I": Daphne Marlatt's Feminist Poetics', *The American Review of Canadian Studies* 15/4 (1985), 481–96.

——, 'Listening for the Silence: Native Women's Traditional Narratives', *The Native in Literature: Canadian and Comparative Contexts*, ed. Thomas L. King, Cheryl Calver and Helen Hoy (Toronto: ECW Press, 1987), 133–58.

Goldie, Terry, *Fear and Temptation: The Image of the Indigene in Canadian, Australian and New Zealand Literatures* (Kingston: McGill-Queen's University Press, 1989).

——, 'Indigenous Stages: The indigene in Canadian, New Zealand and Australian drama', in *The Native in Literature*, ed. Thomas King, Cheryl Calver and Helen Hoy (Toronto: ECW Press, 1987), 5–20.

Goldring, Philip, 'Cypress Hills Massacre', in *Canadian Encyclopedia*, Historica Dominica Institute <http://www.thecanadianencyclopedia.ca/en/article/cypress-hills-massacre-feature> accessed 19 August 2013.

Gould, William Buelow, *Gould's Sketchbook of Fishes*, Online, Tasmania Heritage Collection, Tasmania Images Database <http://images.statelibrary.tas.gov.au> accessed on 31 October 2006.

Granatstein, J. L., *Who Killed Canadian History?* (Toronto: HarperCollins Publishers, 1998).

Griffiths, Gareth, 'The Myth of Authenticity', in *The Post-Colonial Studies Reader*, ed. Bill Ashcroft, Gareth Griffiths and Helen Tiffin (London: Routledge, 1995), 237–42.

Griffiths, Tom, *Hunters and Collectors: The Antiquarian Imagination in Australia* (Cambridge: Cambridge University Press, 1996).

Grisé, C. Annette, '"A Bedtime Story for You, Ina": Resisting Amnesia of the Maternal in Daphne Marlatt's *Ana Historic*', *Tessera* 15 (Winter 1993), 90–8.

Guattari, Pierre-Félix, *The Guattari Reader*, ed. Gary Genosko (Oxford: Blackwell Publishers Ltd, 1996).

Harasym, Sarah, 'EACH MOVE MADE HERE (me) MOVES THERE (you)', *boundary 2* 18/1 (1991), 104–26.

Harris, Wilson, *Ascent to Omai* (London: Faber and Faber, 1970).

——, *The Eye of the Scarecrow* (London: Faber and Faber, 1965).

——, *Fossil and Psyche* (Austin: University of Texas, 1974).

——, *The Four Banks of the River of Space*, in *The Carnival Trilogy* (London: Faber and Faber, 1993).

——, *The Infinite Rehearsal* (London: Faber and Faber, 1987).

——, *The Infinite Rehearsal*, in *The Carnival Trilogy* (London: Faber and Faber, 1993), 169–260.

——, *The Palace of the Peacock* (London: Faber and Faber, 1960).

——, *The Radical Imagination: Lectures and Talks*, ed. Alan Riach and Mark Williams, Université de Liège: L³ (Liege, 1992), 114.

——, *The Tree of the Sun* (London: Faber and Faber, 1978).

Hassall, Anthony J., *Dancing on Hot Macadam: Peter Carey's Fiction* (St Lucia: University of Queensland Press, 1994).

Heiland, Donna, 'History and Sublimity in Keneally's *The Playmaker*', in *Australian & New Zealand Studies in Canada* 11 (June 1994), 12–22.

Hewett, Dorothy, *The Chapel Perilous*, 1971 (Sydney: Currency Press, 1972).

——, 'Shirts, Prams, and Tomato Sauce: The All-Australian Theatre' [1976], *Contemporary Australian Drama*, ed. Peter Holloway [1981] (Sydney: Currency Press, 1987), 108–19.

Hibberd, Jack, '*A Toast to Melba*', in *Three Popular Plays* (Collingwood, Victoria: Outback Press, 1976).

Highway, Tomson, *Caribou Song*, illustr. Brian Deines (Toronto: HarperCollins, 2001).

——, *Comparing Mythologies* (Ottawa: University of Ottawa Press, 2003).

——, *Dry Lips Oughta Move to Kapuskasing* (Saskatoon: Fifth House, 1989).

——, *From Oral to Written: A Celebration of Native Canadian Literature, 1980–2010* (Vancouver: Talonbooks, 2017).

——, 'An Interview with Tomson Highway', by Barbra Nahwegahbow, *A Voice for First Nations* 1/4 (1991), 7–17.

——, *Kiss of the Fur Queen* (Toronto: Doubleday/Random House, 1999).

——, *The Rez Sisters* (Saskatoon: Fifth House, 1988).

Hinz, Evelyn, 'Mimesis: The Dramatic Lineage of Auto/Biography', in *Essays on Life Writing: From Genre to Critical Practice*, ed. Marlene Kadar (Toronto: University of Toronto Press, 1992), 195–212.

Hornby, Richard, *Drama, Metadrama, and Perception* (Cranbury, NJ: Associated University Press, 1986).

Huggan, Graham, *Peter Carey* (Oxford: Oxford University Press, 1996).

——, *The Post-Colonial Exotic: Marketing the Margins* (London: Routledge, 2001).

Hughes, Robert., *The Fatal Shore: A History of the Transportation of Convicts to Australia, 1787–1868* (London: Collins Harvill, 1987).

Hunt, Linda, 'Convict sketchbook makes UNESCO world register', *ABC News. Australian Broadcasting Corporation*, 1 April 2011 <http://www.abc.net.au/news/2011-04-01/convict-sketchbook-makes-unesco-world-register/2631788> accessed 22 January 2017.

Hutcheon, Linda, 'Canadian Historiographic Metafiction', *Essays on Canadian Writing* 30 (1984), 228–38.

——, *The Canadian Postmodern: A Study of Contemporary English-Canadian Fiction* (Toronto: Oxford University Press, 1988).

——, *Narcissistic Narrative: The Metafictional Paradox* (London: Methuen, 1980).

——, *The Politics of Postmodernism* (London: Routledge, 1989).

'Impersonate', *Oxford English Dictionary*, 2nd edn (1989) <http://www.oed.com. ez.library.latrobe.edu.au/view/Entry/92330?rskey=eXx7wa&result=2&isAdv anced=false#eid> accessed 3 July 2012.

Intolerance, dir. D. W. Griffith, perf. Lillian Gish, Mae Marsh, Robert Harron, 1916, Republic Pictures Home Video, 1991.

Irigarary, Luce, *Ce sexe qui n'en est pas un (This Sex Which Is Not One)*, trans. Catherine Porter and Carolyn Burke [1977] (Ithaca, NY: Cornell University Press, 1985).

Iser, Wolfgang, *The Fictive and the Imaginary: Charting Literary Anthropology* (Baltimore, MD: Johns Hopkins Press, 1993).

——, 'The Play of the Text', in Sandford Budick and Wolfgang Iser, eds, *Languages of the Unsayable: The Play of Negativity in Literature and Literary Theory* (New York: Columbia University Press, 1989), 325–39.

Jackson-Harper, Renée, 'Forests, Clearings, and the Spaces in Between: Reading Land Claims and the Actuality of Context in *Ana Historic*', *Studies in Canadian Literature/Etudes en Littérature Canadienne* 40/2 (2015), 128–42.

Jacobs, Melville, *The Content and Style of an Oral Literature: Clackamas Chinook Myths and Tales* (Chicago: University of Chicago Press, 1959).

Jakobson, Roman, 'On Linguistic Aspects of Translation', *Selected Writings: Word and Language* 2 (The Hague: Mouton, 1971), 260–6.

Jameson, Frederic, 'Postmodernism and Consumer Society', in E. Ann Kaplan, ed., *Postmodernism and its Discontents: Theories and Practices* (London: Verso, 1988), 13–29.

Janes, Daniela, 'Truth and History: Representing the Aura in *The Englishman's Boy*', *Studies in Canadian Literature* 27/1 (2002), 88–104.

Jarman, Robert, 'At the Edge', in *Island Magazine* 68 (1996 Spring), 54–61.

Johnson, Paulina, 'The Nêhiyawak Nation through Âcimowina: Experiencing Plains Cree Knowledge through Oral Narratives', *Totem: The University of Western Ontario Journal of Anthropology* 23/1 (2015), 70–81.

Johnston, Basil H., 'Is That All There Is? Tribal Literature', in *An Anthology of Canadian Native Literature in English*, ed. Daniel David Moses and Terry Goldie [1991] (Toronto: Oxford University Press, 1998).

Jones, Jo, '"Dancing the Old Enlightenment": *Gould's Book of Fish*, the Historical Novel and the Postmodern Sublime', *Journal of the Association for the Study of Australian Literature* (May 2008), 114–29.

Jones, Radhika, 'Peter Carey: The Art of Fiction No. 188', in *The Paris Review* 177 (Summer 2006), 119–47.

Jordan, Robert, *The Convict Theatres of Early Australia 1788–1840* (Sydney: Currency Press, 2002).

Jung, Carl Gustav, *The Archetypes and the Collective Unconscious* [1875–1961]. (Princeton, NJ: Princeton University Press, 1980).

Kane, Paul, 'Post-colonial /Postmodern; Australian Literature and Peter Carey', in *World Literature Today* 67/3 (1993), 519–22.

Kanehsatake: 270 Years of Resistance, dir. Alanis Obaomsawin, perf. Jack Burning, Herbie Barnes, Alanis Obomsawin, Ethel Blondin, 1993, Montreal: National Film Board of Canada.

Kearful, Frank J., 'Spanish Rogues and English Foundlings: On the Disintegration of Picaresque', in *Genre* 4 (1971), 376–91.

Kellaway, Kate, 'Hook, Line and thinker', *The Guardian*, 9 June 2002 <https://www.theguardian.com/books/2002/jun/09/fiction.australia> accessed 21 January 2017.

Kelly, Veronica, 'Melodrama, an Australian pantomime, and the theatrical constructions of colonial history', *Journal of Australian Studies* 17/38 (1993), 51–61.

Keneally, Thomas, *Bring Larks and Heroes* (London: Cassell, 1967).

——, *The Chant of Jimmie Blacksmith* (Sydney: Angus and Robertson, 1972).

——, *The Playmaker* (London: Hodder and Stoughton, 1987).

——, *Schindler's Ark* (London: Sceptre, 1986).

King, Thomas, ed., *All My Relations: An Anthology of Contemporary Canadian Native Writing* (Toronto: McClelland & Stewart, 1990).

——, 'Godzilla vs Post-colonial', in *World Literature Written in English* 30/2 (1990), 10–16.

King, Thomas, Cheryl Calver and Helen Hoy, eds, *The Native in Literature* (Oakville, ON: ECW Press, 1984).

Kossew, Sue, 'History and place: An interview with Daphne Marlatt', *Canadian Literature* 178 (Autumn 2003), 49–56.

Krasner, David, ed., *Method Acting Reconsidered: Theory, Practice, Future* (New York: St Martin's, 2000).

Kristeva, Julia, *Revolution in Poetic Language*, trans. Margaret Waller (New York: Columbia University Press, 1984).

Kureishi, Hanif, *The Buddha of Suburbia* (New York: Penguin Books, 1991).

Labaune-Demeule, Florence, 'Anita Nair's Aesthetics of Hybridity; *Mistress* as Narrative Kathakali', in *Hybridity: Forms and Figures in Literature and the Visual Arts*, ed. Vanessa Guignery, Catherine Pesso-Miquel and Francois Specq (Newcastle: Cambridge Scholars Publishing, 2011), 223–36.

Landy, Marcia, *Cinematic Uses of the Past* (Minneapolis: University of Minnesota Press, 1996).

Lawson, Alan, 'A Cultural Paradigm for the Second World', *Australian-Canadian Studies* 9/1–2 (1991), 67–78.

Lever, Sue, 'Heroes, Certainly: Review of *The Narrow Road to the Deep North*' by Richard Flanagan, in *Sydney Review of Books* <http://sydneyreviewofbooks. com/heroes-certainly/> accessed 26 November 2013.

Lewis, Krishna Ray, 'The Infinite Rehearsal and Pastoral Revision', in *Callaloo* 18/1 (1995), 83–92.

Litvak, Joseph, *Caught in the Act: Theatricality in the Nineteenth-Century English Novel* (Oakland: University of California Press, 1992).

Loiperdinger, Martin, 'Lumière's *Arrival of the Train*: Cinema's Founding Myth', *The Moving Image* 4/1 (Spring 2004), 89–118.

Long, William Stuart, aka Vivian Stuart, *Australians Series*, 12 vols (New York: Dell, 1979–90).

Lusty, Terry, 'Dance Me Outside Maintains Stereotypes', in *Windspeaker* (April 1995), 18.

Lutz, Hartmut, 'Canadian Multicultural Literatures', in Klaus Martens, ed., *The Canadian Alternative* (Würzburg: Konigshausen & Neumann, 2003).

——, ed., *Contemporary Challenges: Conversations with Canadian Native Writers* (Saskatoon: Fifth House Publishing, 1991).

McCallum, John, 'The Development of a Sense of History in Contemporary Australian Drama' [1981], *Contemporary Australian Drama*, ed. Peter Holloway (Sydney: Currency Press, 1987), 148–60.

MacCannell, Dean, *The Tourist: A New Theory of the Leisure Class* [1976] (New York: Schocken Books, 1989).

MacDonald, Larry, 'I Looked for It and There It Was – Gone: History in Postmodern Criticism', *Essays on Canadian Writing* 56 (Autumn 1995), 37–50.

MacFarlane, Robert, 'Con Fishing', in *Observer*, 26 May 2002 <http://books.guardian. co.uk/reviews/generalfiction/0,6121,722129,00.html> accessed 10 March 2014.

McGillick, Paul, *Jack Hibberd: Australian Playwright Series* (Amsterdam: Rodopi, 1988).

McKeough, Duncan, 'The Storyteller: Tomson Highway', in *Info Culture Magazine*: Special Coverage <http://www.infoculture.cbc.ca/archives/special_coverage/ special_coverage_tomsonhighway.html> accessed 12 November 2001.

McLeod, Neal, *Cree Narrative Memory: From Treaties to Contemporary Times* (Purich Publishing Limited: Saskatoon, Saskatchewan, 2007).

Maes-Jelinek, Hena, 'Wilson Harris', in *Post-war Literatures in English: A Lexicon of Contemporary Authors*, ed. Hans Bertens, Theo D'haen, Joris Duytschaever, Richard Todd (Alphen aan den Rijn: Samsom and Graningen; Wolters-Noordhoff, 1988 et seq.) Loose-leaf <https://orbi.ulg.ac.be/bitstream/2268/201008/1/ Maes_Wilson-Harris_Post-War-Literatures-in-English_1997.pdf > accessed 19 February 2017.

Maes-Jelinek, Hena, and Bénédicte Ledent, *Theatre of the Arts: Wilson Harris and the Caribbean* (Amsterdam: Rodopi, 2002).

Magarey, Susan, Sue Rowley and Susan Sheridan, eds, *Debutante Nation: Feminism Contests the 1890s* (St Leonards, NSW: Allen & Unwin, 1993).

Magelssen, Scott, 'Making History in the Second Person: Post-touristic Considerations for Living Historical Interpretation', in *Theatre Journal* 58 (2006), 291–312.

Manuel, George, and Michael Posluns, *The Fourth World: An Indian Reality* (New York: The Free Press, 1974).

Marks, Laura U., *The Skin of the Film: Intercultural Cinema, Embodiment, and the Senses* (Durham: Duke University Press, 2000).

Marlatt, Daphne, *Ana Historic* (Toronto: Coach House Press, 1988).

——, *Frames of a story* (Toronto: Ryerson, 1968).

——, *The Gull: The Steveston Noh Project*, trans. Toyoshi Yoshihara (Vancouver: Talonbooks, 2009).

——, 'In the Month of the Hungry Ghosts', *Capilano Review* 16/17 (1979), 45–95.

——, 'Self-Representation and Fictionalysis', *Collaboration in the Feminine: Writings on Women and Culture from Tessera*, ed. Barbara Godard (Toronto: Second Story, 1994).

——, *Touch to My Tongue and musing with mothertongue* (Edmonton: Longspoon, 1984).

Maron, Jeremy, 'Affective Historiography: Schindler's List, Melodrama and Historical Representation', *Shofar* 27/4 (2009), 66–94.

Marowitz, Charles, *The Other Way: An Alternative Approach to Acting and Directing* (New York: Applause, 1999).

Massumi, Brian, 'The Autonomy of Affect', *Cultural Critique, 31, The Politics of Systems and Environments, Part II* (Autumn 1995), 83–109.

Metherell, Mark, and Tim Dick, 'New citizens face test on 200 questions', *Sydney Morning Herald*, 12 December 2006.

Meyer, Lisa, and Peter Carey, 'An Interview with Peter Carey', in *Chicago Review* 43/2 (Spring 1997), 76–89.

Mojika, Monique, *Princess Pocahontas and the Blue Spots: Two plays* (Toronto: Women's Press, 1991).

Moses, Daniel David, and Terry Goldie, *An Anthology of Canadian Native Literature in English* [1991] (Toronto: Oxford University Press, 1998).

Moss, John, 'The Opposite of prayer: An Introduction to Tomson Highway', Introduction, in Tomson Highway, *Comparing Mythologies*, Charles R. Bronfman Lecture in Canadian Studies (Ottawa: University of Ottawa Press, 2002).

Muecke, Stephen, 'Discourse, history, fiction: language and Aboriginal history', *Australian Journal of Cultural Studies* 1/1 (1983), 71–80.

Musgrave, David, *Glissando: A Melodrama* (Collingwood: Sleepers Press, 2010).

——, *Grotesque Anatomies: Menippean Satire since the Renaissance* (Cambridge: Cambridge Scholars Publishers, 2014).

Nadjiwon, Roland, 'Harvesting the Colonies', *ASAIL* Notes 13/3 (1996), 7–9 <http://www.richmond.edu.faculty/ASAIL/newsletter/13,3.html> accessed 13 July 2005.

Naipaul, V. S., *The Engima of Arrival: A novel in five sections* (London: Viking, 1987).

Narogin, Mudrooroo, *Writing from the Fringe: A Study of Modern Aboriginal Literature* (Melbourne: Hyland House, 1990).

Nora, Pierre, 'Memory and History: Les Lieux de Memoire', *Representations* 26 (Spring 1989), 9.

Nosferatu, dir. F. W. Murnau, perf. Max Schreck, Greta Schröder, Ruth Landshoff, Jofa-Atelier Berlin-Johannisthal, 1922.

Nothof, Anne, 'Cultural Collision and Magical Transformation: The Plays of Tomson Highway', in *Studies in Canadian Literature* 20/2 (1995), 34–43.

Nowra, Louis, *Cosi* (Sydney: Currency Press, 1992).

Oliver, Kelly, *Julia Kristeva: The Johns Hopkins Guide to Literary Theory and Criticism*, ed. Michael Grodin and Martin Kreiswirth (Baltimore, MD: Johns Hopkins University Press, 1997), 1–4.

Olson, Charles, 'Human Universe', in *The Poetics of the New American Poetry*, ed. Donald Allen and Warren Tallman (New York: Grove, 1973), 161–74.

Ondaatje, Michael, *The Collected Works of Billy the Kid* (Concord, ON: Anansi Press), 1970.

O'Reilly, Nathanael, 'Mythology, History, and Truth: Teaching Peter Carey's *True History of the Kelly Gang*', *Antipodes* 29/1 (June 2015), 71–81.

——, 'The Voice of the Teller: A Conversation with Peter Carey', *Antipodes* (December 2002), 164–7.

O'Sullivan, E. W., 'Coo-ee; or, Wild Days in the Bush' (Brisbane: University of Queensland, 1906), microfilm.

Pearson, Bill, 'Witi Ihimera and Patricia Grace', in *Critical Essays on the New Zealand Short Story*, ed. Cherry Hankin (Auckland: Heinemann, 1982).

Petrone, Penny, *Native Literature in Canada: From the Oral Tradition to the Present* (Toronto: Oxford University Press, 1990).

Pierce, Peter, *Australian Melodramas: Thomas Keneally's Fiction* (St Lucia: University of Queensland Press, 1995).

Pollock, Della, 'Performing Writing', in Peggy Phelan and Jill Lane, eds, *The Ends of Performance* (New York: New York University Press, 1998), 73–103.

Quartermaine, Peter, *Thomas Keneally: 'The Bookmaker: The Playmaker'*, Modern Fiction Series (London: Hodder & Stoughton, 1991).

Reed, Helen H., *Cervantes: Bulletin of the Cervantes Society of America* 7/2 (1987), 71–84.

Richon, Olivier, 'Representation, the Despot and the Harem', in *The Block Reader in Visual Culture* [1985] (London: Routledge, 1996).

Robertson, Patricia, 'Deadwood North: CBC TV shoots Western mini-series', in *The Globe and Mail*, 21 August 2006 <http://www.theglobeandmail.com/arts/deadwood-north/article1102337/> accessed 23 August 2007.

Robinson, Harry, *Write It On Your Heart: The Epic World of an Okanagan Storyteller*, comp. and ed. Wendy Wickwire (Vancouver: Talonbooks/Theytus, 1989).

Rogers, Robert, *Ponteach: A Tragedy* [1766] (New York: Bart Franklin, 1971).

Rokem, Freddie, *Performing History: Theatrical Representations of the Past in Contemporary Theatre* (Iowa City: University of Iowa Press, 2000).

Rushdie, Salman, *Midnight's Children* [1981] (Toronto: Vintage, 1987).

——, *The Satanic Verses* (New York: Viking, 1989).

Ryan, Sue, 'Metafiction in *Illywhacker*: Peter Carey's Renovated Picaresque Novel', in *Commonwealth: Essays and Studies* 14/1 (Autumn 1991), 33–40.

Ryga, George, *The Ecstasy of Rita Joe* (Toronto: New Press, 1971).

Salzman, Paul, 'Narrative Contexts for Bacon's New Atlantis', in Bronwen Price, ed., *Francis Bacon's New Atlantis* (New York: Manchester University Press, 2002).

Sanders, Scott Russell, *Audubon Reader: The Best Writing of John James Audubon* (Bloomington: Indiana University Press, 1986).

Sarkar, Parama, 'Performing Narrative: The Motif of Performance in Arundhati Roy's *The God of Small Things*', *South Asian Review* 28/2 (2007), 217–36.

Sears, Djanet, *Afrika Solo* (Toronto: Sister Vision, 1990).

Seiler, Tamara Palmer, 'Multi-vocality and national literature: Toward a post-colonial and multicultural aesthetic', *Journal of Canadian Studies* 31/3 (Autumn 1996), 148–65.

Shainberg, Lawrence, 'Exorcising Beckett', in *Playwrights at Work: The Paris Review* [1987], intro. John Lahr (New York: The Modern Library, 2000), 50–86.

Shakespeare, William, *Henry V*, ed. T. W. Craik (London: Routledge, 1995).

——, *A Midsummer Night's Dream*, ed. Roma Gill (Oxford: Oxford University Press, 1981).

Shaw, George, ed., *1988 and All That: New Views of Australia's Past* (St Lucia: University of Queensland Press, 1988).

——, 'Bicentennial Writing: Revealing Ash in the Australian Soul', in Introduction, in George Shaw, ed., *1988 and All That: New Views of Australia's Past* (St Lucia: University of Queensland Press, 1988), 1–15.

Shipway, Jesse, 'Wishing for modernity: temporality and desire in *Gould's Book of Fish*', *Australian Literary Studies* 21/11 (May 2003), 43–53.

Singer, Ben, *Melodrama and Modernity: Early Sensational Cinema and Its Contexts, Film and Culture* (New York: Columbia University Press, 2001).

Slipperjack, Ruby, *Honour the Sun* (Winnipeg: Pemmican Publications, 1987).

Smethurst, E. William, Jr, 'Imaginative reflections on art, nature and corruption', in *Chicago Tribune*, 28 April 2002 <http://articles.chicagotribune.com/2002-04 28/entertainment/0204270054_1_natural-world-richard-flanagan-con-man> accessed 2 January 2017.

Snodgrass, Mary Ellen, *Peter Carey: A Literary Companion* (Jefferson, NC: McFarland & Company, 2010).

Söderlind, Sylvia, 'The Contest of Marginalities', *Essays on Canadian Writing* 56 (Autumn 1995), 96–109.

Stanislavski, Constantin, *An Actor Prepares*, ed. and trans. Elizabeth Reynolds Hapgood [1936] (London: Methuen Drama, 1986).

Stanislavskiy, Konstantin, *My Life in Art*, trans. G. Ivanov-Mumjiev [1924] (Moscow: Foreign Languages Publishing, 1970).

States, Bert O., *Great Reckonings in Little Rooms: On the Phenomenology of Theater* (Berkeley: University of California Press, 1985).

Stephenson, M. A., and Suri Ratnapala, *Mabo: A Judicial Revolution. Aboriginal Land Rights Decision and Its Impact on Australian Law* (St Lucia: University of Queensland Press, 1993).

Stroppel, Elizabeth C., 'Reconciling the Past and the Present: Feminist Perspectives on the Method in the Classroom and on the Stage', in David Krasner, ed., *Method Acting Reconsidered: Theory, Practice, Future* (New York: St Martin's, 2000), 111–23.

Sturgess, Charlotte, ed., *Politics and Poetics of Passage in Canadian and Australian Culture and Fiction* (Nantes: University de Nantes CRINI/CEC, 2006).

Suleri, Sara, *The Rhetoric of English India* (Chicago: University Chicago Press, 1992).

Surname Viet, Surname Nam, dir. Trinh T. Minh-ha, 1989, Vancouver, B. C., Idera Films.

Tedlock, Dennis, 'On the Translation of Style in Oral Narrative', in *The Journal of American Folklore* 84/331 (January–March 1971), 114–33.

Ten Commandments, The, dir. Cecil B. DeMille, perf. Theodore Roberts, Charles de Rochefort, Estelle Taylor, Famous Players/Lasky Corporation, 1923.

'Theatricality and Performance in Victorian Literature and Culture', ed. Beth Palmer, *Victorian Network* 3/2 (2011).

Thein, Madeleine, *Certainty* (New York: Little Brown and Company, 2007).

Theobald, Elizabeth, and Drew Hayden Taylor, 'Storytelling to stage: The growth of native theatre in Canada', in *The Drama Review* 41/3 (Autumn 1997), 140–53.

Thiong'o, Ngugi Wa, *Writers in Politics* (London: Heinemann Educational Books, 1981).

Thomas, D. M., *The White Hotel* (New York: Viking Press, 1981).

Tiffin, Helen, 'Post-Colonial Literatures and Counter-Discourse', in Bill Ashcroft, Gareth Griffiths and Helen Tiffin, eds, *The Post-Colonial Studies Reader* (London: Routledge, 1995), 95–8.

Tompkins, Joanne, 'Celebrate 1988? Australian Drama in the Bicentennial Year', *Australian & New Zealand Studies in Canada* 11 (June 1994), 103–13.

——, '"Spectacular Resistance": Metatheatre in Post-Colonial Drama', *Modern Drama* 38/1 (1995), 42–51.

——, '"The story of rehearsal never ends": Rehearsal, performance, identity in settler culture drama', *Canadian Literature* 144 (Spring 1995), 142–61.

Tostevin, Lola Lemire, 'Daphne Marlatt: Writing in the Space That Is Her Mother's Face', *Line* 13 (Spring 1989), 32–9.

Tremblay, Michel, *Albertine in Five Times: A play* (Vancouver: Talonbooks, 1986).

Turner, Graeme, *Making it National: Nationalism and Australian Popular Culture* (Sydney, NSW: Allen and Unwin, 1993).

Twain, Mark, *The Adventures of Huckleberry Finn* [1884] (New York: Dover Publications, 1994).

Van Essen, Angela, 'nêhiyawaskiy (Cree Land) and Canada: Location, Language, and Borders in Tomson Highway's *Kiss of the Fur Queen*', in *Canadian Literature* 215 (Winter 2012), 104–18.

Vanderhaeghe, Guy, *The Englishman's Boy* [1997] (London: Anchor/Transworld Publishing, 1998).

——, 'History and Fiction', *Canadian Journal of History* 40/ 3 (2005), 429.

——, 'Writing History vs Writing the Historical Novel', in *Drumlummon Views* (Spring/Summer 2006), 136–47.

Vernon, Denise, 'The Limits of Goodwill: The Values and Dangers of Revisionism in Keneally's "Aboriginal" Novels', in Ashok Bery and Patricia Murray, eds, *Comparing Postcolonial Literatures: Dislocations* (London: Macmillan Press, 2000), 159–76.

Vizenor, Gerald, *Manifest Manners: Postindian Warriors of Survivance* (Lincoln: University of Nebraska Press, 1994), vii.

Wachtel, Eleanor, '"We Really Can Make Ourselves Up": An Interview with Peter Carey', in *Australian and New Zealand Studies in Canada* 9 (1993), 103–5.

Wang, Mei-Chuen, 'Wilderness, the West and the national imaginary in Guy Vanderhaeghe's *The Englishman's Boy*', *British Journal of Canadian Studies* 26/1
(2016), 21–38.

Weir, Zach, 'Set Adrift: Identity and the Postcolonial Present in *Gould's Book of Fish*',
Postcolonial Text 1/2 (2005) <http://postcolonial.org/index.php/pct/article/
view/345/803> accessed 12 November 2016.

Wertenbaker, Timberlake, *Our Country's Good* [1988] (London: Methuen Drama,
The Royal Court Writer's Series, 1991).

Wheeler, Winona, 'Cree Intellectual Traditions in History', in Ute Lische and David
T. McNab, eds, *Walking a Tightrope: Aboriginal People and their Representations*
(Waterloo: Wilfrid Laurier University Press, 2010), 189–213.

White, Hayden, *The Fiction of Narrative: Essays on History, Literature, and Theory,
1957–2007*, ed. Robert Doran (Baltimore, MD: Johns Hopkins University Press,
2010).

——, 'The Historical Event', *differences: a Journal of Feminist Cultural Studies* 19/2
(2008), 9–34.

——, 'The Modernist Event', in Vivian Sobchack, ed., *The Persistence of History:
Cinema, Television and the Modern Event* (New York: Routledge, 1996), 17–38.

Whitlock, Gillian, 'White Diasporas: Joan (and Ana) Make History', *Australian and
New Zealand Studies in Canada* 12 (1994), 90–100.

Whitman, Walt, *Leaves of Grass*, ed. Malcolm Cowley [1855] (New York: Penguin
Books, 1976).

Whitmore, Ashley Rose, 'Reconfigurations of History and Embodying Books in
Gould's Book of Fish', *Postcolonial Text* 7/2 (2012), 1–16.

Wicks, Ulrich, 'The Nature of Picaresque Narrative: A Modal Approach', in *PMLA:
Publication of the Modern Language Association of America* 89/1 (1974), 240–9.

Wiesel, Elie, 'Art and the Holocaust: Trivializing Memory', in *The New York Times*,
11 June 1989, section 2.

Willbanks, Ray, 'Peter Carey', *Speaking Volumes: Australian Writers and their Work*
(Ringwood: Penguin, 1992), 43–57.

Willett, John, ed. and trans., *Brecht on Theatre: The Development of an Aesthetic* by
Bertolt Brecht (London: Methuen, 1964).

Willett, John, and Ralph Manheim, 'Introduction', in *Collected Plays: One*, ed. Bertolt
Brecht, John Willett and Ralph Manheim (London: Methuen, 1970), vii–xvii.

Williamson, Geordie, 'A Spiritual Superiority: Glissando Review', *The Australian*,
Arts, 24 April 2010 <http://www.theaustralian.com.au/arts/books/review-
musgrave-glissando/story-e6frg8nf-1225856027192.> accessed 10 August 2016.

Worthen, W. B., 'Drama, Performativity and Performance', *PMLA: Publication of the
Modern Language Association of America* 113/5 (1998), 1093–107.

Wright, Chris, 'Swimming to Tasmania', The Phoenix.com, 2–9 May 2002 <http://
     www.bostonphoenix.com/boston/news_features/other_stories/multipage/
     documents/02253069.htm> accessed 12 November 2016.
Wyile, Herb, 'Dances With Wolfers: Choreographing History', in *The Englishman's
     Boy, Essays on Canadian Writing* 76 (Spring 1999), 23–52.
——, *Speaking in the Past Tense: Canadian Novelists on Writing Historical Fiction*
     (Waterloo: Wilfrid Laurier University Press, 2007).
Young-Ing, Greg, 'Aboriginal Peoples' Estrangement: Marginalization in the Pub-
     lishing Industry', in *Looking at the Words of Our People: First Nations Analysis
     of Literature* (Penticton: Theytus Books, 1993), 177–88.
Zarrilli, Phillip B., 'kathakali', in *The Oxford Companion to Theatre and Performance*,
     ed. Dennis Kelly (Oxford: Oxford University Press, 2010).
Zwicker, Heather, 'Daphne Marlatt's *Ana Historic*: Queering the Postcolonial Nation',
     ARIEL 30/2 (1999), 161–75.

Index

CULTURAL HISTORY AND LITERARY IMAGINATION

EDITED BY CHRISTIAN J. EMDEN & DAVID MIDGLEY

EDITORIAL BOARD: RODRIGO CACHO, SARAH COLVIN, KENNETH LOISELLE AND HEATHER WEBB

This series promotes critical inquiry into the relationship between the literary imagination and its cultural, intellectual or political contexts. The series encourages the investigation of the role of the literary imagination in cultural history and the interpretation of cultural history through literature, visual culture and the performing arts.

Contributions of a comparative or interdisciplinary nature are particularly welcome. Individual volumes might, for example, be concerned with any of the following:

- The mediation of cultural and historical memory,

- The material conditions of particular cultural manifestations,

- The construction of cultural and political meaning,

- Intellectual culture and the impact of scientific thought,

- The methodology of cultural inquiry,

- Intermediality,

- Intercultural relations and practices.

Acceptance is subject to advice from our editorial board, and all proposals and manuscripts undergo a rigorous peer review assessment prior to publication. The usual language of publication is English, but proposals in the other languages shown below will also be considered.

For French studies, contact Kenneth Loiselle <kloisell@trinity.edu>

For German studies, contact Sarah Colvin <sjc269@cam.ac.uk>

For Hispanic studies, contact Rodrigo Cacho <rgc27@cam.ac.uk>

For Italian studies, contact Heather Webb <hmw53@cam.ac.uk>

Vol. 1   Christian Emden & David Midgley (eds): Cultural Memory and Historical Consciousness in the German-Speaking World Since 1500. Papers from the Conference 'The Fragile Tradition', Cambridge 2002. Vol. 1.
316 pp., 2004. ISBN 3-03910-160-9 / US-ISBN 0-8204-6970-X

Vol. 2   Christian Emden & David Midgley (eds): German Literature, History and the Nation. Papers from the Conference 'The Fragile Tradition', Cambridge 2002. Vol. 2.
393 pp., 2004. ISBN 3-03910-169-2 / US-ISBN 0-8204-6979-3

Vol. 3   Christian Emden & David Midgley (eds): Science, Technology and the German Cultural Imagination. Papers from the Conference 'The Fragile Tradition', Cambridge 2002. Vol. 3.
319 pp., 2005. ISBN 3-03910-170-6 / US-ISBN 0-8204-6980-7

Vol. 4   Anthony Fothergill: Secret Sharers. Joseph Conrad's Cultural Reception in Germany.
274 pp., 2006. ISBN 3-03910-271-0 / US-ISBN 0-8204-7200-X

Vol. 5   Silke Arnold-de Simine (ed.): Memory Traces. 1989 and the Question of German Cultural Identity.
343 pp., 2005. ISBN 3-03910-297-4 / US-ISBN 0-8204-7223-9

Vol. 6   Renata Tyszczuk: In Hope of a Better Age. Stanislas Leszczynski in Lorraine 1737-1766.
410 pp., 2007. ISBN 978-3-03910-324-9

Vol. 7   Christian Emden, Catherine Keen & David Midgley (eds): Imagining the City, Volume 1. The Art of Urban Living.
344 pp., 2006. ISBN 3-03910-532-9 / US-ISBN 0-8204-7536-X

Vol. 8   Christian Emden, Catherine Keen & David Midgley (eds): Imagining the City, Volume 2. The Politics of Urban Space.
383 pp., 2006. ISBN 3-03910-533-7 / US-ISBN 0-8204-7537-8

Vol. 9   Christian J. Emden and Gabriele Rippl (eds): ImageScapes. Studies in Intermediality.
289 pp., 2010. ISBN 978-3-03910-573-1

Vol. 10   Alasdair King: Hans Magnus Enzensberger. Writing, Media, Democracy.
357 pp., 2007. ISBN 978-3-03910-902-9

Vol. 11   Ulrike Zitzlsperger: ZeitGeschichten: Die Berliner Übergangsjahre. Zur Verortung der Stadt nach der Mauer.
241 pp., 2007. ISBN 978-3-03911-087-2

Vol. 12 Alexandra Kolb: Performing Femininity. Dance and Literature in German Modernism.
330pp., 2009. ISBN 978-3-03911-351-4

Vol. 13 Carlo Salzani: Constellations of Reading. Walter Benjamin in Figures of Actuality.
388pp., 2009. ISBN 978-3-03911-860-1

Vol. 14 Monique Rinere: Transformations of the German Novel. *Simplicissimus* in Eighteenth-Century Adaptations.
273pp., 2009. ISBN 978-3-03911-896-0

Vol. 15 Katharina Hall and Kathryn N. Jones (eds): Constructions of Conflict. Transmitting Memories of the Past in European Historiography, Culture and Media.
282pp., 2011. ISBN 978-3-03911-923-3

Vol. 16 Ingo Cornils and Sarah Waters (eds): Memories of 1968. International Perspectives.
396pp., 2010. ISBN 978-3-03911-931-8

Vol. 17 Anna O' Driscoll: Constructions of Melancholy in Contemporary German and Austrian Literature.
263pp., 2013. ISBN 978-3-0343-0733-8

Vol. 18 Martin Modlinger and Philipp Sonntag (eds): Other People's Pain. Narratives of Trauma and the Question of Ethics.
252pp., 2011. ISBN 978-3-0343-0260-9

Vol. 19 Ian Cooper and Bernhard F. Malkmus (eds): Dialectic and Paradox. Configurations of the Third in Modernity.
265pp., 2013. ISBN 978-3-0343-0714-7

Vol. 20 Kristina Mendicino and Betiel Wasihun (eds): Playing False. Representations of Betrayal.
355pp., 2013. ISBN 978-3-0343-0867-0

Vol. 21 Guy Tourlamain: *Völkisch* Writers and National Socialism. A Study of Right-Wing Political Culture in Germany, 1890–1960.
394pp., 2014. ISBN 978-3-03911-958-5

Vol. 22 Ricarda Vidal and Ingo Cornils (eds): Alternative Worlds. Blue-Sky Thinking since 1900.
343pp., 2015. ISBN 978-3-0343-1787-0